CONTEMPORARY ANTHROPOLOGY

CONTEMPORARY ANTHROPOLOGY

Edited by

Dr. Nanjunda D.C.

Director
National School for Advanced Research
Coor Dist., Karnataka
(India)

DISCOVERY PUBLISHING HOUSE PVT. LTD.

NEW DELHI-110 002

Published by:
Tilak Wasan
DISCOVERY PUBLISHING HOUSE PVT. LTD.
4831/24, Ansari Road, Prahlad Street
Darya Ganj, New Delhi-110002 (India)
Phone: +91-11-23279245, 43764432
Fax: +91-11-23253475
E-mail: parul.wasan@gmail.com
info@discoverypublishinggroup.com
web: www.discoverypublishinggroup.com

***First Edition:* 2011**
ISBN: 978-81-8356-759-6

Contemporary Anthropology

Printed at:
Shree Balaji Art Press
Delhi

Dedication

To the

Indian Defence Force

PREFACE

The Anthropological study of social renovate has often been driven by the large to give track to it by analyzing its cases and circumstances. In the early years of Independence, a large amount of expectation was placed on the transformation of society through cognizant and planned effort. The country had fashioned a new Constitution that set its back on the old hierarchical order. Planners, policy-makers, and educators applied themselves to the removal of poverty, illiteracy, superstition, inequality, oppression and exploitation, and to the creation of a new social order based on equality, justice and freedom and material richness. Unsurprisingly enough, Indian Social Scientists did not wish to fall behind in this exhilarating endeavor.

In all this, the lead was taken among social scientists by economists, for it was extensively assumed then that social change would be driven in the desired direction by economic development. But economic development itself had to be broadly conceived, and in any case it could not be understood or managed without taking into account its social causes and consequences. Hence sociologists and social anthropologists were associated from the beginning, though not as major players, with research on development and change.

The intention is to critically discuss the history of development theory, with a special attention to the political context and content of each model, alongside anthropological models of culture change and development. After a historical assessment, the course looks at the relation between anthropology and the development machine. It traces the paradigm shifts in development models as the global political and economic landscape shifted: the end of the cold war and the neoliberal world system. The will ask if anthropology should draw a line between development cooperation and intervention, and provides the methodological toolbox to analyse neo-colonial practice.

Any work and editing a book can rarely be done individually. It is only with the inspiration, guidance and cooperation of individuals that such an effort is possible. It would therefore, be failing if I do not acknowledge the valuable contributions of the very persons and friends who have helped me in completing this endeavor. Basic resources are greatly acknowledged. First I would like to thank for the blessings of Sri Siridi Sai Baba. I owe a special debt to all the contributors and editors of various journals. Next I am very thankful to Dr. Steven Wind (USA) and Prof. Fleming Just (Netherland). I am thankful to Dr. B.R. Ghosh, Prof. M. Annapurna, M. Prof. Ramesh, Dr. Lancy D Souza, and Venugopal P.N. for their help. I deeply indebted to Linga Raju, Ms Jyothi Lakshmi S., Suresh Kumar M. S.

CONTENTS

LIST OF CONTRIBUTORS

- **Prof. Binod C. Agrawal,** Director, TALEEM Research Foundation, Sterling City Bopal, Ahmedabad-380058
- **Prof. Muzaffar Assadi,** Professor, Dept. of Studies in Political Science, University of Mysore, Karnataka
- **Dr. Alok Chantia,** Lecturer, Dept. of Anthropology, Sri Jai Narain Post-Graduate College, Lucknow, U.P., India
- **Dr. G. Sreeramulu,** Reader, Department of Political Science, Gulbarga University, Gulbarga–585 106
- **Dr. V. Rama Krishna,** Research Student, Department of Political Science, Gulbarga University, Gulbarga–585 106
- **Dr. K.A. Pradeep Kumar,** Lecturer, Mar Baselios College of Education, Bathery, Wayanad, Kerala
- **Dr. Gandham Bulliyya,** Assistant Director, Regional Medical Research Centre, Indian Council of Medical Research, Chandrasekharpur, Bhubaneswar-751 0230, Orissa
- **Dr. Md. Mosiur Rahman,** Lecturer, Department of Population Science and Human Resource Development, University of Rajshahi, Rajshahi-6205, Bangladesh
- **Dr. S.K. Lakhera,** Reader, Dept. of Education, B.C.C. H.N.B. Garhwal University, Srinagar, Garhwal
- **Dr. N. P. Uniyal,** Lecturer, Dept. of Education, B.C.C. H.N.B. Garhwal University, Srinagar Garhwal
- **Dr. Md. Rafiqul Islam,** Associate Professor, Department of Population Science & Human Resource Development, University of Rajshahi, Bangladesh
- **Md. Nure Alam Siddiqi,** Research Fellow, Department of Population Science & Human Resource Development, Rajshahi University, Bangladesh
- **Dr. K. Damodaran,** Lecturer, Dept. of Economics, Annamalai University, Chidambaram, Tamil Nadu
- **Dr. Mohammad Nasser Modoodi,** DOS in Environmental Science, University of Mysore, Mysore-570 006, India

- **Dr. M.H. Rahmani Doust,** DOS in Mathematics, University of Ilam, Ilam, Iran
- **Dr. Subba Reddy,** Programme Officer, Poverty Learning Foundation, No. 12-5-149/6A, Vijayapuri, Tarnaka, (AP)
- **Dr. Ashis Kumar Das,** Department of Anthropology, Vidyasagar University 35/2/1, Bhattacharyya Para Lane, Howrah –711104, Kolkata
- **Dr. Lev Yakobson,** State University– Higher School of Economics, Illinois, USA
- **Dr. Md. Mustafa Kamal Akand,** Associate Professor, Department of Anthropology, Rajshahi University, Bangladesh
- **Prof. A.B. Subhashini,** Dept. of Anthropology, S.V. University, Tirupati, India
- **Prof. A.B. Srilatha,** Dept. of Home Science, S.V. University, Tirupati, India
- **Nagamani,** Dept. of Home Science, S.V. University, Tirupati, India
- **Dr. Nanjunda D.C.,** National Academy for Public Policy and Management, Kushalnager-34, Kodagu Dist., Karnataka-India
- **Prof. Venkateshkumar, G.,** Dept. of Psychology, Mysore University, Mysore, Karnataka, India
- **Dr. Manjunatha P.,** KSO University, Mysore, Karnataka, India
- **Dr. Nahid Sarikhani,** Department of Sociology, Mysore University, Mysore, Karnataka, India
- **Venugopal P.N.,** Junior Research Fellow, Anthropological Survey of India (ASI), Mysore, Karnataka
- **Prof. Annapurna M.,** Dept. of Anthropology, University of Mysore, Mysore, Karnataka
- **Dr. Subramanya C. E.,** Independent Researcher, Mysore, Karnataka
- **Aneela Sultana,** Department of Anthropology, Quaid-i-Azam University (QAU), Islamabad, Pakistan
- **Dr. Rana Ejaz Ali Khan,** Assistant Professor, Department of Economics, The Isamia University of Bahawalpur (Pakistan)
- **Dr. Tannim Khan,** Chairperson, Department of Economics, The Islamia University of Bahawalpur (Pakistan)
- **Dr. Md. Irvani,** Lecturer, Islamic Azad University, Iran.

Documenting India's Cultural Heritage for Posterity: The Use of Communication Anthropology

—Binod C. Agrawal

Introduction

The aim of this chapter is three-fold: (*i*) to discuss the concept and meaning of the term "communication anthropology" and "visual anthropology" in the cultural context of India, (*ii*) to discuss its evolution, growth and expansion in the wake of the communication technology revolution for mass dissemination of diverse and multiple continuing civilisational heritage of India, and (*iii*) to discuss ways and means of its audio and visual documentation and preservation for future generations of the world to appreciate, admire and assimilate the uniqueness of the Indian civilisation in its multiplicity of colours and shades from stone age living to jet set satellite based communication age.

The first time that the term "communication anthropology" was used, to the best of my remembrance, was during the first Ethnographic and Folk Culture Society Annual Conference, 1975. During this conference, a special session on communication anthropology was organised, in which a band of young anthropologists belonging to six different universities of India presented their preliminary findings of communication study of rural India (for details see Agrawal ed. 1985). In more than one way, this was an interesting period in the history of Indian Anthropology, where a great deal of emphasis was laid on applications of anthropology for rural and tribal development.

Communication was seen as an essential ingredient to reach out to remote and isolated tribal and rural communities. The aim was to accept new ways of living and adopting technologies that would help the rural and tribal population produce more food and be part of those who live in better material comfort. In other words, economic development was at the core of the national ethos for the betterment of remote rural and tribal areas identified for change in agriculture, nutrition and family planning. Education was seen as a precondition for adoption of innovation. The entire national climate was charged with centralised planning to bring about desired change. It was a time when India had reaped the fruits of the green revolution in large parts of the country, in which communication had played a significant role. More than anthropologists, technologists were greatly enthused about the prospect of using satellite communication for better living conditions and elevating lives of the miserable millions. Many young anthropologists joined hands in the applications of anthropology for communication that would eventually lead to development. Due to lack of appropriate professional growth within the field of anthropology, several anthropologists migrated to mass media organisations like All India Radio and Doordarshan in search of jobs where opportunities existed. A few, who were interested in music, art and dance, also became part and parcel of the growing number of anthropologists interested in communication. In the last three decades, there has been no looking back for the students of communication anthropology in India. The story is somewhat narrated in an article entitled "Anthropological Applications in Communication Research and Evaluation of SITE in India" (Agrawal 1981). Vidyarthi (1978), in his two-volume book *"Rise of Anthropology in India"*, devoted a small section on "space anthropology" instead of "communication anthropology" and indicated the work carried out by all those anthropologists who were involved in the Satellite Instructional Television Experiment (SITE) (Vidyarthi 1978). Since then, communication anthropology has moved into the areas of Information and Communication Technology, broadening its scope of research and teaching. Agrawal, assisted by Joshi, in collaboration with a number of anthropologists carried out the first study in the field of Information Technology (see Agrawal 1996). Anthropologists in India have continued their efforts in this direction (see Anonymous 2004).

Another significant development in the last three decades relate to the emergence of visual anthropology, particularly after the *Xth International Congress of Anthropological and Ethnological Sciences*, New Delhi, 1978. It may not be out of place to mention that the first Indian to serve on the commission of Visual Anthropology (1973-78) during the conference was Professor K.N. Sahay of Ranchi University. The Anthropological Survey of India has been contributing in visual anthropology in a significant way, but with little dissemination of their efforts in the country. Historically, an organised effort to discuss and document achievements of visual anthropology in the country was jointly organised by Anthropological Survey of India and the Indian National Trust for Art and Cultural Heritage (INTACH) at Jodhpur, India, December 15-19, 1987. The author had assisted the organisers in planning and scheduling of the seminar and later on collated the entire proceedings on the request of INTACH.

Visual Anthropology and India

(Singh ed. 1992) was the outcome of this effort. At present, visual anthropology has moved into the commercial arena of television, and has even been monopolised by 24-hour news channels. News channels are keen to depict the cultural uniqueness and diversity of India in its vivid colours and manifestations. Digital technology has further helped television channels to produce and transmit the many facets and cultural dimensions of the Indian civilisation. In the international arena, key interests in visual and communication anthropology remained an important pre-occupation of American anthropologists, who made tireless efforts to document and preserve the vanishing tribal cultures of North America and elsewhere. The *Visual Anthropology* Journal, published in cooperation with the Commission on Visual Anthropology, remained one of the major sources of reporting, as well as theoretical and methodological discussions in the field. After the completion of the conference, I was nominated as Chairman of Visual Anthropology Commission, which was never ratified due to a number of geo-political problems; the only meeting that was ever held of Indian anthropologists was at Space Application Centre, Indian Space Research Organisation, Ahmedabad. A number of anthropologists presented their work of visual documentation of tribal and rural life. After that, not much happened, except that Mr. K.N. Sahay continued his interest and wrote some articles. On the communication anthropology front, a whole lot of work has been carried out in the last 30 years, having direct applications in development communication and education. These are based on five basic premises of anthropology–a holistic view, process analysis, 'emic' approach, comparative perspective and methods of participant observation (Agrawal 1981: 136-146).

Anthropology and Communication

More than 70 years ago, in the *Encyclopaedia of Social Sciences*, Edward Sapir wrote the first article on "communication". He observed, "every cultural pattern and every single act of social behaviour involves communication in either an explicit or implicit sense" (Sapir 1931: 4). It still remains a classic writing on communication by an anthropologist that marked the beginning of a new discipline called communication. The author took inspiration from Sapir, who was one of the greatest anthropologists who brought in linguistic dimension to the analysis of culture. Levi-Strauss (1953) thought of multiple layers of interactions between culture and communication. Three different levels of communication were thought to operate in any society. These included women, goods and services and messages.

Hence, it is believed that culture does not consist exclusively of communication through language, since there is a dynamic and integral relationship between kinship and communication. These thoughts helped in expanding the scope of anthropological applications in communication for development. The first time a large number of anthropologists were recruited was to help conduct Satellite Instructional Television Experiment (SITE) communication research. It is here that the notion of communication anthropology was advanced, for which a reference has already been made.

Three aspects of SITE that helped in setting the research agenda for the anthropologists were:

1. Preparation of audience profile
2. Needs assessment study
3. Holistic or ethnographic study to evaluate the effects of SITE on the first generation television viewers.

Beyond Anthropology

The pioneering work of Karve (1953) on kinship, and Bose's (1961) study on material culture in India came handy while preparing audience profile. Within Indian "cultural mosaic", according to them, there are ecological, agro-climatic, and linguistic regions. Within each such region there are a number of sub-regions in terms of linguistic zones. The principles of categorisation were adopted in the communication research. In the process, the task became more difficult due to two contradictory needs : (*a*) a generalised audience profile acceptable to all the regions of India, and (*b*) non-existence of such a generalised profile in real life. The anthropological team stopped searching for a generalised farmer and village in the Indian civilisation. Instead, the team thought of region-specific audience profile. But even for this, there was no data or theoretical framework for writing the audience profile. So it was decided to take Benedict's (1934) configuration approach. The basic idea was that a culture could artfully be described without analysing various aspects of its configuration. Around this configuration, the total culture can be described giving a psycho-cultural portrayal, which was needed for television programme production.

Audience Profile

An anthropologist's role, could well beyond Anthropology. A view could be taken that an Indian village and an Indian family must be conceived as a cultural microcosm of the macrocosm of the Indian civilisation. The concept of "whole" was thought of as a basis for developing audience profile for television production. Since the aim of the audience profile was to provide useful socio-cultural material for TV production, generalised ethnographic descriptions of the village culture for each of the seven states were attempted. The audience profile briefly provided, among others:

(1) Social structure

(2) Occupational pattern and development issues

(3) Rural material culture

(4) Language and exposure to mass media

(5) Special cultural uniqueness

Keeping in mind the objectives of SITE, the following development issues were also discussed and highlighted.

(1) Agricultural activity

(2) Health and hygiene

(3) Family planning

(4) Education, especially primary education, and

(5) Problems related to rural development

Here is an illustration on how the configuration approach was used for describing rural cultural regions of the country. In Chhattisgarh, for example, a paddy growing state, the status of women was observed to be higher than that of men. After careful analysis of existing data and field work, the author developed a "woman-dominated rice-eating configuration". Keeping this configuration in mind, the audience profile of Chhattisgarh having a number of interesting implications for those who were involved in television production. Later discussions with a number of anthropologists who had not worked there also confirmed the author's observations, although their data had not been analysed in this framework.

Implications

Anthropologists involvement in the field of communication is relatively new in India. Yet, they were able to provide authentic material culture and depiction of the Indian cultural traditions. The team was also more in a position to influence ideas and views of those creative persons, who were responsible for changing the lives of millions through television. The ideological justification of such an involvement lay in providing realism in the depiction of true cultural visual images for meaningful communication. It also provided credibility to the medium and helped in preserving those traditions that would have died out in the wake of communication revolution. Similar descriptions could be provided for other researches that were carried out during SITE. But this serves as an illustration of how anthropology went beyond the confines of traditional teaching and research.

Visual Anthropology

According to Mead (1978: 278), "How to cultivate and cherish the conditions under which very small and fragile cultures could at least be properly recorded and preserved for their own sake, and possibly cultivated to the point of some enrichment and new spontaneity, came out, for example, in the emphasis on what could be done today with TV. If anthropologists could be present to guide the TV cameramen when they go out to pick up all sorts of 'folk' materials, these materials could be both enriched and refined into genuine materials and preserved as archives to be studied, and in some cases, when they were fed back to the people, stimulate what they did also."

Visual documentation allows a broader and holistic comprehension of cultural reality, and to a large extent, breaks the language barrier. While visuals give accurate depiction, the selection of a sequence of events, its juxtaposition with other events and the very selection of live events creates a composite visual mosaic that could create an illusionary or distorted comprehension of culture. What we have is a mediated understanding between the technology, the person documenting it and the people whose cultures are being documented. Without going into discussion of how these mediated images cannot truly reflect culture, it could be said that even with this limitation, visual documentation provides an understanding far superior than does written description help in preservation of culture.

An Approach to Visual Documentation

The visual documentation of culture for posterity essentially means describing culture on celluloid or on videotape or digitally, while keeping a holistic view. A holistic view involves

This part of the chapter has been largely drawn from Agrawal, 1995, *Computerising Cultures. Kapila Vatsyayan and Baidyanath Saraswati (eds.), New Delhi: New Age International (P) Limited* describing not only different aspects of a culture in its totality but also the interrelationships and interdependence among aspects of culture as a dynamic phenomenon. Translating such a conception of culture into visuals raises a basic issue of identifying salient categories or elements that should be recognised for the purpose of description and for demonstrating the relationships. As it is well established that each culture has its own categories and classification systems, which may or may not have comparable categories in other cultures, there arises the issue of whose categories should be utilised in visual documentation.

While reviewing the efforts at documenting cultures of some of the administratively and socially identifiable groups referred to as 'caste' and 'tribe' in India, one finds an impressive list of nearly a hundred documentaries. But when compared with the total number of such groups, the size of the country, and the time duration, it is a miniscule effort. The leadership for producing such 'ethnographic films' came from the Anthropological Survey of India over more than a quarter of a century. Sinha feels that these films produced "complementary ethnographic data for the purpose of research and not for making less-known people known to the wider national society and the world" (Sinha 1987: xv).

Units of Visual Documentation

At any given time, even with unlimited resources, it would be extremely difficult to document every part of the civilisation, cultural or linguistic groups. This problem is further compounded in a multi-religious, multi-ethnic and multi-linguistic India, with built-in historical continuities and multi-layered social formations. Therefore it would be most desirable to have visual documentation of cultures that could be referred to as broad patterns, or themes and aspirations of life, as Benedict mentioned in the thirties (Benedict 1934). At the second level, within a linguistic region, linguistically distinct social groups or units should have their special characteristics separately documented. At the third level, the unit of visual documentation should be the groups identified as distinct and special by the people, like a caste or tribe. At this level, visual documentation should be as exhaustive as possible, to incorporate almost all aspects of culture, which could be referred to as a total way of life.

No matter how open-ended or eclectic the approach to visual communication, some ordering is inevitable, either by conscious effort of the filmmaker or through the sequence of events and the selection of certain parts. It is essential that efforts be made to follow a logical sequence, and that logic should emerge from the people. In addition, still photographs must be taken and natural sound should be recorded. Supplementary written documents providing technical details like kind of film used, aperture, shutter speed, time of day, and so on should be documented. An ethnographic note on the event should be recorded and transferred to the computer. This holds true both for still photographs and movies.

More than visual documentation, appropriate techniques for the preservation and retrieval of visual material are of great importance. Appropriate computer software and hardware are available and ought to be procured for this purpose. Given the cost dimension of such a system, a centralised facility at the regional level is recommended, with proper arrangement for acquisition, duplication and distribution.

Given its technological complexity and interdisciplinary nature, a critical input in the creation of such a facility will be the training of personnel and the continuous updating of their knowledge. Also, all efforts should be made to evolve a common technical specification for the recording, storage and retrieval of documents to minimise incompatibilities in the future. In practical terms, it means a continuous information flow among the participating institutions and individuals to indicate the adoption of any new communication technology, which may facilitate or hinder the transfer of visual data.

Professional Cooperation for Visual Documentation

A brief mention has been made of the technical cooperation required for such an effort. But a more important form of cooperation will be required for capturing cultures on celluloid. Given the cost and complexity of filmmaking, any effort to visually document cultures in the way that filmmakers usually work will lead nowhere. It will also permit the documentation of cultural realities in their 'emic' categories. If we go along the classical ethnographic filmmaking path, we will end up producing films on a few specialised topics of great interest to anthropologists (Hockings ed. 1975). What is required is a professional, multi-disciplinary team. The authenticity of cultural data should be identified by cultural anthropologists who have a holistic view and an 'emic' approach, which then should be documented *in situ* without altering any sequence of events. The team should also include an expert if the aim is to document a particular aspect of art. Such a visual documentation also promotes understanding, besides being a resource, where every frame ought to be preserved.

There are several tribal groups living all along the international boundaries of many South Asian countries. Countries need to cooperate on initiating joint country-specific documentation projects. Cooperation in specialised training in visual documentation requires attention as well and institutions for such skill development identified. Also crucial is the theoretical and conceptual training of professionals involved. National, regional and international support and financial allocations will be required for reaching a meaningful goal.

REFERENCES

1. Anonymous 2004, "Digital Equalizer Program—An Impact Evaluation". Unpublished report, TALEEM Research Foundation, Ahmedabad.
2. Agrawal, Binod C. (Assisted by Madhavi Joshi) 1996, *The Pedagogy of Computer Literacy: An Indian Experience*. New Delhi: Concept Publishing Company.
3. Shashikala Vishwanath 1985 (eds.), *Anthropological Methods in Communication Research*. New Delhi: Concept Publishing Company.
4. Benedict, Ruth 1934, *Patterns of Culture*. New York: Houghton Mifflin.

5. Bose, N.K. 1961 (ed.), *Peasant Life in India: A Study in Unity and Diversity*. Calcutta: Anthropological Survey of India, Memoir No. 8.
6. Hockings, Paul 1975 (ed.), *Principles of Visual Anthropology*. The Hague: Mouton Publishers.
7. Karve, Irawati 1953, *Kinship Organisation in India*. Bombay: Asia Publishing House.
8. Levi-Strauss, Claude 1953, *Social Structure in Anthropology Today*. A.L.Kroeber, (ed.), pp. 524-53. Chicago: University of Chicago Press.
9. Mead, Margaret 1978, "Anthropology in Culture Building: Results and Problems of World Anthropology, 1977." In *Anthropology for the Future*, Dimitri B. Shimkim, Sol Tax and John W. Morrison (eds.). Urbana: University of Illinois Press.
10. Sapir, Edward 1931, "Communication". In *Encyclopaedia of Social Sciences*, Volume 4, pp. 78-91. New York: Macmillan Press.
11. Singh, K.S. 1992 (ed.), *Visual Anthropology and India*. Calcutta: Anthropological Survey of India.
12. Sinha, Surajit 1987, *A Portrayal of People; Essays on Visual Anthropology in India*. New Delhi: ASI, INTACH.
13. Vidyarthi, L.P. 1978, *Rise of Anthropology in India*. Vol II, pp. 222. New Delhi: Concept Publishing Co.

Ethnic Groups/Tribals in the Midst of Policy Transfer: Displacement, Rehabilitation and Governance in India—A Critique

—Muzaffar Assadi

Policy transfer refers to the attempt to introduce an external policy to the cultural setting of a country. It is also viewed as movement of ideas or policies between countries. In fact, globalization as well as modernization has increased such tendencies. This is true in the case of India. Couple of policies formulated by the international agencies such as World Bank or ADB on Dams or Ecology/biodiversity have been adopted by India, particularly the policy on Resettlement and Rehabilitation (World Bank: 1993, 2001). The importance of such policies lies in their approach to address the issues of rehabilitation of displaced much more comprehensively than merely as policy prescriptions. However, policy transfer has its own weakness: this lies in the fact that external policies are drawn in a setting which does not takes into cognizance the cultural setting of locality (Anthony Needley: n.d).

Secondly many a time policies are forced upon different countries, particularly this is acute in the case of developing countries. Thirdly, policy transfer is also limited or linked to certain conditions and thereby it becomes imperative on the part of the receiving country to abide the policies dictated by the external agencies. Fourthly policy transfer also becomes a tool to control the countries, particularly the way the funding is linked to larger issues. Fifthly policy transfer does not takes place in a vacuum; rather it involves many procedures and conditions. Most important is the fact that issues of policy transfer also linked to the issues of power relation both between the western and non-western countries on the one hand, different social categories in developing countries, particularly it is seen in terms of domination and dominated relations. Further it is argued that policy transfer does not take into cognizance "history" including historical social categories.

This is the reason why the issues of policy transfer have become the centre of contestation, both by the marginalized groups as well as by the civil society groups in different parts of world. In fact, the debate on North -South, developing /developed world to restructure the relations largely centers around the way the policy transfer has changed or altered the socio-economic structure of large number of people. It is often argued that there is an inbuilt bias in the policy transfer–particularly it is biased towards industrial/ global capital or western capital. It is also biased towards urban areas, landlord categories and rich peasants.

Policy Transfer in fact has become a site of contestation, a site of negotiation, a site of debate and discourse. Many a time Policy Transfer from the west, particularly coming through the Multilateral Institutions has been viewed in suspicion, particularly because of the inherent potentiality to affect the lifestyles of large number of people, particularly the ethnic groups. The affect has been felt in the realm of community life, in the realm of social life, in the realm of culture, in the realm of identity. Secondly the affect is largely felt and expressed through the means of large-scale displacement of ethnic groups particularly the tribals. Thirdly the affect is translated into different forms: it stretched between radical movements and civil society activism. Sometime affect has created spaces for perpetual conflict between the state/multilateral institutes and the ethnic groups.

One of the arenas wherein the issue of policy transfer has been contested is in the arena of displacement. This is because of two important factors: Policy transfer has caused much physical displacement of ethnic groups from their historical places; secondly policy transfer has also not completed the project of rehabilitating the displaced completely. This is apparent in India too.

Broadly there are three forms of displacement: Conflict Induced Displacement, Conservation Induced Displacement and Development Induced Displacement. (Schidt-Soltau: 2004). The latter two become major controversial issue in India (Walter Fernandes et.al: 1998: 264-79; Walter Fernandes and Mohammad Asif, 1997; Walter Fernandes et al. 2001; Smithu Kothari: 1995: 9-28, Cernea: 1995; Cernea: 1999; Thukral, 1995: 93-122). There is no clear-cut number of populations displaced over the years. Planning Commission for example estimated that 21.3 millions have been displaced during 1951-90 (Planning Commission, 2001), which include construction of dams, mines, industries, wildlife etc. (Ministry of Rural Development: 2001). Majority of them come from the category of tribals (85.4%), including women, (Walter Fernandez: 1989) and peasantry. However, not all of them have been rehabilitated. Nearly 75 per cent of them are still waiting for proper rehabilitation.

Our paper will focus on two important projects supported by the World Bank, particularly Eco Development Project and Project on Dams. The first Eco Development Project is a conservation project mainly confined to seven National Parks in India. This project involved reallocation of tribal families from the National Parks to adjacent areas. In the second, the World Bank has been funding construction of Dams in different parts of India. This is apparent when World Bank funded Sardar Sarovar or Almatti Dam.

Displacement in India: Dimension and Nature

Over the past couple of years issues of displacement has become a major contentious issue. In fact there are different perspectives. Some would view "displacement is inevitable, although it is a painful process". Others would argue that effect of displacement could be compensated by adequate rehabilitation package, including monetary package.

Displacement has taken different forms. In Indian context one of the best-known method by which displacement has taken on a massive scale is Development Induced Displacement. There has been major debate about it. Many felt that "development induced displacement" is inevitable and inescaple—as development would usher in economic growth, equity and prosperity. Other, particularly the critical developmentalist would view it differently. They would see the larger power nexus between the state apparatus on the one hand and the ruling class or elites on the other in almost all the Development Projects. The latter's perception goes a step further, and view in every development an inherent bias against the ethnic groups. This is because of following factors: developmental schemes or projects provide little spaces to the ethnic groups particularly the tribals to voice their presence or to contest, and, it takes no cognizance of the presence of ethnic groups either. Most of the time developmental projects are imposed upon, rather than taking into account prior consent of the ethnic groups. Further, developmental projects are decided not in cultural setting of ethnic groups rather "outside their realm"—the realm lies either in the capital cities or in the western multilateral institutions. Fourthly, developmental projects are imposed or introduced in a straightjacket manner without however taking into confidence locality or cultural settings of ethnic groups. Finally the developmental projects are not backed by a proper rehabilitation policy. In other words most of the time, the projects are implemented without a proper rehabilitation package or policy.

One of the major problems confronted while analyzing the displacement is numbering. In fact numbering or estimate is always essential so as to formulate proper rehabilitation policy. This also helps in reducing the number of displacement in due course. Couple of studies has estimated differently. It is stated that between 1951 and 1990 nearly 213 lakhs or 21.3 million populations must have been displaced due to development (Walter Fernandes, 2001: 87). This number might have increased to more than 30 million due to increasing development projects that the Indian government has introduced in recent years.[1] Conservative estimates put the number of families displaced by development projects alone (displacement due to processes such as urbanization are not included) at over 20 million up to 1991. Various studies have put the figure between 2 million and 56 million. Of them, 75 per cent of families (as per government records) are awaiting rehabilitation. Smitu Kothari, for example, an authority on environment and tribal issues would argue that "development projects under India's Five-Year plans have displaced about 500,000 persons each year–over 40 per cent of those displaced from 1950 to 1990 were from tribal communities" (Smithu Kothari: 1995). On the contrary Satyajit Sinha estimated that 33.7 million by 1348 large Dams have displaced during 1952-79 in India (P. Raghu Ram: 2006: 91). One estimate that[2] "nearly 2.13 crore people have been displaced due to large projects since independence". [3]It is also stated "[4]21.3 million people are internally displaced due to development projects in India.[5]Many a time the official statistics shows less than the independent studies. This is apparent in such studies as [6]Hirakud Dam.

Nonetheless one has to accept the fact that there are varieties of displacement. Although Development Induced Displacement is the larger framework under which the displacement is taking place, however there are different reasons for displacement too. These reasons are: Displacement due to Dams, Mines, Industries, and Wildlife etc. Here too there are contradictory debates. In fact, the Indian state now accepts the presence of various forms of displacement. For example, Ministry of Rural Development. Estimated that between 1951 and 1990 213 lakhs have been displaced. It includes those displaced by dams (16.4 million), mines (2.55 million), industrial development (1.25 million) and wildlife sanctuaries and national parks (0.6 million).

Most important question is which category of population is mostly affected by the displacement. Once again it is estimated that Tribal population constitute the big chunck of population affected by the displacement, despite the fact that they constitute hardly 7.8 per cent of the total population. It is estimated that not less than 4.5-lakh tribal population have been displaced due to Wildlife sanctuaries and National Parks. In fact they constitute 75 per cent of population who were displaced due to Wildlife sanctuaries and National Parks. The second important category is Dalits. Nearly 20 per cent of Dalit populations have become the victims.

Table 2.1. Displacement between 1951 and 1990 (in lakhs)

Sl.No.	Type of projects	Total displaced and percentage	Tribal displacement and percentage	% of Tribals to the total
1.	Dams	164.0 (25.0%)	63.2 (25.0%)	38.5
2.	Mines	25.5 (25.5%)	13.3 (24.8%)	52.2
3.	Industries	12.5 (30.0%)	3.1 (25.6%)	25.0
4.	Wildlife	6.0 (20.8%)	4.5 (22.2%)	75.0
5.	Others	5.0 (30.0%)	1.3 (20.0%)	25.0
	Total	213.0 (25.4%)	85.4 (24.8%)	40.1

Source: As quoted in Planning Commission, *Report of the Steering Committee on Empowering the Scheduled Tribes For Tenth Five Plans",* 2001, p. 3 from Ministry of Rural Development.

Initially the Government of India refused to accept the fact that any displacement is taking place due to Development Projects. This became apparent when Farakka Thermal Power Project was established in West Bengal. Government came to the conclusion that none were affected. However over the years it is slowly but firmly accepting the fact that the large-scale displacement is taking place due to different development policies. This is reflected in different policy documents including Tenth Five-Year Plan document[7]. The latter clearly admits that the, "displacement or forced/voluntary eviction (of tribals) from their land and from their natural habitats and their subsequent rehabilitation has been a serious problem that needs to be addressed". Similar kind of arguments is apparent in the National Policy on Resettlement and Rehabilitation for Project Affected families, 2003. It states that,[8] "Compulsory acquisition of land for public purpose including infrastructure projects displaces people, forcing them to give up their home, assets and means of livelihood. Apart from depriving them of their lands, livelihoods and resource-base, displacement has other traumatic psychological and socio-cultural consequences. The Government of India recognizes the need to minimize large-scale displacement to the extent possible and, where displacement is inevitable, the need to handle with utmost care and forethought issues relating to Resettlement and Rehabilitation of Project Affected Families. Such an approach is especially necessary in respect of tribals, small and marginal farmers and women".

Other than that Planning Commission of India (Planning Commission: 2001: 37) now has come to conclusion that "that 21.3 millions have been displaced, during 1951-90. Of whom 8.54 million (40%) are tribals". Its estimate is almost similar to that of the estimate of Ministry of Rural Development.

Interestingly even World Bank is now accepting the fact of displacement. In 1994 it estimated that 63,325 persons were displaced which include Project Affected Persons too.

Nonetheless one should not overlook the fact that multiple displacements also taking place. This is apparent in different parts of India. In Karnataka, the Soligas and Jenu Kuruba tribes were again and again displaced—once due to the construction of Kabini Dam and later on due to the Declaration of National Park or Wildlife Act. Similarly "the Rihand Dams oustees were displaced not less than four times." In Orissa, the Chikapar village near Sunabeda displaced by HALMIG complex were displaced again by the Uppper Kolab Dam and a third time by the Naval Armament Depot (Walter Fernandes, 2001: 89.

Two important issues have received much focus in recent years while detailing Development/Displacement/Rehabilitation.

Eco Development Project and Policy Transfer

A clear cut policy transfer, which also saw winding up the project on later date, is very much visible in the World Bank sponsored Eco Development Programme or Project in India during the last decade. This has created binary oppositions: contestation and hailing, opposing and welcoming. Most of the time the contestation or opposition came from the stakeholders particularly the tribal population, as they saw in this policy transfer the loss of their social, cultural identity, loss of the self and most importantly, they saw in it the larger design of the global capitalism mediating through multilateral institutions to displace the tribals enmasse.

World Bank has the major concern in this respect. In fact the World Bank has been the largest financier for the protection of biodiversity.[9] "Between 1988 and 2004, World Bank funding for biodiversity has involved over 426 projects with about US $1.5 billion of IBRD/IDA resources, over US $964 million of GEF funds and an additional US $2.2 billion in co-funding from other donors, governments, NGOs, foundations and the private sector; a total Bank-managed biodiversity portfolio of US $4.7 billion". It all started in the year 1996, when World Bank declared the project. However it receive cabinet consent in the year 1997. The project was initially meant for five years, however it was extended by one more year. It is largely seen as a failed project. The total cost involved in the project upto June 2004 was approximately 250 crores.

In India project towards preserving biodiversity was contemplated when World Bank advocated Eco-Development Programme. This is because of the following fact, "India's biodiversity is rich, often unique and increasingly endangered. India is one of the twelve mega diversity countries in the world that collectively account for 0-70 per cent of the world's bio-diversity, second, important reason is economic. This is also apparent in the following: "India's biological resources are economically important, both globally and nationally. India is one of the oldest and largest agricultural societies, India has an impressive diversity of crops species and varieties. At least 166 species of crop plants and 320 species of wild relatives of cultivated crops originate on the subcontinent. About 90 per cent of all medicines in India come from plant species many of which are harvested in the wild." (World Bank, 1996: 1)

The project had five basic objectives: (*a*) Improve protected Area Management; (*b*) Eco development of villages (*c*) Development of more effective and extensive support for PA Management and eco development; (*d*) Overall Project management and finally preparation of future biodiversity. There are two important reasons why Eco Development Project was introduced. One of the major concern was to cover seven states in India. This is apparent in the following: "This is a 70 million dollar project covering seven projected areas (PA) in seven states in India–Bihar, Gujarat, Karnataka, Madhya Pradesh, Rajasthan, and West Bengal–and covers five tiger reserves (Buxa, Weste Benga; Palamau, Bihar; Pench, Madhya Pradesh; Periyar, Kerala; Ranathambore, Rajasthan) and one elephant reserve (Rajiv Gandhi National Park).

Nonetheless the Eco-Development Project was designed to target the "tribal people, and forest fringe villages belonging to the poorest section of society. In this particular project" tribal development concerns are addressed in an integral fashion under the fabric of social impact participation and equity, rather than as a subsidiary tribal development plan or component" Project also "incorporates specific measures to safeguard the interests of landless and women through participation in village committees, employment preference and ongoing social assessment review and other monitoring". Nevertheless it had identified five core areas as its main objectives: to improve the capacity of PA Management and activities and decisions, reduce negative impact of PAs on local people in conservation efforts, more effective and extensive support for PA eco-development to ensure effective management and finally prepare biodiversity to ensure effective management and finally prepare biodiversity project.

Policy transfer in the case of eco development lies not only in the rationale for fund but also "enhancing, participation, increasing women's role in managing productive resources", Policy also aims at incorporating local people into PA management activities, benefit sharing, and planning, and "emphasize consideration of the needs and welfare of forest dwelling people". (World Bank, 1996: 7). Policy transfer also aims at voluntary resettlement of forest dwellers or the ethnic groups to the fringes.

However what went wrong with this policy transfer is the poor governance and subsequent contestation. In Many places particularly Nagarhole and Kudremukh in Karnataka tribal opposed the Eco-Development Programme—they opposed their rehabilitation including resettlement in different place. Policy transfer of Eco Development was seen and viewed as a larger ploy to displaces tribals from their forest dwelling. Secondly since the policy transfer also demanded local consultation, the same was not adhered to while displacing or resettling the tribal population. Thirdly the policy transfer although advocated a comprehensive rehabilitation package for the tribal or ethnic groups, the same was not implemented. Policy transfer in this context was seen and viewed in terms of "larger ploy", an attempt to displace, an attempt to create cultural genocide, or eco-terrorism, and an attempt to further marginalize the tribals.

This is the reason why tribals went on to agitate against such project. In fact in some places it provided spaces for radical politics to enter in. However the attempt to rehabilitate all the tribals remain incomplete. Even in some cases the World Bank withdrew from further funding. This shows that the local population does not always welcome the policy transfer, as the policy transfer has the larger consequences of displacement, cultural loss and loss of the identity of the social categories. Contestation also emerged due to the fact that the rehabilitation of the displaced, sometime forcible, has been without taking into account the cultural setting of the social categories.

Big or Large Dams

Big Dams in Indian context once were hailed as symbols of Indian Modernity, particularly first Prime Minister of India, Jawaharlal Nehru called them as symbols of Indian modernity, without understanding the fact that the same modernity became a contesting terrain, a site of conflict, a location of and for cultural loss and the loss of the identity. Today India is one of the top most country which has big dams numbering around 4291—this is nothing but competing with China and USA. Nonetheless there are couple of arguments either in favour or against the Large or Big Dams in India. In fact, Taneja, Bansuri and Thakkar, Himanshu in their study estimated that a total of 4,387,625 persons have been displaced across the 140 large and medium dams in India. (Taneja n.d)

One perspective tries to view *essentiality* of Large Dams, as they would help in the irrigation, water supply, power generation and flood control (Shripad Dharmadikari, 2001: 104). Here lies the argument of Developmentalism. This particular perspective would give scant respect to the people who would be affected. Even it makes hardly any reference to the International rules and regulations. Other important perspective tries to see the essentiality of big or large dams in creating food security (IIM: 2002). It is true that, the big dams have increased the food production, from 51 million tons in 1950-51 to 208 million tons in 1999-2000 (MOWR, 2002). However it does not mean that the big dams do not have other face too. Most important perspective tries to view in the larger dams an attempt to expedite the capitalist development. Here the capitalist mode cares less for the rehabilitation of the victims (P. Raghu Ram: 2006: 318).

In fact the issue of large dams have created conditions for large-scale conflict between the Indian state on the one side and the masses, particularly the ethnic groups, on the other. The best example is the way Narmada Bachao Andolan is agitating against the rehabilitation package given to the Tribals. There are other places where trend of opposing the big dams is apparent: Tehri Dam, earlier Silent Valley Project, Kabini in Karnataka. Large Dams are no more seen as temples of modern India. As Bandopadhya argues, "The long history of involuntary displacement and inadequate resettlement and rehabilitation of the project-affected people (particularly the tribals) has been the single most important factor behind the dams losing their status as temples" (IIM: 2002).

Table 2.2. Independent estimate of total persons displaced by dams during 1950-90 (in lakhs)

Category	Number (in lakhs)	Percentage (%)
Total number of persons displaced	164	100
Total number resettled	41	25
Backlog	123	75
Total number of tribal persons displaced	63.21	38
Total tribal persons resettled	15.81	25
Backlog	47.40	75

(**Source:** Fernandes and Paranjpye, 1997)

Nonetheless while detailing rehabilitation and resettlement of the displaced, India often banks on the World Bank Policies. This is because of the fact that World Bank is the greatest source of funding for large number of Dams in India and other parts of the world. The World Bank, has provided more than US $50 billion (1992) for construction of more than 500 large dams in 92 countries. Its funding is apparent in the case of Narmada or Sardar Sarovar Project. Its involvement in the Project dates back to the decade of 1980s. It was not possible then to Indian government to go alone to take up the gigantic task. World Banks' involvement is apparent in the following:"[10] that it was not possible for India to go ahead with this project without the Bank involvement, and, that this project offered the best opportunity for modernization of India's irrigation in the direction desired by the Bank!" In fact in 1985 the World Bank advanced two loans. In 1985, the World Bank approved and agreements were signed for two loans to the project totaling 450 million US dollars. Nonetheless when policy transfer failed to reflect the ground reality, the World Bank withdrew from further funding. Similar case is the Almatti Dam in Karnataka. In fact World Bank funding for large dams has come under sever contestation for various reasons:[11]

Over the years its policies have displaced more than ten million population from their homes. Majority of them are tribals, followed by farmers, and dalits etc. It is true that social cost is much more than the total cost incurred due to the construction of Dams. Its projects are in the ultimate analysis support the big industries, urban areas than the tribes including the fact that its irrigation projects ultimately meant to create export-oriented production than for local consumption.

Thirdly it has created binary opposition with regard to the rehabilitation: effective rehabilitation and poor rehabilitation. The effective rehabilitations are confined to one or two localities such as Almatti Dam in Karnataka wherein the governance has been very effective. Narmada is a classic case of failure where the ethnic groups have been constantly struggling for retaining their identity.

However unlike in the eco-development, the categories involved in the debate on rehabilitation or resettlement are tribals, but also peasants, backward castes, women etc.

Displacement in fact has not confined to Dams or Eco development alone, rather different development projects such as Mining, establishment of satellite towns also have induced displacement. Most of the time displacements have been backed by violence, although many a time the state has advocated the "voluntary allocation" or resettlement. The examples of and for forcible displacement are plenty. The recent example include forcible acquire of land in Orissa and Maharashtra for bauxite mining by Sterlite Industries, and Sahara Groups Amby Valley Lake City Project. Land has been acquired mainly through Land Acquisition Act of 1894. This has become one of the major contentious issues. Large number of civil society groups demanding the repealing of act.

Policy Transfer and Resettlement and Rehabilitation

Rehabilitation is one of the major issues, which is much debated (Hari Modi, 2006: 246-67) in recent years. The received policies from the international agencies although have been for a proper and an effective rehabilitation of displaced, the same has not been done in many cases. It is estimated that nearly 75 per cent of the total population, who have been displaced over the years are yet to be rehabilitated—this is true in the case of Tehri Dam *(B.K.Sinha and H.C Pokhiyal: 2001: 110-43)* "In the case of Hirakud Compensation amounting to Rs. 154,146,994 was not paid after years" (Mahapatra, 1990)". In fact, World Commission on Dams indicated that more than one time people have been displaced. This is apparent in the case of Dam projects such as Rihand, Koyna, and Sardar Sarovar. However World Commission on Dams has recommended that the stakeholders particularly the ethnic groups in the development projects should be taken into confidence; that before implementing any project assessment should be made with all "options strategically and comprehensively"...

This is almost echoed in the Policy of Asia Development Bank. The Bank policy states, "affected[12] people should be fully informed and closely consulted on resettlement and compensation options". "Consultation with APs is the starting point for all activities concerning resettlement. People affected by resettlement may be apprehensive that they will lose their livelihoods and communities, or be ill-prepared for complex negotiations over entitlements. Participation in planning and managing resettlement helps to reduce their fears and gives APs an opportunity to participate in key decisions that will affect their lives. Resettlement implemented without consultation may lead to inappropriate strategies and eventual impoverishment. Without consultation, the people affected may oppose the project, causing social disruption, substantial delay in achieving targets or even abandonment, and cost increases. Negative public and media images of the project and of the implementation agency may develop. With consultation, initial opposition to a project may be transformed into constructive participation. Holding public meetings and identifying focus groups can foster consultation. Planners might draw on participatory problem-solving methods, supplemented by use of the media in scattered or broad areas. Household surveys represent an opportunity for direct consultation. Community workers can be engaged to foster a process of group formation and development, possibly through a social preparation phase".

Interestingly the policy transfer from the World Bank is apparent many times. For example, as we said earlier it is apparent in the Eco-Development Project at the time of "voluntary resettlement" or "consultation by the stakeholders". Over the years it has evolved seven basic elements for the purpose of resettlement of displaced. This include: minimizing the displacement or avoidance; two, whenever there is unavoidable displacement the objective should be to improve or at least restore the earlier standard of life including living capacities; "In order to achieve this objective borrowing governments should prepare and execute resettlement plans as development plans", three, displaced should be compensated for their losses at replacement cost, which include giving share in the project benefits, four, there should be minimal distance between the displaced area and resettled areas; the new areas should provide them economic opportunities; fifth, both planners as well as displaced should take into account socio-cultural specificities; sixth, new communities or resettles should be designed as viable settlement systems equipped with infrastructure and services, host communities should be assisted to overcome the possible adverse impacts from the increased population densities and finally "indigenous people ethnic minorities pastoralists and other groups that don't have legal land titles but informal customary rights should not be denied compensation and rehabilitation" (K. Raghu Ram, 2006: 222).

The policy transfer is also apparent even in the context of Land Acquisition Act; the latter has been used by different states, in the absence of a Compressive Resettlement Act, to acquire land for the national purpose. In this context policy transfer is visible in the following:[13] Notification of land to be acquired within specific time period; inviting public opinion before the acquition of land for the national purpose; payment of cash directly to the land loosers, while awarding compensation adding inflatory prices so as to give the landloosers particularly the farmers the market price etc.

Indian government including its different units at provincial level has formulated different rehabilitation policies. Some of the policies reflect the arguments of international agencies, particularly the World Bank, and ADB. In fact, National Policy on Resettlement and Rehabilitation for Project Affected Families, 2003 is one such policy which recognizes the need to minimize the displacement, including a dialogue for effective implementation of packages. However, this policy has come under sever contestation. Its first draft came in the year 1993 and many a time the same has been revised. This has been treated as regression from the earlier policy. This is because of the fact that earlier policy believed in "total rehabilitation". On the contrary the new Policy document does not fix a time frame for rehabilitation.[14] Further it limits each family to 500 in plain land and 250 in hilly region.

The central government in recent years has introduced a Scheduled Tribes (Recognition of Forest Rights) Bill; 2005—this is the first time that historical rights of the tribals have been recognized. This is where it comes closer to World Bank and United Nations; the latter recognizes the rights of indigenous population. Here is an attempt to rehabilitate the tribals in their own locality can be seen. Even different ministries have formulated different policies: in 1994, the Water Resource Ministry came out with "Draft Policy for the rehabilitation for reservoir project affected persons (Ministry of Water Resources, 1994).

There are different states too, which have introduced rehabilitation policies. Maharashtra, for example, has Maharashtra Rehabilitation Act, 1986, Karnataka has introduced Karnataka Resettlement of Project Displaced Persons Act, 1987, and, Orissa is now having Draft Resettlement and Rehabilitation Policy. (Manipadma Jena, 2006) Other states such as Bihar, Madhya Pradesh, Gujarat, Punjab, and Andhra Pradesh too have resettlement policy. Here the policies try to be comprehensive so as to minimize the agony of displacement. Some states have further liberalized their policies. [15]Gujarat and Madhya Pradesh falls into this category. In other states the issues of land general or project-specific directives basically govern acquisition and resettlement. Other than that there are sectoral policies (e.g., Coal India Ltd., Maharashtra State Electricity Board) and several parastatal policies (National Thermal Power Corporation).

All these shows the policy transfers from international to national and then to the local. It shows that the concern for the rehabilitation is not only confined to locality but also a growing international phenomenon. All these do not mean that the policy transfer from international to national or to local has completely changed the lifestyle of the ethnic groups including the fact that it has enhanced the Social and Human Development of Displaced. Only in some cases the social and Human Development has increased. This is visible in those places wherein governance has become effective, accountable, and responsive. For example, in the case of Almatti Project the Human and Social Development of all the social categories has increased. This is not the same with some social categories such as Scheduled Tribes in other parts of India. It is observed that "There is a relative difference of 32 per cent between the human development indices (HDI) at the national level and those of Scheduled Tribes,—this became a fact mainly due to the loss of productive resources to the construction of dams and mining (The Hindu: April 29, 2006). Barring one or two cases in majority of the cases studies point towards the increasing impoverishment of the Displaced persons (Walter Fernanades, 2001: 88). There are reasons why such a trend is growing.

Firstly, the received policies have not been able to focus on the major issues. One important issue is the absence of recognizing the community land. In fact, the land, which has been acquired under Land Acquisition Act of 1894, recognizes only the individual Patta than the community right. It is true that there are large number of tribals who have been living inside the National Parks are without any title deeds. The Wild Life Act of

1972, for example, has either converted them as "encroachers" or non 'titled" categories. This situation has made the task of large-scale displacement much easier.

Secondly, ineffective governance including the fact that deviation from received policies has further marginalized the already marginalized ethnic groups. This is apparent whenever the displaced have been rehabilitated in far off places, wherein the economic opportunities are not available. In many places, such as National Park or Dam (Kabini, Rajiv Gandhi National Park) the displaced have been rehabilitated in such places wherein they would not get anything for their own sustainability. They have been rehabilitated in barren or dry land or far off places from their original habitat. There are hardly any employment opportunities available in the newly rehabilitated places. The new places have become centers of cultural crisis, centers for identity crisis including the crisis of the self. Many a time the rehabilitations packages are defeated, and in the process tribals or displaced are further marginalized.

Thirdly, absence of political commitments also defeats the rehabilitations. Given the slow nature of functioning of bureaucracy or the government, the packages are seldom introduced in one go or in meaningful way. Most of the time packages are announced as a political gimmick or ploy rather than due to the real concern. This is the reason why the packages take years to reach the affected one (classic case is the case of Kudremukh National Park in Karnataka wherein Karnataka government thrice declared packages to contain Naxalites, however it is yet to reach the tribals living inside the National Park).

Most important is the power relations. This has further placed the displaced in disadvantageous position. Given their relative weak nature, the displaced ethnic groups have not been able to demand effectively for their rehabilitation. Whenever they demanded their rights, displaced have been treated as those challenging the edifice of the state or political structure. Some time they are branded as radicals supporting the cause of Naxalites. This has increased the friction between the state on the one hand and the ethnic groups on the other.

However the policies have no clear-cut idea about the growing poverty. Poverty is not only rooted in the absence of a comprehensive rehabilitation policy, but also in the hold-over land. In many places the issue of land has become contentious issue—the tribals are demanding the right over land; the other ethnic groups are also demanding adequate land. Recognizing the historical right over land would help in alleviating the poverty level of tribals.

However if there is any definition of poverty, lack of entitlement, calories intake, purchasing power, distribution of land etc. all these definitions of poverty will suit large number of displaced, especially thwe ethnic groups. It is here the paradox of development lies–on one side it should help protect and alleviate the ethnic or tribals from their poverty level, and on the other it should help in development. It does not do both the things simultaneously. Large number of displaced ethnic groups still struggle to retain their identity, struggle to "enlist" their presence in the political discourses and struggle to remain as social categories.

NOTES

1. http://www.infochangeindia.org/analysis33.jsp
2. http://www.landaction.org/display.php? Article=59
3. There is one more estimate- 85.39 lakh tribals have been displaced since 1990
4. http://www.idpproject.org/Sites/IdpProjectDb/idpSurvey.nsf/wViewSingleEnv/IndiaProfile+Summary
5. http://www.fmreview.org/text/FMR/08/08.htm
6. It is estimated that the number of persons displaced by the Hirakud dam was between 1.1 lakh and 1.6 lakh. This is the estimate of an individual scholar. On the contrary the official figures are only 1.1 lakh. Interestingly World Bank accept the fact that as many as many as 0.6 million people who are displaced out of 192 projects of big have not been accounted for in project planning. Meanwhile it also states that each time a new dam constructed it displaces 13,000 population
7. Tenth Five Year Plan, p. 458
8. http://rural.nic.in/rrpolicy.doc
9. http://web.worldbank.org/WBSITE/EXTERNAL/TOPICS/ENVIRONMENT/EXTBIODIVERSITY/0,menuPK: 400959~pagePK: 149018~piPK: 149093~theSitePK: 400953,00.html
10. http://www.ieo.org/world-c13-p2.html
11. See Manibelli Declaration http://www.ieo.org/world-c13-p2.html
12. http://www.adb.org/Documents/Handbooks/Resettlement/consultation00.asp
13. http://www.his.com/~mesas/resindia.htm
14. http://www.infochangeindia.org/analysis33.jsp
15. Now the Gujarat government has recognized the major sons as joint holders. Even it is preparing to give to two hectares of land for encroachers, including the landless agricultural labourers, it is now allotting one ha agricultural land to each of the landless outstees. Madhya Pradesh is now advancing Rs 40,000 for all the outstees particularly landless agricultural labourers, SCs/STs Even it has declared major unmarried daughters as separate family. See http://www.nvda.nic.in/policies.htm

REFERENCES

1. http://www.infochangeindia.org/analysis33.jsp
2. http://www.adb.org/Documents/Handbooks/Resettlement/consultation00.asp
3. http://www.infochangeindia.org/analysis33.jsp
4. http://www.landaction.org/display.php?article=59
5. http://www.idpproject.org/Sites/IdpProjectDb/idpSurvey.nsf/wViewSingleEnv/IndiaProfile+Summary
6. http://www.fmreview.org/text/FMR/08/08.htm
7. http://rural.nic.in/rrpolicy.doc
8. http://web.worldbank.org/WBSITE/EXTERNAL/TOPICS/ENVIRONMENT/EXTBIODIVERSITY/0,,menuPK:400959~pagePK:149018~piPK:149093~theSitePK:400953,00.html.
9. Anthony Nedly, *Policy Transfer and the Developing Country Experience Gap: Taking a Southern Perspective*, see http://www.york.ac.uk/depts/poli/news/sem3esrc/nedley.pdf#search='policy%20transfer'.

10. B.K. Sinha and H.C. Pokhriyal, 2001, "Rehabilitation in Tehri DAM: An Evaluation," *Social Change*, Vol. 31, No.1&2, March-June, pp. 110-143.

11. Bansuri Thakkar Taneja and, Himanshu *Large Dams and Displacement in India*, Document Serial No: SOC166; n.d.

12. Cernea, M.M.1995. "Understanding and Preventing Impoverishment from Displacement", *Social Action,* Vol. 45, No. 3, pp. 261-76.

13. Cernea, M.M., *Involuntary Settlement in Development Projects*, World Bank Technical Paper No. 80.

14. Ganguly Thukaral, et al, 1995, "Dams and the Displaced in India": in Hari Mohan Mathur Ed, *Development and Rehabilitation: Focus on Asian Experience*, New Delhi, Vikas, pp. 93-112.

15. Hari Modi, 2006, 'Managing Resettlement in India: Approaches, Issues and Experiences" *Journal of Refugee Studies.* 19: 264-267.

16. J. Bandyopadhya, B. Mallik, M. Mandal and S. Perveen, 2002, *Report on a policy dialogue on Dams and Development,* Indian Institute of Management, Calcutta, July.

17. Ministry of Rural Development, 2001, *Empowering the Scheduled Tribes For Tenth Five Plans*".

18. Ministry of Water Resources, 2002, *National Water Policy,* April (New Delhi).

19. P. Raghu Ram, 2006, Rehabilitation and the Rights of the Displaced Persons: A Study of Public Policy in Karnataka, (Unpublished Thesis), JNU, CPS/SSS, and New Delhi.

20. Planning Commission, 2001, *Report of the Steering Committee on Empowering the Scheduled Tribes For Tenth Five Year Plans"* New Delhi.

21. Shripad Dharmadhikary, 2001, Displacement, Development and Large Dams, *Social Change*, March-June, Vol. 31, Nos 1 & 2, pp. 104-109.

22. Smitu Kothari, 1998, "Development, Displacement and Official Policies: A Critical Review, *Lokayana Bulletin,* Vol. 11, No. 5, pp. 9-28.

23. Smitu Kothari, 1995, Development and Displacement: Whose Nation Is It? "*PCDForum Column #77*, Release Date July 10.

24. Walter Fernandes and Mohammad Asif, 1997, *Development Induced Displacement in Orissa 1951-1985: A Data Base on its Extent and Nature*, Indian Social Institute, New Delhi.

25. Walter Fernandes et al, 1989. "The Extent and Prospects of Displacement " *Social Action,* Vol. 38 July–Sept., pp. 264-79.

26. Walter Fernandes et al, 2001, *Development Induced Displacement, Deprivation and Rehabilitation in Andhra Pradesh, 1951-1995 A Quantitative and Qualitative Study of Its extent and nature*, ISI, New Delhi.

27. Walter Fernandes, 2001, "Development Induced Displacement and Sustainable Development, *Social Change*, March-June, 2001, Vol. 31, Nos. 1 & 2, pp. 87-103.

28. World Bank, 1993, *Early Experience with Involuntary Resettlement Overview,* Washington DC, World Bank.

29. The World Bank, 1996, Staff Appraisal Report, *India, Eco Development Project.*

Human Rights, Marriage, Woman and Anthropology

—Alok Chantia

Every creature begins its life with nature but human being became distinct, when he formed an artificial nature for his protection and needs in the form of culture. Among all cultural peculiarities marriage is his diversified effort which regulates sexual behavior according to circumstances. Culture as first effort of human being for smooth survival may be assigned as human rights which were assured from nature. This journey was continued until nation/state concept came. This concept further developed with the protection of human rights. Since 1948, the United Nations has been promoting and codifying human rights through the Universal Declaration of Human Rights, which is a common standard of achievement for all peoples and nations. Over the years the concept of human rights has continuously expanded. The first generation concept of political and civil rights, having been broadened with the input of socialist states and states of third world, to incorporate a wide range of economic social and cultural rights, a right to development and the right of indigenous people. This ongoing effort to establish a global human community based on universal and evolving standard of human decency, morality and dignity is considered a significant achievement. (Messer 1993).

Anthropologists have been selectively involved in these discussions given the initial insistence on cultural relativism, anthropologists generally resisted the universal formulation of the concept of human rights. Gradually, however, they moved from the criticism of universalism and expanded the scope of human rights, filling in the content in the changed circumstances. Human rights are problematic in their own way and broaden the international discourse on human rights. They contributed to this continuing effort in two ways: First by providing cross cultural research on the twin questions of 'what are right' and the concept of 'womanhood', that is "who is counted as a full person or human being entitled to enjoy them"; and second by inquiring into multiple source of human right violation and monitoring compliance with human rights standards mainly by highlighting violations or abuse (ibid).

In the process, these studies have also inquired into whether the religion and societal notions (or ideologies) of behavior and rights in different societies confirm or come in conflict with the secular and universalistic approach of human rights. The perspective generally incorporated non-legal or extra-legal approaches to human rights and identified the religious and social code of behavior that identified the religious and social code of behavior that conflicted with or supported the universal rights. In this context some have considered the UN human rights framework to be the particular expression of secular humanists against which other religions and social perspectives are examined and compared (ibid).

In this paper an attempt has been made to evaluate the impact of Universal Declaration of Human Rights which ensures dignified life, equality before law and liberty and practice of polyandary in global perspective, while focusing on tribal women.

Marriage is a social institution that formalizes certain aspects of the relationship between males and females. It is an institution that evolves in us deep seated emotions about questions of right and wrong, good and evil, and traditional versus modern. Within families, arguments may be about what is appropriate premarital behavior? What is a proper marriage ceremony and how long a marriage should last? Although these arguments may be traumatic for parents and their off springs from a cross cultural perspective, they generally involve minor deviations from the cultural norms. In contrast anthropology text-books describe an amazing variety of marriage systems that fulfill biological and social functions. This selection will show just how different things could be. Many types of marriage are in practice across the globe but polyandry and polygyny are slight different because these make an analysis of woman's place in the men's world regarding human right which encompasses the soul of dignified and free life.

In an example of Tibet, the form of marriage—'fraternal polyandry' in anthropological parlance—is one of the world's rarest forms of marriage but is not uncommon in Tibetan society, where it has been practiced from time immemorial. For many Tibetan social strata, it traditionally represented the ideal form of marriage and family. The mechanics of fraternal polyandry are simple, two, three, four, five or more brothers jointly take a wife who leaves her home to live with them. Generally marriage is arranged by parents, women can't deny to accept such marriage traditionally. The eldest brother is normally dominant in terms of authority that is, in managing the household, but all the brothers share the work and participate as sexual partner, off springs are treated similarly. There is no attempt to link children biologically to any particular brother, and a brother shows no favoritism towards his child even if he knows he is real father. He loves every child equally. In some respect Tibetan polyandry and others across the globe are thus in many ways analogous to the way primogeniture functioned in nineteenth century England. Primogeniture dictated that the eldest son inherited the family while younger sons had to leave home and seek their own employment for example, in the military or the clergy. Primogeniture maintained family estates intact over generations permitting only one heir per generation. Fraternal polyandry also accomplishes this but does so by keeping all the brothers together with just one wife so that there is only one set of heirs per generation.

Two reasons have commonly been offered for the perpetuation of fraternal polyandry in Tibet : That Tibetans practice female infanticide and therefore have to marry polyandrous, owing to a shortage of females; and that Tibet lying at extremely high altitudes is so barren and bleak that Tibetans would starve without resort to this mechanism. Both explanations are wrong however, not only has there never been institutionalized female infanticide in Tibet, but Tibetan society gives female considerable rights including inheriting the family estate in the absence of brothers. In such cases, the woman takes a bridegroom who comes to live in her family and adopts her family's name and identity. Morever there is no demographic evidence of a shortage of females up to 1974, many adult females were unmarried (Goldstein 1976). The second reason is also incorrect, the climate in Tibet is extremely harsh and ecological factors do play a major role perpetuating polyandry, but polyandry is not a means of preventing starvation. It is characteristic, not of the forest segments of the society, but rather of the peasant land owning families.

In the old society, the landless poor could not realistically aspire to prosperity, but they did not fear starvation. There was a persistent labour shortage throughout Tibet, and very poor families with little or no land and few animals could subsist through agricultural labour, tenant farming, craft occupations such as carpentry, or by working as servants. An alternative reason for the persistence of fraternal polyandry is that it reduces population growth (and thereby reduces the pressure on resources by relegating some females to life-time spinsterhood. In his study Godstein has pointed out logically sex ratio among Tibetans who practice polyandry. Fraternal polyandrous marriages averaged 2.35 men per woman and not surprisingly, 31 per cent of the females of child bearing age (twenty to fortynine) were unmarried. These spinsters either continued to live at home, set up their own households, or worked as servants for other families. They could also become Buddhist nuns. Being unmarried is not synonymous with exclusion from the reproductive pool. Discreet extramarital relationships are tolerated, and actually half of the adult unmarried women in time (Tibet) had one or more children. While Polyandry helps regulate population, this function of Polyandry is not consciously by Tibetans and is not the reason they consistently choose it.

When all above reasons are not true explanations of practice of polyandry among Tibetans, what motivates brothers to opt for this system of marriage? From the perspective of the younger brother in a land holding families, the main incentive is the attainment or maintenance of the good life. He can expect a more secure and higher standard of living with access not only to his family's land and animals, but also to its inherited collection of cloths, jewelry, rugs, saddles and horse. Among all these pleasures Tibetans regulate their life around the latent sacrifice of a woman who surrenders all her liberty, freeness, psychological pressure free life and her sole identity as human being. (ibid.)

Apart from Tibetan polyandry example when we focus African continent from where human evolution took its place and pace, women get pressure to regulate culture on their shoulders. Ford and Beach (1951), found that in 84 per cent of the 185 cultures they studied, men were permitted to have more than one wife at a time, whereas Anthropologists tell us that monogamy is the norm around the world (Fisher 1992) In her many years of study, Sudarkasa (1982) pointed out African social organization, it is her opinion that widespread in Africa is the preference for a system of co-wives rather than one, where women bear children outside of marriage or where women may choose to live as childless (Spinsters). Many studies in African continent on practice of polygyny (Ware 1979, Lwanga 1976, Maiden 1989-1992, Moller and Welch 1990) reveal that African continent is an evidence of many tribal groups. Zulu of Southern Africa is one of those, who practice polygyny.

In the process of acculturation, modernization it is not easy to practice polygyny. Polygyny has become more problematic in today's deteriorating economic climate. Many men still want the respect they can gain by having many wives and children, but women emphasize the difficulties of polygyny due to a shortage of land and labour and an increasing need for money for school fees, clothing, labour and food. (Whyte, 1980) Whyte has pointed out that Polygyny has never been popular with women. It is even less so at present because the resources of individual men are becoming less adequate. Thus, there is an increase in competition for the already scarce resources of the Polygynous husband. (ibid.)

One of the frequently mentioned circumstances resulting in Polygyny is the practice of labour migration, in which many African travel away their home areas in search of cash income. For these men, Polygyny provides a solution to the problem of being required to spend lengthy periods away from their home families. Thus one wife may visit the husband in town while the other one cares for rural homestead. Polygynist wives may also share labour and keep each other company in the rural area when the husband is away (Meller and Welch 1990).

How does react a woman about polygyny? And how much she desires for it, is explained in Perlez (1991) study. "She reports about an African postgraduate student in French at Nairobi University and a former school teacher. She sees herself ten years from now as a single parent with a male companion, but not a husband. She points out, that this is a choice made not only by herself but by many of her over 30 female friends with occupations ranging from television producers to professors. For example many educated women are delaying marriage; more than half of the 16 female law graduates of Nairobi University are still single. She admonishes that traditionally, men looked after their women, but today the average man contributes to the rent if one is lucky while using the rest for mistresses and beer. According to Perlez, anecdotal evidence from Kenya abounds concerning professional women who have been previously married but have left their husbands because they can't tolerate the restrictions imposed by these men, eventually these women seek a relationship of some kind with a Man. African postgraduate lady points out that it is difficult to raise a child without the financial help of a man. By the age of 35, however, most of her economically self sufficient, single, female friends have decided to have children even though they are married. Some choose to have a child by a younger man because he is less likely to "boss them around" than would an older man". Women possess a pressure which she compensates with bearing cultural value system. Polyandry or polygyny is nothing but encroachment of liberty of men is woman's life which creates question mark on the real meaning of dignified life and equality.

The Indian peninsula contains a total of 437 tribal groups, out of which 40 are polyandrous. They can be classified as 28 being fraternal polyandrous, 5 are non-fraternal polyandrous, 7 are mixture polyandrous. But polyandry in the Himalayan region of Garhwal is well-known to every-one. It is also a matter of discussion that most tribal groups are engaged in agriculture. So tribal should be included in the rural society. Due to heavy population, scarcity of food, unemployment, tribalization has increased. In 1967, the government declared Khasa as a tribe in the light of their queer characteristic polyandry. After seeing the parameter-polyandry, in deciding a group as a tribe, the people of an adjacent area of Khasa tribe declared themselves a tribe with a strange name *Jaunsar Bawar*. While Dr. Majumdar described only one tribe in Garhwal Himalaya, (*i.e.,* Khasa), who engaged in polyandry.

Jaunsar Bawar lies in the Chakrata tehsil of district Dehradun, Jausarr lies in the Dhanaulti tehsil of Tehri district and Rawain in the Purola and Barkot tehsil of Uttarkashi district. Lying adjacent to each other, these tracts constitute a geographic-cultural chunk of polyandry in the Garhwal Himalaya in Uttaranchal. They lie in an inaccessible mountainous terrain, the topographical regions of which make life exacting, and as assumed in the academics of polyandry functional.

Here it is notable that the inhabitants of Jaunsar Bawar are a Schedule Tribe, but not those of Rawain Jaunpur though like the former, they also practice polyandry and are structured in a similar caste-stratification. In Chakrata tehsil of Dehradun, the local caste structure is discernible into three stratification levels, *i.e.,* the upper (land-owning castes–Rajputs and Brahmins), the middle (artisan castes—Nath, Bajgi, Mistri and Lohar), and the lower (unclean castes–Kolta, Chamar and Dom). Among these, the castes of the upper and the lower levels are more numerous than those of the middle level. They also show a higher incidence of polyandry. Because of these changes, this correlation between caste-structure and polyandry is now changing, though not evenly.

Jaunsar Bawar claims their association with the Pandavas. Is it true? Do women normally union with several husbands? In the *Mahabharat,* Draupadi is *bahubhartrika,* but not Subhadra, the second wife of Arjuna. Other wives whom the Pandava brothers individually, like Hidimba (Bhim's wife), were also not shared. Only Draupadi was shared by common consent. The inhabitants of these tracts claim spiritual and mythical affinity with the Pandava of the *Mahabharata*. The Pandava dance and the worship of Draupadi in certain areas in the biannual ritual celebration (at the time of each harvest) evidently symbolize this relationship. But here, unlike Draupadi, the wife is not won in a competition of archery. Nor has she the right to *swayamvar* as such. She is rather purchased and shared as a wife.

A comparison of the similarities and variations in the practices of polyandry in the Rawain Jaunpur and Jaunsar Bawar throws much light on the ways of polyandry, its dynamics and a woman's place in it. Jaunsar Bawar show a higher incidence (48.3%) of polyandry than the Rawain Jaunpur (30.56%).

Disparity of the sexes is wider in Jaunsar Bawar, here being 820 females for 1000 males, as against 996.56 females for 1000 males in the Rawain Jaunpur. The correlation between wider disparity of sexes and higher incidence of polyandry is obvious, though not casual. Showing a wider disparity of sexes, the castes of the middle level don't register a corresponding higher incidence of polyandry. In Rawain Jaunpur, two brothers generally born one after another, generally share one, two or three wives. In Jaunsar Bawar, two to five brothers have been found sharing one to four wives.

Both in Jaunsar Bawar and the Rawain Jaunpur, a woman has to compensate her husband, if she forces the dissolution of marriage. Even a widow has to acquire freedom to remarry, by compensating her deceased husband's family-in certain cases, even her son. In Jaunsar Bawar, she compensates for the expenses incurred on marrying her and in Rawain Jaunpur for the price paid for her. Sometimes, expenses incurred on the wife's maintenance and treatment may also be demanded and added to the compensation charged. Depending on the negotiations and consequent agreement, interest on the amount of bride price paid and/or on the expenses incurred in marriage may also be charged.

In all these tracts, a daughter is viewed as an asset of her father, a wife of her husband and a widowed woman of her son and the deceased husband's family. In the exigencies of life, to look to her father, brother and brother's son is a woman's privilege, which is honoured as her right. The tradition allows a woman the right to remarry, but the traditional liability to compensate the husbands, she divorces *(choot ka paisa dena)* also constraints this right. She plays a vigorous role in the local household and agricultural economy. Yet she is viewed as impure and, like an untouchable is denied temple entry.

The worldwide view about woman is a more meaningful social reality relating to woman in polyandry. Woman is a dependable source of labour needed for agriculture and household work. She is needed to procreate sons, for whom there is definite preference. She is a possession, an asset. As a daughter, she is to be given in marriage for a price. As wife she can be fraternally shared like land, if brothers sharing her agree to do so. This also explains sexual sharing of a set of wives by a set of brothers, though wives may be brought and kept in the individual names of the brothers.

Why polyandry? The question is not purely academic, when examined in the perspective of *dam vivah* and woman's place in it and in polyandry. The directive principles of Indian Constitution relating to uniform civil code and the amelioration of the weaker sections (to which women belong) lead to this question as its political undertones. It is said "polyandry is a functional consequence of disparity of sexes, scarcity of land, difficult mountainous terrain, labour intensive agriculture, coupled with sheep and goat rearing and domestication of cattle. This setting necessitates joint living at the level of household, of which sharing of wife is the most outstanding feature." The growing politics of being polyandrous tribal is a consequence of that, on the basis of polyandry and the claim of not practicing Hinduism and untouchability. The elite of Jaunsar Bawar could wrest for the region, the political status of Scheduled Tribe under an irrelevant fragile title, the Jaunsari tribe—and the advantages of protective discrimination flowing there from (Bhoria 1975). This smacks of a muffled political compromise on the woman's status as *bahubhartrika.*

However, this political move has been challenged since then, the status of a Scheduled Tribe for all the Jaunsari, it is pointed out, promotes the interest of the elitist castes (the Brahmin and the Rajput) at the cost of those of the middle and the lower strata, the have-nots. Since then, a bill has also been pending to exclude the Brahmin and the Rajput from the status of Scheduled Tribe. To retain the status of Schedule Tribe, the elite in Jaunsar Bawar lift arguments from the writing of academicians. They argue that the custom of polyandry or making woman *bahubhartrika* is functional to the social economy. It need not be disturbed, meaning thereby that their status as a Scheduled Tribe should be secured. Following the Jaunsaris, the inhabitants of Rawain Jaunpur have also been demanding and politically lobbying for the status of Scheduled Tribe.

In this politics, a woman's position as *bahubhartrika* and problems associated there with get relegated to the background. It is tending to reinforce polyandry as a vested elitist interest. The crumbling facade of polyandry has tended to become a sort of political lever to retain or attain the status of Scheduled Tribe. In the light of status of woman of the Garhwal Himalaya in a polyandrous society, women suffered due to the judgment of Supreme Court. In case of *Dr. Surajmani* vs. *Durgacharan* 2001 (42) ALR-847, in which the honorable judge said, "Hindu Marriage Act, 1955 covers whole India, but those groups are excluded who do their marriage with special custom". In this regard polyandry cannot be challenged. So the whole geographical chunk of Garhwal Himalaya for polyandry has been protected by court. But this judgment makes worse the position of those women who are not tribal but practicing polyandry (Brahmin and Rajput). This is a real picture of rural woman in the Garhwal Himalaya, who are the victim of customs, politics and the judiciary.

All these three examples from different geographic and culture show a comparative position of woman across the globe in the light of anthropology and "Human Right".

REFERENCES

1. Bhatt, G.S. (1992): *Women in Polyandry in Rawain and Jaunpur.* Jaipur, Rawat Publications.
2. Bhona, K.S., (1975): The Case of Jaunsaries as a Scheduled Tribe. *Journal of Lal Bahadur* Shastri, National Academy of Administration, XX (2).
3. Bierreman, G.G., (1963): *Hindus of the Himalayas.* Bombay, Oxford.
4. Majumdar, D.N., (1944): *The Fortunes of Primitive Tribes.* Lucknow, Universal Publishers.
5. Messer, Ellen (1993): Anthropology and Human Rights quoted in the *Hindu Social System & Human Rights of Dalits* by Sukhadeo Thorat, 2004, Critical Quest, New Delhi.
6. Melvyn C. Goldstein (1987): When Brothers Share A Wife. *Natural History,* Vol. 96 No. 3 American Museum of Natural History, N.Y.

7. Fisher, H.E. (1992): *Anatomy of Love: The Natural History of Monogamy, Adultery and Divorce*, W.W. Norton and Company, New York.
8. Ford, C and F. Beach (1951): *Pattern of Sexual Behavior*. Harper & Row, New York.
9. Lawanger, G. (1976): *Report on the Health Education of Clan Health Workers*. Nangina Hospita,. Nangina, Kenya.
10. Moller, V and G.H. Welch (1990)—Polygamy, Economics Security and Well Being of Retired Zulu Migrant Workers, *Journal of Cross Cultural Gerontology*, vol. 5, pp. 205-216, New York.
11. Mulder M. (1989)—Polygyny and the Extent of Women's Contributions to Subsistence: A Role to White, *American Anthropologist*, 91: 178-180, N.Y.
12. Mulder M. (1992)—Women's Strategies in Polygynous Marriage, *Human Nature* 3(1) : 45-70, N.Y.
13. Perlez., J. (1991)—*Elite Kenyan Women Avoid a Rite : Marriage*, The New York Times March 3, p. 14.
14. Sudarkasa, N. (1982)—African and Agro American Family Structure In *Anthropolgy for the Eighties* (ed.) J. Cole, p. 132-16, Free Press, New York.
15. Ware. H. (1979)—Polygyny, Women's Views in a Traditional Society, Nigeria 1975. *Journal of Marriage and the Family* (1): 185-195.
16. Whyte. S. (1980)—*Wives and Co-wives in Marachi*, Kenya Folk 21-22, 134-136.
17. Kilbridge, P.L. and J.K. Kilbridge (1990)—*Changing Family Life in East Africa Women and Children at Risk*. University Park Pennsylvania State, University Press.

Development of Weaker Sections and Panchayat Raj Institutions: New Dimension for Political Anthropology?

—G. Sreeramulu and V. Rama Krishna

The present paper intends to discuss the theoretical aspects of panchayat raj system in India in general and the growth of PRIs in Karnataka in particular. It also focuses on the provisions for the involvement of weaker sections in PRI's after the 73rd Amendment Act, in the development process and political participation. It analyses the status of weaker sections in the institutions of PRI's in Gulbarga district. The objectives of this paper are to discuss the status of weaker sections in panchayat raj institutions and in the process of development. It also intends to discuss the implementation of welfare policies through the representatives of weaker sections. In order to assess the effective functioning of weaker section's representatives in panchayat raj institutions and the involvement after 1993 Act of Karnataka, the case study and analytical methods have been employed in this study. In the study the collected sample is 75 in total, covering of 3 type's panchayat raj institutions. Thus, the paper focuses on the political participation of weaker sections in the process of development in Gulbarga district through the Panchayat Raj Institutions in Karnataka.

Introduction

The political participation of weaker sections in panchayat raj institutions i.e. Zilla Panchayats, Taluk Panchayats and Village Panchayats facilitated for the involvement of weaker sections in the process of development. In the state of Karnataka the two major panchayat raj Acts (1983 and 1993) were designed in accordance with rural development and for the involvement of weaker sections in the institutions of panchayat raj institutions. The act of 1983 was to bring about more meaningful developmental plans, in which mass participation of the rural population was assumed. The act of 1993 was designed in tune with the rural development by providing reservation provisions to weaker sections.

Since from the India's independence the Government of India made many attempts for developing its people *i.e.,* educationally, socially, and culturally. As the Government of India has been preparing and implementing a number of policies and programmes for its integrated development. On the other hand, the evaluation reports of all these programmes viewed that, the intensified development has not taken place. And at the same time, some sections of society developed in the areas such as educationally, socially, culturally and politically. But the weaker sections are far behind, the reasons are more. The foremost reason for the backwardness of these weaker sections is political. The opportunities and involvement of these sections in politics comparatively to the higher sections of society is very low. In a democratic state like India, the political actions are related to development. Since, the developmental policies and programmes are being formulated in state legislatures and in Parliament and the involvement of weaker sections in these institutions are very less. The policies and programmes for the development of these sections might not been formulated and implemented by the upper castes. By recognizing these lacunas after the 73rd Amendment Act the political participation of weaker sections was provided. Through this Act, the weaker sections are entering into the institutions of Panchayat Raj, and thus, they are formulating and implementing the schemes and programmes for the development of weaker sections.

Panchayat Raj Institutions in Karnataka

If we look the major objectives of Local Bodies which are working since from the number of years in the country. One could ascertain that there was an attempt to achieve the development. Therefore, it is necessary to evaluate the provisions of different acts pertaining to the working of local bodies time to time.

Before reorganization of Karnataka state on linguistic basis, the parts of state were under Mysore state, Madras presidency, the Bombay presidency, and the state of Hyderabad. In all parts the local Governments were working *i.e.,* under Mysore Local Bodies Act of 1902. There were three tier structures of Union Panchayat, Taluk Boards, and District Boards. In princely Mysore state the local governments were given limited powers. In these two provisions to some extent there was the provision of rural development with the involvement of weaker sections.

Under Madras Presidency, the Local governments were established by the Madras District Boards Acts, 1920 and in the Madras Panchayat Act, 1920. These Acts facilitated only two tier systems of local governments *i.e.,* District Boards were relating to education public health maintenance of roads etc. It is evident that all these powers are to concentrate on local problems and thus to achieve rural development. In the Bombay presidency the local governments were established and further enlarged by series of amendments. Such as the Bombay Village Panchayat Act, 1920 facilitated the introduction of panchayat raj system in Bombay presidency. The other acts were 1928, 1933, 1939 and 1947. These acts extended for the local bodies with the powers to supervise and the control of primary and secondary education.

After independence, the development of panchayat raj institutions in Karnataka has taken place in different phases. The recommendations of Balwantroy Mehta Committee and the implementation of its reports provided a new impetus and a new rationale for panchayat raj. Based on the recommendations of the Balwant Rai Mehta Committee, the government of Mysore enacted a new legislation in 1959 called as "the act facilitated for the three tier system of panchayat raj institutions in Karnataka." There are 1. Village Panchayat 2. Taluk Board (these two are with directly elected representative's), the third one was the Constitution of the District Development Council (CDC, nominated members). This act further authorized with the powers and assigned functions only to village panchayat and taluk development board. The functions of village panchayats were limited and powers of levying some local taxes were also assigned. On the other hand the primary powers and functions were assigned to taluk development board (TDB). The TDB's with the intention of achieving rural development through TDB's the act provided powers to TDB's for collecting revenue. Unless and until the power of levying to taxes through the rural developmental programmes would not be implemented. The financial powers of the TDB's were to meet the needs of rural areas only. TDB's were empowered to levy a surcharge on stamp duty. The state government transferred 50 per cent of land revenue collected in the local area and 10 per cent of total collection of land revenue in the state to these local bodies. During this period there was considerable popular enthusiasm among the people towards PRI's. It is mainly because of satisfactory functions carried by PRI's and these PRI's were able to make people including weaker sections to participate actively in developmental process.

Weaker Section's Involvement in PRI's

The term 'Weaker Sections' has been defined differently by different authorities. The study group on the welfare of weaker sections was of the view that "we should not however, be wrong if the agriculture labours, petty cultivators and village artisans also constitute weaker sections". As a matter of fact the value the weaker sections consist of all such people who because of socio-political, socio-religious reasons, have become suppressed, depressed and oppressed.

The people of the weaker sections are those who are subject to both social and economic disabilities and are denied the opportunities to equip themselves to participate in administrative, political, social and cultural affairs. Weaker sections consist of vulnerable groups of society needing special care and protection. They are the alienated section of the society. For the purpose of the present study the SCs, STs and OBCs as identified by the Government of Karnataka are taken as the weaker sections of the society.

The Karnataka Panchayati Raj system based on 1983 Act has been recognized as important in making effort in the process of democratic decentralization. Firstly, the Act give status and stature to the panchayat raj bodies, secondly, the Act entrust the Panchayati Raj bodies with all those welfare, development and civic functions and responsibilities. Thirdly, the Act equips Panchayati Raj bodies with resources by way of budgetary support and staff, fourthly, the Act entrusted powers to perform the entrusted functions satisfactorily with statutory autonomy of decision-making, and fifthly, the Act also called for involvement in socio-economic rural development with distributive justice.[5]

As per the amendment Act of 1993, following are the reservation provisions provided for weaker sections in PRIs:

1. Reservation of seats in favour of SCs and STs in proportion of their population subject to minimum of 15 to 3 per cent respectively in all levels.
2. Reservation of 1/3 of seats for women at all levels.
3. Reservation of 1/3 of seats to persons belonging to backward classes.
4. Reservation of 1/3 of seats in each category (SCs, STs and Backward classes and general) at all levels for women.
5. The office of the chairpersons and Deputy Chairpersons are also reserved at all levels for persons belonging to SCs, STs and OBC and women.[6]

As a result of 73rd Constitutional Amendment and the subsequent Panchayati Raj Acts in 1993, the Karnataka Government extended the reservation of seats in PRIs to people belonging to OBC and women on par with SCs and STs. In fact this Act facilitated the political reservation for weaker section in all types of PRIs.

Need for Local Governments and Decentralized Development

The Local Government, both of indigenous and colonial forms, with certain exceptions had one common characteristic. Both were largely instruments for control concerned with the maintenance of status quo and collection of revenue and keeping captive forces in check respectively. Like national governments, local authorities have shifted their concern from law and order to the promotion of the general welfare of the community and thereby have become partners of the Governments in national/social and economic development. They are involved in projects that have distinctly political goals such as promoting popular participation in public affairs, those that were designed to spur economic development, and others that were clearly intended to bring about radical social change. They are changed with the equitable distribution of the fruits of economic and social development among all parts of the country. In short; they perform four-fold development functions in addition to the traditional regulatory functions:

(*i*) promotion of popular participation:

(*ii*) spurring of economic development;

(*iii*) social transformation; and

(*iv*) equitable distributions of the fruits of development.

Karnataka Panchayati Raj Act of 1993 and the Development

Karnataka State was one of the very few States in India to act early on obligation set by the 73rd Amendment Act.[8] In Karnataka an Act was passed in the year 1993 and accordingly a three tier panchayats (TP) at the taluka level and Gram Panchayats (GP) at the village level has been established in the year 1994 and 1995.

A large number of important functions have been assigned to the panchayats in Karnataka, under Karnataka Panchayat Raj Act 1993. Schedule I assigns 29 subjects to the GPs, Scheduled II assigns 28 functions to TPs and Schedule assigns 29 functions to VPs. These functions include basic amenities, infrastructure and development sectors like agriculture, horticulture, fisheries, health, education etc. In fact, the functions delegated to the PRIs include almost all the functions enumerated under 248 (G) of the Eleventh Schedule of the Constitution. The State government has transferred more than 400 states and centrally sponsored schemes to panchayats for implementation. All the three bodies should be elected bodies with appropriate powers and functions. These powers and functions are for greater participation of the people in all the three tier system of panchayat raj institutions and for more effective implementation of rural development programmes. The gram panchayat has to concentrate on the developmental activities as the function of gram panchayat will be carried out by the three standing committees. All the three standing committees are established in tune with the development and social justice in the village. They are 1. Production Committee 2. Social Justice Committee. 3. Amenities Committee.[11] The production committee was meant to perform functions related to agricultural production, animal husbandry, rural industries and poverty alleviation programmes. Second one was the social justice committee is meant to perform functions related to promotion of educational, economic, social, cultural and other interests of SC/ST's OBC's and welfare of women and children. Thirdly, the amenities committee is entrusted with functions in respect of education, public health, and public works. There is no doubt if the gram panchayats performs the responsibilities that were assigned to different standing committees definitely there will be an improvement in the areas of gram panchayat and thus rural development will take place.

The intermediatory tier of panchayat raj system is taluk panchayat, the 73rd act recognize the taluk panchayat as co-operating agency between Zilla panchayat and gram panchayat.[13] The most important function of taluk panchayat are relating to establishment, communications, building rural housing, village extension relief works and water supply. All these powers are also designed with the intention of attaining rural development only.

Another important body of panchayat raj system is Zilla parishad. The Zilla parishad performs the functions through its standing committees. There are (*a*) general standing committee (*b*) finance, audit and planning committee (*c*) social justice committee (*d*) education and health committee (*e*) agriculture and industries committee.

1. The general standing committee performs the functions which are assigned to general standing committee of taluk panchayats. But these are in accordance with the need of the entire district.

2. The finance and planning committee perform the functions relating to budget and through the plan priorities.

3. The social injustice committee performs functions relating to the promotion interests of SC/ST's, OBC, women and child particularly, protecting them from social injustice and exploitation.

4. The education and health committee performs the functions relating to education, adult literacy, cultural activities, health services, hospitals, water supply and family welfare.

5. The agriculture and industry committee performs the functions relating to agricultural production, animal husbandry, co-operation, soil conservation, village and cottage industries.

It is evident from the above functions of standing committees of Zilla panchayat, that all these are designed only to meet the problems of rural areas and to achieve the rural development through the Zilla panchayats.

Development Functions of PRI's

As per the 73rd Amendment Act the following are the developmental functions, which are transferred to the Eleventh Schedule of the Constitution. The following are added to the Eleventh Schedule:[15]

1. Agriculture, including Agricultural Extension.
2. Land Improvement, Implementation of Land Reforms, Land Consolidation and Soil Conservation.
3. Minor Irrigation, Water Management and Watershed Development.
4. Animal Husbandry, Dairying and Poultry.
5. Fisheries.
6. Social Forestry and Farm Forestry.
7. Minor Forest Produce.
8. Small Scale Industries, including Food Processing Industries.
9. Khadi, Village and Cottage Industries.
10. Rural Housing.
11. Drinking Water.
12. Fuel and Fodder.
13. Roads, Culverts, Bridges, Ferries, Waterways and other means of Communication.
14. Rural Electrification including Distribution of Electricity.
15. Non-Conventional Energy Sources.
16. Poverty Alleviation Programme.
17. Education, including Primary and Secondary Schools.
18. Technical Training and Vocational Education.
19. Adult and Non-Formal Education.
20. Libraries.
21. Cultural Activities.
22. Markets and Fairs.
23. Health and Sanitation, including Hospitals, Primary Health Centres and Dispensaries.
24. Family Welfare.

25. Women and Child Development.
26. Social Welfare, including Welfare of the Handicapped and Mentally Retarded.
27. Welfare of the Weaker Sections, and in particular, of the Scheduled Castes and the Scheduled Tribes.
28. Public Distribution System.
29. Maintenance of Community Assets.

Review of Related Literature

There are quite number of publications on the development of weaker sections such as political, educational, economic, cultural, social etc; along with the reports of various committees on political participation of weaker section in general and in particularly Panchayat Raj Institutions in Karnataka. Apart, from the publications made by the Government, a number of scholarly works have been carried out by individuals and institutions on *"Development of Weaker Sections Through Panchayat Raj Institutions: - A study in Karnataka"* at the national and also international level.

Though, several studies and research works have been conducted on the issue of development of weaker sections through Panchayat Raj Institutions in India, which focuses on the status and problems of weaker sections in the process of political participation and development. Thus, present study is entirely a different one comparatively to the studies carried out by other individuals and organizations.

Prabhat Datta (1998) is a collection of articles on grassroots development in India. It calls for decentralization of powers and functions and empowerment of the people. The 73rd Amendment Act which is widely recognized as a significant and mighty effort towards revitalization of Panchayats has been critically reviewed in the light of development in rural India. The review is conducted critically but constructively, having faith in the power of the people who are the real actors and change-agents.

Dhirendra Vajpeyi (1990), *"Local Government and Policies in the Third World: Issues and Trends"* is a collection of nine scholarly papers. These essays attempts to raise questions and analyze issues related to changes taking place in local governments in Asia and Africa. The authors realize that there are no easy answers to these crucial issues. However, there is also concern expressed here that success or failure of local level institutions would have serious implications for nation-building, political development, democratic decentralization, elite recruitment and policy formulation in the Third World. A quest for a common direction or broad vision is desired.

T.K. Lakshman, B.K. Narayan (1987) *"Rural development in India"* considers various issues and projects, the views of many writers on a wide variety of problems, such as neglected sectors in integrated rural development, planning and rural poverty, rural industrial development, rural assets accumulation, socio-economic typology of villages, land reforms, agricultural price policy, economic development of weaker sections, dairy development, rural education, evaluation programme of rural development. It also suggests the various steps that may be taken to ensure rural development in the eighties.

Nagendra Ambedkar (2000), in his book on *"Panchayat Raj at Work"*, explained the origins and growth of panchayat raj institution in India and structural patterns of panchayat raj in Rajasthan. The author also has given importance to electoral system of the local bodies. Further, he analyzed the socio-economic and political background of the panchayat raj elite, their perceptions and orientations of various issues, pertaining to the panchayat raj institutions; finally he analyzed the leadership in panchayats and the qualities, attitude of the leaders towards weaker section of the society.

Shymala (2001) conducted study on 594 Zilla Panchayat Members in Karnataka, of which 232 were females and 362 males. Specific purpose of the study was to know (a) socio-economic, political and cultural background of the members, and (b) their perceptions and aspirations about the working of Panchayats in relation to the expectations of the people and the villagers in general. However, the above mentioned studies have their fingers either to ideology, the social or economic problems of weaker sections. But the present study is focusing rightly on the attempts being made by the weaker section representatives in PRIs.

Objectives and Methodology

The objective of this paper is to discuss the development of weaker sections through the representatives of weaker sections in the institutions of panchayat raj. In order to assess the attempt of weaker sections representatives in the panchayat raj institutions for the development of weaker sections, the case study and analytical methods have been employed in this study.

Analysis

Figure 1 discusses the caste-wise distribution of representatives in Gram Panchayats in Gulbarga Taluk. Out of the total 645 representatives, the SCs are 233, STs 126, OBCs 115 and 171 are from General category. Among the general category there are representatives belonging to weaker sections also. It is observed in the figure that more than 73.49 per cent representatives are from weaker sections. Therefore in Gulbarga Taluk the developmental programmes intended for the welfare of weaker sections are being implemented successfully.

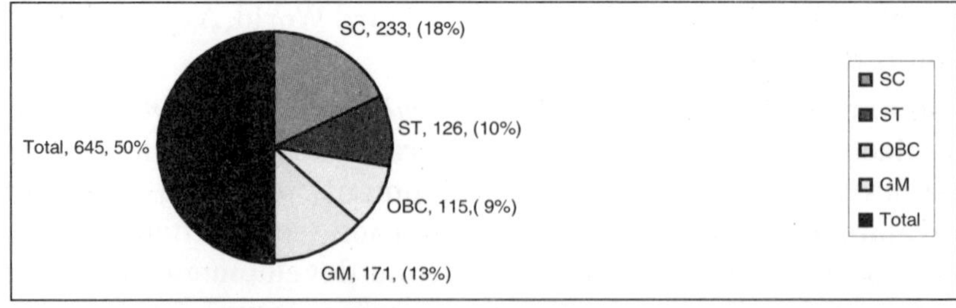

Fig. 4.1. Caste-wise Distribution of Members in PRIs in Gulbarga Taluk

Figure 2 discusses the caste-wise and gender-wise distribution of representatives in Gram Panchayats of Gulbarga Taluk. The figure shows that out of the total, the weaker sections representatives belonging to male community are 268 with 72.24 per cent and female representatives are 206 with 75.18 per cent. From the figure it is identified that male and female representatives consists of more number than the general category. This is the indication that in the study area the representation of weaker sections in Gram Panchayats is around 72 per cent to 75 per cent.

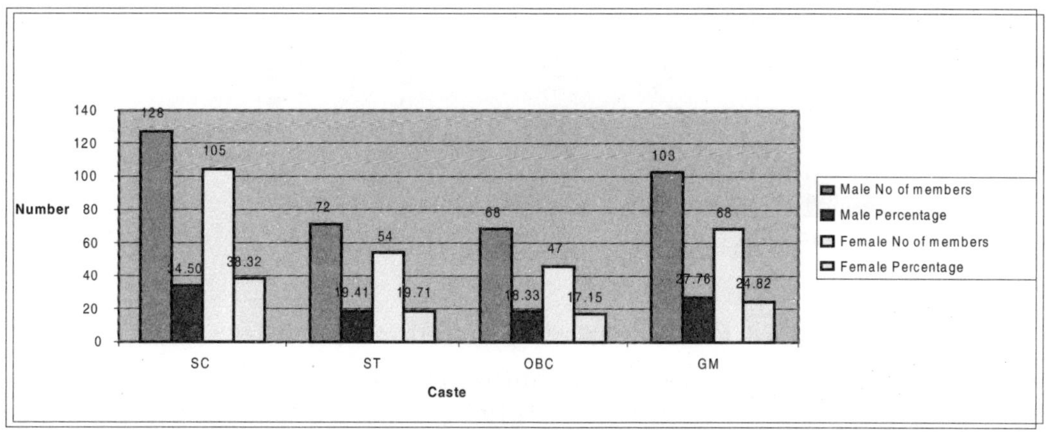

Fig. 4.2. Male, Female Wise Distribution of Members in Gulbarga Taluk

Figure 3 reveals the caste-wise representation of the Gram Panchayat in Afjalpur Taluk. It is observed in the figure that out of the total 412 representatives, OBCs are 138, SC 69, ST 27 and 181 representatives from general category. In total, the weaker sections consist of 234 with 56.80 per cent, which relatively more than general category.

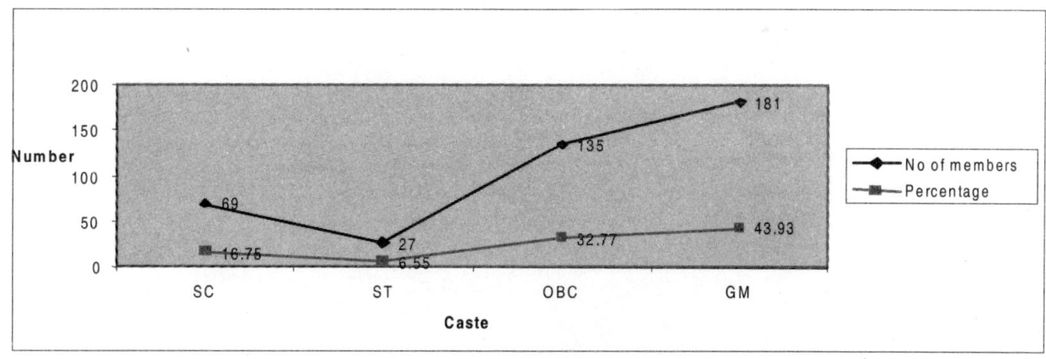

Fig. 4.3. Caste-wise Members in Afjalpur Taluk

Figure 4 discusses the caste-wise and Gender-wise distribution of representatives in the Gram Panchayats of Afzalpur Taluk. From the SCs 39 are male and 30 are female. Representatives from STs are only 08 number from male and 28 from female. So for as concern of OBCs, 85 are male and 51 female from the General Category. 102 are from male and 69 from female. It is observed from the figure that female are more number of representatives belonging to weaker sections both from male and female. It indicates that the women welfare programmes are also being implemented for women beneficiaries. The representation of male members in total are 132 with 56.45 per cent and female representatives are 108 with 61.24 per cent.

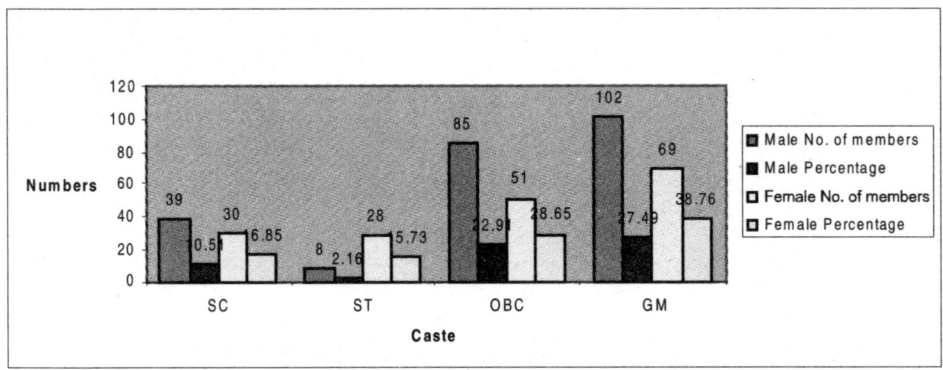

Fig. 4.4. Male, Female wise Members in Afjalpur Taluk

Figure 5. reveals the caste-wise distribution of respondents opinion towards the awareness of objectives of panchayat raj institutions. It is evident from the figure that the majority of representatives belonging to weaker sections have awareness of the objectives of Panchayat Raj Institutions. Therefore, it is viewed that in the study area majority of representatives are actively involving in the working of Panchayat Raj Institutions and involving for the development of weaker sections through the institutions of panchayat raj.

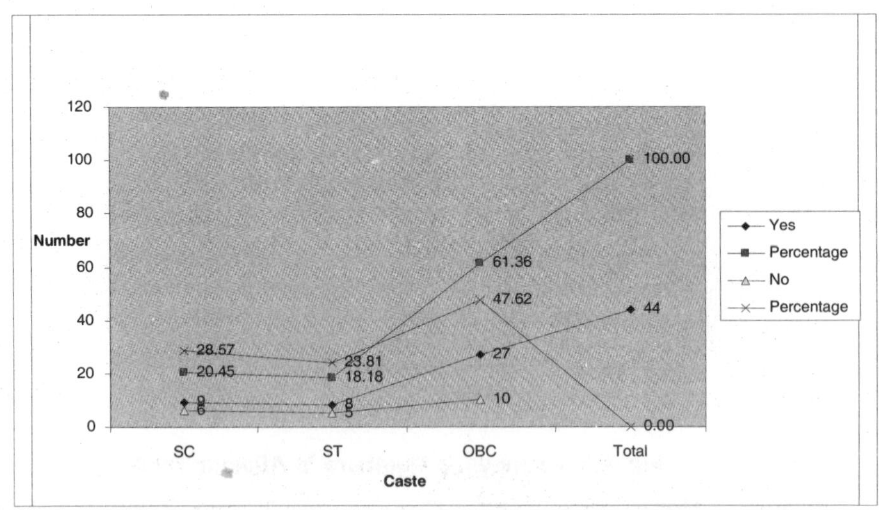

Fig. 4.5. Caste-wise Opinion of Respondents

Source: Compiled from the Information collected from the Field Work in the study area

Figure 6 discusses that the Education-wise distribution of representatives opinion towards the objectives of Panchayat Raj Institutions. The figure shows that except illiterate representatives, the majority of representatives from all the categories have the awareness about objectives of Panchayat Raj Institutions. From the illiterates only 9 representatives have awareness, 24 representatives who have studied up to 10th have awareness, 12 representatives studied up to PUC have awareness and all the representatives with graduation as their qualification have awareness.

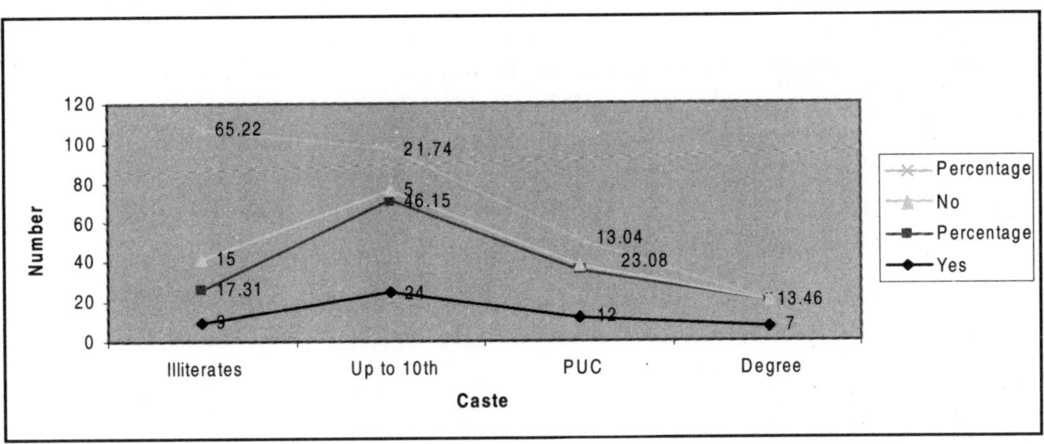

Fig. 4.6. Education-wise Opinion of Respondents

Source: Compiled from the Information collected from the Field Work in the study area.

Table 1. Reveals that the caste-wise distribution of respondent's opinion towards specific earmark of allocations and expenditure for the welfare of SC, ST, and OBC in Panchayat Raj Institutions. It is evident from the table that the majority (76%) of respondents belonging to SCs, wanted a specific earmark of allocations and expenditure for the welfare of SC and STs in the institutions of Panchayat Raj, and 24 per cent of respondents opined that their should not be a special earmark for SC and STs in Panchayat Raj Institutions. Respondents belonging to STs opined that the highest number (70%) wanted a special earmark and 30 per cent does not want a special earmark of allocations and expenditure for the welfare of SC and STs. The highest number (75%) respondents belonging to OBC wanted a special allocations and expenditure whereas 25 per cent are not in favour of special earmark for the welfare of SC and STs in Panchayat Raj Institutions.

Table 4.1. Caste-wise Distribution of Respondent's Opinion towards Specific Earmark of Allocations and Expenditure for the Welfare of SC, ST and OBC in Panchayat Raj Institutions

Sl.No.	Opinion	SC	%	ST	%	OBC	%	Total	%
1.	Yes	19	76	7	70	30	75	56	74.67
2.	No	6	24	3	30	10	25	19	25.33
3.	Total	25	100	10	100	40	100	75	100.00

Source: Compiled from the data collected from the field work.

The over all observation of the table is that the majority of respondents belonging to weaker sections wanted a special allocations and expenditure for the welfare of SC, ST and OBC's in Panchayat Raj Institutions.

Table 2 reveals that caste-wise distribution of respondent's opinion towards their reaction if the funds intended for weaker sections are not implemented by Panchayat Raj Institutions. The table shows that 72 per cent of SC expressed that they will keep quite and 28 per cent opined that they protest in different forms in case the funds from Central and State Governments intended for the welfare of these sections are not utilized by Panchayat Raj Institutions. The respondents belonging to STs, the highest number 80 per cent of respondents opined that they will keep quite and only 20 per cent of respondents will protest in various forms. The respondents belonging to OBC's, the highest number (62.5%) of respondents will keep quite and 137.5 per cent of respondents opined that they will protest in different forms in case funds intended for the welfare of weaker sections by Centre or State governments are not implemented.

Table 4.2. Distribution of Opinion by Caste Towards their Reaction if the Funds intended for Weaker Sections are not Implemented by Panchayat Raj Institutions

Sl.No.	Opinion	SC	%	ST	%	OBC	%	Total	%
1.	Yes	18	72	8	80	25	62.5	56	74.67
2.	No	7	28	2	20	15	37.5	19	25.33
3.	Total	25	100	10	100	40	100	75	100.00

Source: Compiled from the data collected from the field work.

The over all observation of the table is that the majority of respondents across the castes in Panchayat Raj Institutions are not committed for the utilization of funds given by Central and State Governments for the welfare of weaker sections.

Findings of the study

1. Development of weaker sections is being done by the representatives belonging to these sections.
2. As the number of developmental programmes are assigned to Panchayat Raj Institutions, the representatives in the institutions of Panchayat Raj belonging to weaker sections are concentrating on the welfare of these sections.
3. In the study area it is found that the representatives of OBCs are also contesting and won from the seats reserved for general category. Thus, there exists the more number of representatives belong to weaker sections in PRIs and are able to insist more number of schemes for development of weaker sections across the institutions of Panchayat Raj Institutions.
4. In the study area it is found that the representatives of weaker sections are committed for the development of weaker sections.

5. The representatives of weaker sections are moving the resolutions intended for the welfare of weaker sections and are also pursuing for getting the approval of the respective bodies in Panchayat Raj Institutions.
6. It is found in the study area that unless the weaker sections involvement in Panchayat Raj Institutions there will not be the development of weaker sections. Because, the political representation is necessary for the preparation, earmark of Budget and for the execution of schemes and programmes for the welfare of weaker sections.
7. It is found in the study area that the majority of representatives in Panchayat Raj Institutions are known the provisions of the 73rd Amendment Act and thus they are insisting for the preparation and implementation of schemes for the development of these sections.
8. The majority of representatives belonging to weaker sections in Panchayat Raj Institutions are demanding for specific allocation of funds and expenditure for the welfare of weaker sections.

Conclusion

After the 73rd Amendment Act in the state of Karnataka these representatives belonging to weaker sections are entering in the working of panchayat raj institutions. Since the development activities have been taken place through the institutions of panchayat raj, the involvement of weaker sections in these institutions as representatives certainly facilitating in the process of development. Thus, by the representatives of weaker sections causes for the specific preparation of plans earmark of budget and execution of there programmes with the intention of the development.

REFERENCES

1. Sivanna, N. "Decentralized Governance and Planning in Karnataka: A Historical Review", *Social Change*, Vol. 28, No. 1, March 1988, p. 29.
2. Subka, K. "Panchayat Raj in Karnataka: Some Significant Developments", *Gandhian Perspectives*, Vol. VII, No. 2, 1994.
3. Rajesh Kumar, "Political Empowerment of Weaker Sections: A Study of Municipal Bodies in Hariyana", *The Indian Journal of Political Science*, Vol, LXII, No. 3., July-Sep., 2006, p. 457.
4. Madhusudhan Bandi, "Emergence of OBC Leadership in Karnataka: An Assessment", *The Indian Journal of Political Science*, Vol, LXII, No. 4., Oct-Dec, 2006, p. 890.
5. The Karnataka Zilla Parishads, Taluk Panchayat Samithis, Mandal Panchayats and Nyaya Panchayats Act, 1983.
6. Cited in www.kar.nic.in, Panchayat Raj Act of Karnataka, 1993.
7. Local Government Reform, op. cit., p. 4.
8. Cited in www.kar.nic.in, Panchayat Raj Act of Karnataka, 1993.
9. Cited in www.kar.nic.in, Panchayat Raj Act of Karnataka, 1995.

10. Cited in www.rural.nic.in

11. Anand Inbanathan, "Decentralisation and Affirmative Action: The Case of Panchayats in Karnataka", *Journal of Social and Economic Development*, Vol. 11, No. 2, 1999, pp. 269-86.

12. Bhargava, B. S., and Vidya K. C., "Position of Women in Political Institutions (With Special Reference to Panchayat Raj System in Karnataka), *Journal of Rural Development*, Vol. II, No. 5, September 1992, p. 602.

13. Satpal Puliani, ed., "The Karnataka Raj Manual", *Karnataka Law Journal Publication*, 1998, pp. 133-34.

14. Gopinath Reddy, M. & Madhusudana Bandhi, "The Status of PRI's in Andhra Pradesh and Karnataka: A Comparison", *Grassroots Governance*, Academy of Grassroots Studies and Research in India, Vol. I. No. I, January-June 2003, pp. 88-95.

15. Prabhat Datta "*Major Issues in the Development Debate:- Lessons in Empowerment from India*", Kanishka Publishers, Distributors, New Delhi, 1998.

16. Dhirendra Vajpeyi ed., "*Local Government and Politics in the Third World: Issues and Trends*", Heritage Publishers, New Delhi, India. 1990, pp. 8-10.

17. T. K. Lakshman, B. K. Narayan, "*Rural Development in India: A Multi Dimensional Analysis*" ed. T. K. Lakshman, B. K. Narayan, Himalaya Publishing House, Bombay, 1987.

18. Nagendra Ambedkar, *New Panchayat Raj at Work*, ABD Publishers, Jaipur, India, 2000.

19. Shyamala, C.K. (2001): "Evaluation of Decentralized Governance and Planning in Karnataka", *Man and Development*, June.

20. "Panchayat Raj Institutions in Select States: An Analytical Study", National Institute of Rural Development, Hyderabad, 1995; pp. 81-82.

Human Rights Awareness among Tribal and Non-tribal Higher Secondary School Students in Wayanad District, Kerala

—Pradeep Kumar K.A.

Abstract

The present study was conducted to compare the Human Rights awareness among the tribal and non-tribal higher secondary students with respect to their subject (Science and Humanities) management categories of school (government, private and open school) and gender. An intact sample of 612 students from 15 Higher Secondary Schools was selected. The investigator used stratified Random sampling technique for taking sample from the population of Higher Secondary School Students. Due representation was given to the factors while selecting the sample: Cast of the Students (Tribal and Non-Tribal), Sex of the students (boys and girls), Management of Schools (Govt., Private and Open school), subject of specialization (Science, Humanities). The present study made use of the tool for data collection under the title, "Human Right Awareness Test for Higher Secondary Students", developed by the investigator. T-test was used to analyse the data. It was found that:-

Human Rights Awareness among non-tribal students are more as compared to tribal students at Higher Secondary level, boys are more aware about Human Rights compared to Girls among the Non-tribal students at Higher Secondary level and there was no difference in Human Rights Education Awareness between Tribal boys and Tribal girls at Higher Secondary level.

Introduction

Human Rights education enables us to respect each other and live with each other. In other words, they are not only rights to be requested or demanded but rights to be respected and be responsible for. The rights that apply to you also apply to others. The denial of Human Rights and fundamental freedoms not only affect individual and personal tragedy, but also creates conditions of social and political unrest, sowing the seeds of violence and conflict within and between societies and nations.

For the Protection of Human Rights, it is very essential that people know their rights and are fully conscious of them. Ignorance of the people in this regard has often remitted their sufferings. Students occupy the key positions in every programme of education and for promoting world peace and Human Rights. Since the ultimate aim of education is the all round development of the child, students need to be sensitized as to how the observance of Human Rights in their day to day life enhances equality of life in the society. Teachers can raise the awareness of Human Rights in their students and make them respectful to others rights. Only in such a society the Human Rights would be protected.

Human Rights are those requirements that allow as to develop to the fullest extent and satisfy our basic human needs. Human Rights affect the daily life of each individual. They are to be enjoyed by all without discrimination with regard to race, gender, language, religion, political or social origin, property, birth or other status.

All "claims" of the individual cannot be treated as Human Rights. Only those claims which are essential for the development of one's personality and recognized as such by the "society" constitute rights. But one has to recognize the fact that this idea is not the reality and that what is conceptually recognized as rights, is often not legally enforced or enforceable. So one must distinguish between what is morally and universally accepted as rights and what constitute 'legal rights' established according to the law-creating process and judicially enforceable in a given society.

Objectives of the Study

(1) To adapt a tool to assess the Human Right Awareness among tribal and non-tribal students at higher secondary level.

(2) To study the Human Right Awareness among tribal and non-tribal students.

(3) To study the significant difference if any in the Human Right Awareness among tribal and non-tribal students with regards to their gender.

(4) To study the significant difference if any in the Human Right Awareness among tribal and non-tribal students with regards to their elective subjects opted in higher secondary course.

(5) To study the significant difference if any in the Human Right Awareness among tribal and non-tribal students belongs to schools of different management.

Hypotheses of the Study

There will not be significant difference in Human Right Awareness between Tribal and Non-tribal students with respect to their gender, their elective subjects opted in higher secondary course and students belongs to schools of different management.

Design of the Study

The study employed was normative survey wherein human right education awareness between tribal students and non-tribal students at higher secondary level with respect to their subject (Science and Humanities) Management Categories of School (Government, Private and Open School) and gender was compared.

Sampling Techniques

The population for the present study was Higher Secondary School Students in Wayanad district. There are around 45 Higher Secondary Schools in Wayanad district. From this a representative sample of 612 students from 15 Higher Secondary Schools were selected. The investigator used stratified Random sampling technique or for taking sample from the population of Higher Secondary School Students in Wayanad district.

Due representation was given to the following factors while selecting the sample.

1. Tribal and Non-Tribal students
2. Sex of the students (boys and girls)
3. Management of Schools (Govt., Private and Open school)
4. Subject of specialization (Science, Humanities)

Tool used for the Collection of Data

The present study made use of the tool for data collection under the title, "Human Right Awareness Test for Higher Secondary Students", prepared by the investigator with the help of his supervising teacher.

Human Rights Awareness Test

This test was used to measure the Human Rights Awareness among the Higher Secondary Students. The major areas selected to give awareness are Natural Rights, Human Rights, and Legal Rights. Each major dimension has subdivisions of different Human Rights components.

Descriptive Data of Students with Regard to Human Rights Awareness

The scores obtained by the pupils covered in the sample were subjected to descriptive statistical treatment. Data related to Human Rights Awareness were collected from 306 tribal and 306 non-tribal students. As descriptive statistics, the investigator applied Mean, Standard deviation, skewness and Kurtosis calculations. The results obtained from descriptive analysis are presented in the table 5.1.

From the table 5.1 it is obvious that the mean, median, mode, standard deviation, skewness and Kurtosis of Human Rights Awareness score are 22.93, 23.87, 25.75, 9.22, –0.31, 0.19 respectively. The skewness value and Kurtosis value of the present distribution are more or less coincide with the value of normal distribution curve (Sk = 0.00, and Ku = 0.263).

Table 5.1. Descriptive data of students with regard to Human Right Awareness

Sl.No.	Statistics	Value
1.	Total Sample	612
2.	Mean	22.93
3.	Median	23.87
4.	Mode	25.75
5.	Standard Deviation	9.22
6.	Skewness	-0.31
7.	Kurtosis	0.19

Differential studies are always help in studying the difference between the two groups of samples. Analysis has been done to test different hypotheses framed. The test of significance of mean differences was directed to examine whether there exists a significant difference in the Human Rights Awareness between tribal and non-tribal higher secondary students in Wayanad district. The data and result of test of significance in mean scores of Human Rights Awareness between the tribal and non-tribal higher secondary students are presented in the Table 5.2.

Table 5.2. Human Rights Awareness of Tribal and Non-tribal students

Category	Sample size	Mean	S.D.	S.E.	't' Value
Tribal (total)	306	21.55	9.5	0.74	3.75*
Non-tribal (total)	306	24.32	8.75		

*Significant at 0.01 level

From the table 5.2, it is clear that the mean score of Human Right Awareness of Non-tribal student (24.32) is greater than that of tribal student (21.55). The 't' value calculated (3.75) is found to be greater than the 't' table value (2.58) at 0.01 significance level. Hence the null hypothesis is rejected, an alternative hypothesis states that 'there will be significant difference in Human Right Awareness between Tribal and Non-tribal higher secondary students is upheld.

Major Findings of the Study

On the basis of the discussions and interpretations of the results, the following findings have been emerged out of the study:

(1) Human Rights Awareness among Non-tribal students is found to be more as compared to tribal students at Higher Secondary level.

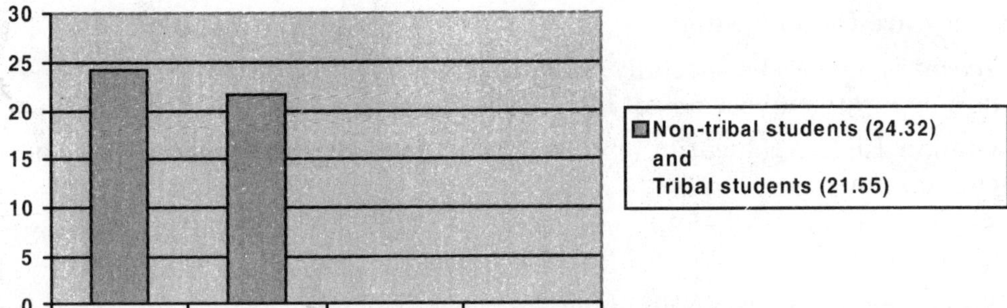

Fig. 5.1. Bar diagram showing the difference between the awareness of Human Rights among Tribal and Non-tribal Higher secondary students.

(2) It is found that boys are more aware about Human Rights compared to Girls among the Non-tribal students at Higher Secondary level.

(3) There is no difference in Human Rights Awareness between Tribal boys and Tribal girls at Higher Secondary level.

(4) Non-tribal students are found to be more aware about Human Rights in the Government, Private and Open schools compared to the Tribal students at the Higher Secondary level.

(5) There is no difference in Human Rights Awareness between Tribal and Non-tribal students who are opted Humanities as a subject of study at Higher Secondary level.

(6) Human Rights Awareness among the Humanities students are found to be more when compared to the science students at Higher Secondary level.

Educational Implications of the Study

From the present study it was found that there is a significant difference between tribal and Non-tribal students in Human Rights Education Awareness with respect to their gender and subjects opted. The tribal students are less aware of Human Rights Awareness. The reason being they are educationally and culturally backward. So the government should provide some intervention programs to tribal students to develop their Human Rights Awareness.

The humanities students are more aware than the science students. This may be the fact that the humanities students are studying about Human Rights Awareness in their humanities curriculum. So the study of Human Rights Awareness should be included as a separate subject in schools and colleges.

The present study thus revealed that the subject of specialization has significant influence on Human Rights Awareness among higher secondary schools pupils. Therefore necessary steps should be taken to provide Human Rights Education to all higher secondary students like Humanities curriculum.

On the basis of results obtained from the present study several implications can be derived, they are the following:

1. Teachers have to be specially trained to teach Human Rights Education Awareness as a separate subject for all higher secondary students.
2. Human Rights Education should be included in the secondary teacher training curriculum.
3. Special classes to provide the awareness about Human Rights violation in school level.
4. Special education to be provided for tribal students through awareness of right to education and health and an adequate livelihood including food, water and housing, to just a favourable condition of work to security and freedom from violence.

REFERENCES

1. Best John W., *Research in Education*, Prentice Hall, New Delhi, 1986.
2. Bini Borgahan, *Human Rights: Social and Political Challenge*, Kanishka Publishers, New Delhi, 1999.
3. Deshmukh B.A., *Tribal Education*, Sonali Publications, New Delhi, 2004.
4. Goutam Ashwanikant, *Human Rights and Justice System*, A.P.H. Publishing, New Delhi , 2001.
5. Hill Dilys M., *Human Rights and Foreign Policy Principles and Practices*, Macmillan Press, Southamplan, 1989.
6. Iyer Krisnhna V.R., *Human Rights and Human Wrongs*, B.R. Publishing Corporation, New Delhi, 1990.
7. Kalaiah A., *Human Rights in International*, Deep and Deep Publication, New Delhi, 1986.
8. Narasimhan R.K., *Human Rights and Social Justice*, Common Wealth Publishers, New Delhi, 1999.
9. Naseema C., *Human Rights Education*, Kanishka Publishers, New Delhi, 2004.
10. Patil V.T. and Sastry, *Studies in Human Rights*, P.R. Books, New Delhi, 2000.
11. Ramachandran K., *Gupta and Sharma*, Political Science, NCERT, New Delhi, 2000.

Ethnographic and Health Profile of the Dongria Kondhs: A Primitive Tribal Group of Niyamgiri Hills in Eastern Ghats of Orissa (India)

—Gandham Bulliyya

Of the 461 scheduled tribes in India, Orissa has declared 62 tribal communities and 13 as primitive tribal groups (PTG). Dongrias, a major sect of the great Kondh tribe, mostly stay on high hills known as Dongar. The Dongria Kondh is one of the officially designated PTG in Orissa. They are the original inhabitants of Niyamgiri hilly region which extends to Rayagada, Koraput and Kalahandi districts of south Orissa. The Dongria population is confined to three community development blocks namely Bissamcuttack and Munuguda of Gunpur sub-division and Kalyansinghpur Block of Rayagada sub-division. Dongria Kondhs have an estimated population of about 10,000 and are distributed in around 120 settlements, all at an altitude up to 5,000 feet above the sea-level.

They speak a language, called the Kuvi, which is of Dravidian linguistic ancestry that has no script. They are patrilineal and patriarchal; they have nuclear families, extended families, lineage and clans. Unlike other tribal groups of India, Dongria Kondhs are known for their deep knowledge and skill in horticulture. They largely rely on hunting, gathering and shifting cultivation in the Niyamgiri hills for survival. However, due to development, education, medical facilities, irrigation, plantation and so on and so forth, they have started adapting to the great tradition of modern civilization standards in many ways. Their traditional lifestyle, customary traits of economy political organization, norms, values and worldview have been drastically changed over a long period of time. Their population is around 10,000 spread over 120 villages with a sex ratio of 1352 females/ 1000 males. Literacy rate is less than 10 per cent, particularly female literacy is only 3 per cent. Dongria Kondh is an endogamous group and within them the clans are exogamous divided into several patrilineal clans forming socio-cultural territorial organizations. The health status is poor due to high level of poverty, poor environmental sanitation and hygiene, and increased morbidity from water-borne and vector-borne infections. Poor knowledge of availability and access to public health care facilities resulting in increased severity and duration of illnesses. Moreover, social barriers and taboos preventing utilization of healthcare services increase vulnerability to specific endemic and communicable diseases.

Malnutrition is fairly common, especially young children and women debilitating their physical condition and lowering resistance to disease, leading at times even to behavioural impairment. More than 70 per cent of households are protein-energy deficient with a wide range of seasonal variation. Preotein-energy malnutrition is more common, 66 per cent, 63 per cent and 21 per cent of preschool children are underweight, stunting and wasting respectively indicating growth retardation. Malnourishment is seen in 60 per cent of schoolage children and 50 per cent of adolescents. Low body-mass index (BMI<18.5 kg/ m^2) reflected in 55 per cent of adults shows chronic energy deficiency. Micronutrient deficiencies particularly iron, vitamin A and iodine are of public health significance. Iron deficiency anaemia is widespread problem among all the age groups. Iodine deficiency disorders are endemic in the Niyamgiri region with a high goitre rate and low urinary iodine excretion, while 10 per cent of households are using iodized salt. There is certainly an urgent need to focus on this social isolate community in formulating specific programs and strengthening existing schemes to improve the health and nutritional status at par with mainland population.

Introduction

India has the second largest concentration of tribal population in the world next to Africa. According to Article 432 of the Constitution of India, the Scheduled Tribes (ST) refers to specific indigenous peoples whose status is acknowledged to some formal degree by appropriate national and state legislation. As per 2001 Census, ST population was 84.3 million representing 8.2 per cent of Indian population. A total of 461 ST groups have been identified, who are scattered throughout the length and breadth of the country (Singh, 1994). There are 6 predominantly tribal states where more than 50 per cent population is ST (Mizoram 94.8 per cent, Nagaland 87.7 per cent, Meghalaya 85.5 per cent, Arunachal Pradesh 63.7 per cent, Union Territories of Lakshadweep 93.2 per cent and Dadra & Nagar Haveli 79.0 per cent). More than half of ST population in the country is concentrated in the states of Madhya Pradesh (23.3%), Orissa (22.2%), Gujarat (14.9%), Assam (12.8%), Rajasthan (12.4 per cent), Maharashtra (9.3%), Bihar (7.7%), Andhra Pradesh (6.3 per cent) and Andaman & Nicobar Islands (5.5%). A tribe is a group of families bound together by kinship, usually descending from common mythical or legendary ancestors, living in a common region, speaking a common dialect having a common historical background. These groups are distinct biologically isolates with characteristic cultural and socio-economic background. They inhabit widely varying ecological and geo-climatic setting having different stages of development. These are considered to be the oldest ethnic segments of population and hence, the term 'Adivasi' has been fairly popular in India.

In the Fifth Five-Year Plan (1974-79), Government of India in 1984 classified 75 ST communities as Primitive Tribal Groups (PTG) on the basis of a four-point criteria; (*i*) smallness and diminishing population, (*ii*) backwardness and isolation, (*iii*) pre-agricultural technology for their subsistence, and (*iv*) very low level of literacy. They spread over 15 States/Union Territories with a total population of 1.32 million (1.95%). Their distribution in different states is shown in Table 6.1. Each group is small in number, differentially developed with respect to one another of remote habitat with poor administrative and infrastructure back up. Due to isolation they are untouched by modern civilization and thus their traditions have been left intact through the ages. Their problems and needs are quite different from other ST, hence, priority accorded for protection and development. Though they have put into one category, yet each of PTG is at a different level of development and socio-culturally distinct facing survival problems (Pandey, 2002). PTG like Shompens, Jarawas, Sentinelese of the Andaman and Nicobar Islands, Bondos of Orissa, Cholanaickans of Kerala, Abujhmarias of Chhattisgarh and Birhors of Jharkhand are under the threat of getting of extinction. As they live in more interior inaccessible pockets with declining sources of sustenance and become vulnerable to hunger, starvation and ill-health. For the welfare of PTG, 100 per cent subsidy is being provided for individual family benefit and income generation-oriented schemes, out of special central assistance by Government of India.

Table 6.1. Distribution of Primitive Tribal Groups in Different States of India

State/UnionTerritory (n)	Primitive tribal groups
1. Andhra Pradesh (12)	1. Bodo Gadaba, 2. Bondo Poraja, 3. Chenchu, 4. Dongria Kondh, 5. Gutob Gadaba, 6. Khond Poroja, 7. Kolam, 8. Konda Reddis, 9. Konda Savaras, 10. Kutia Kondhs, 11. Porangi Perja, 12. Tholi.
2. Bihar and Jharkhand (9)	13. Asur, 14. Bishor, 15. Bisjia, 16. Hill Kharia, 17. Korwa, 18. Mal Pharis, 19. Pahasias, 20. Sauria Paharis, 21. Savar.
3. Gujarat (5)	22. Kathodi, 23. Kotwalia, 24. Padhar, 25. Siddi, 26. Kolgha
4. Karnataka	27. Jenu Kuruba, 28. Koraga
5. Kerala (5)	29. Cholanaikayan, 30. Kadar, 31. Kurumba, 32. Kuttunayakan, 32. Koraga
6. Madhya Pradesh and Chattisgarh (8)	33. Abhuj, 34. Maria, 35. Baiga, 36. Bharia, 37. Hill Korwa, 38. Kamar, 39. Saharia, 40. Birhor
7. Maharastra (3)	41. Katkaria (Kathodi), 42. Kolam, 43. Maria Gond
8. Manipur (1)	44. Maram Naga
9. Orissa (13)	45. Birhor, 46. Bondo, 47. Didayi, 48. Dongria-Kondh, 49. Juang, 50. Kharia, 51. Kutia-Kondh, 52. Lanjia-Saura, 53. Lodha, 54. Mankirdia, 55. Paudi Bhuiyan, 56. Saura, 57. Chuktia-Bhunjia
10. Rajasthan (1)	58. Seharia
11. Tamil Nadu (6)	59. Kattinayakan, 60. Kotas, 61. Kurumba, 62. Irula, 63. Paniyan, 64. Toda
12. Tripura (1)	65. Reang
13. Uttar Pradesh (2)	66. Buxa, 67. Raji
14. West Bengal (3)	68. Birhor, 69. Lodha, 70. Tolo
15. Andaman & Nicobar Islands (5)	71. Great Andamanese, 72. Jarwa, 73. Onge, 74. Setenelese, 75. Shompen

Tribal Scenario of Orissa

Of all the states, Orissa has the largest number of tribes, as many as 62 existing today contribute 10.38 per cent to the country's tribal population (Fig. 6.1). Total population of the state is 36,804,660 of which the ST is 81,44,871 forms an impressive 22.13 per cent of the total state population (Census, 2001). Almost 44.21 percent of the total land area of the state has been declared constitutionally as Scheduled Area. The tribals mainly inhabit the Eastern Ghat hill range, which runs in the north-south direction (Patro and Panda, 1994). The districts largely dominated by ST are Malkangiri (58.51%), Mayurbhanj (57.87%), Nawarangpur (55.26%), Rayagada (54.99%), Sundargarh (50.74%), Koraput (50.67%), Phulbani (50.13%), Keonjhar (44.62%), Gajapati (47.88%) and Jharsuguda (33.31%). Although many of the tribes are found in other parts of the country, the Juangs, Saoras, Bondas and Bathudis are exclusive to Orissa. These groups range from small communities like Chenchu, Bonda, Juanga, Didayi, to large tribes like Munda, Santalas, Kondh, Oraon, Saora and Bhuyan. Linguistically the tribes are broadly classified into four categories (Indo-Aryan, Dravidian, Tibeto-Burmese and Austric). In Orissa, the speakers of the Tibeto-Burmese family are totally absent and hence, belong to three divisions. The Indo-Aryan language family includes Dhelki-Oriya, Matia, Haleba, Jharia, Saunti, Laria and Oriya spoken by Bathudi and the acculturated sections of Bhuiyan, Juang, Kondh, Soura, Raj-Gond.

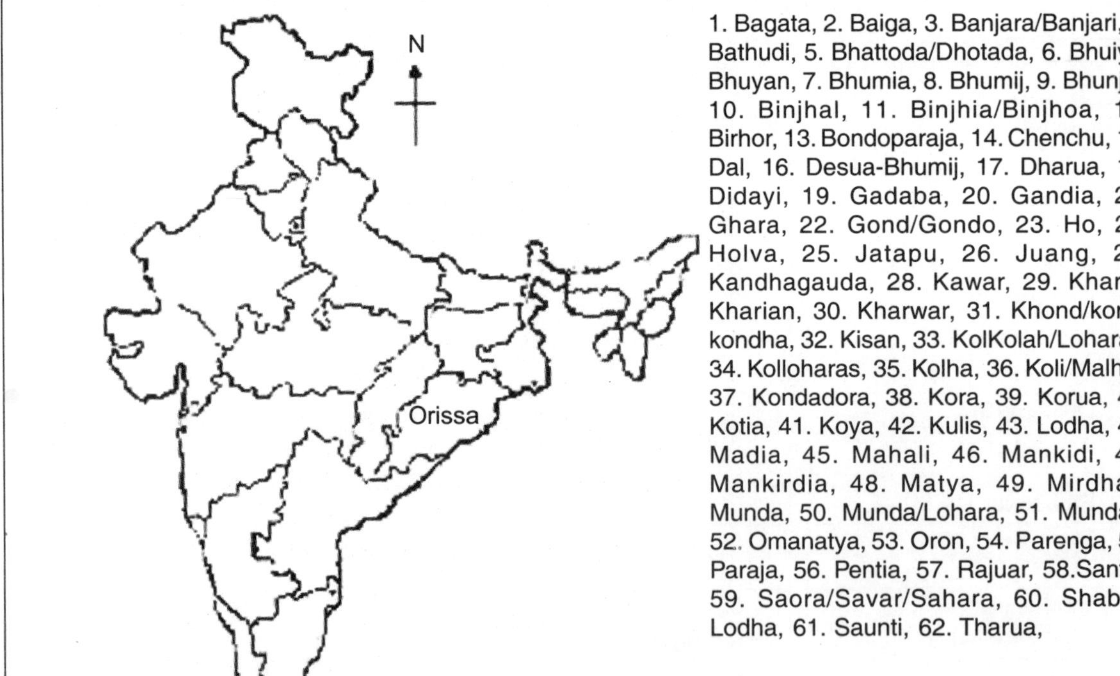

Fig. 6.1. Distribution of Scheduled Tribal Communities in Orissa

The Austric language family includes eighteen tribal languages (Birija, Parenga, Kisan, Bhumiji, Koda, Mahili Bhumiji, Mirdha-Kharia, Ollar, Gadaba, Juang, Bondo, Didayee, Karmali, Kharia, Munda, Ho, Mundari and Savara). And within the Dravidian language family there are nine languages that include Pengo, Gondi, Kisan, Konda, Koya, Parji, Kui, Kuvi and Kurukh or Oraon. Each group has its own distinct language, culture, religion and social custom. They are grouped into hunter-gatherer-nomads, hunter-gatherer and shifting cultivators, artisans, settled agriculturists, industrial and urban unskilled and semi-skilled workers.

Primitive Tribal Groups of Orissa

Out of 75 PTG of the country, Orissa has numerically highest number of 13 PTG (Table 6.1 and Fig 6.2). The 25 lakh PTG population constitutes nearly 3.6 per cent of the state's tribal population and 0.3 per cent of the country's population. They live in undulating hilly terrains and dense forests and far from modern amenities (Nityananda, 2005). The ethnic identities are reflected through their dress pattern, housing structure, ornaments, god, goddess and spirits of both benevolent and malevolent nature. Lack of awareness, ignorance, illiteracy and poverty altogether has affected their lives (Bulliyya, 2006). Considering the general features of their eco-system, traditional economy, supernatural beliefs and practices, and recent impacts of modernization, the PTG are classified into hunting, collecting-gathering, cattle-herders, simple-artisan, hill and shifting cultivation, settled-agriculture, and industrial-workers (Jena, 2002).

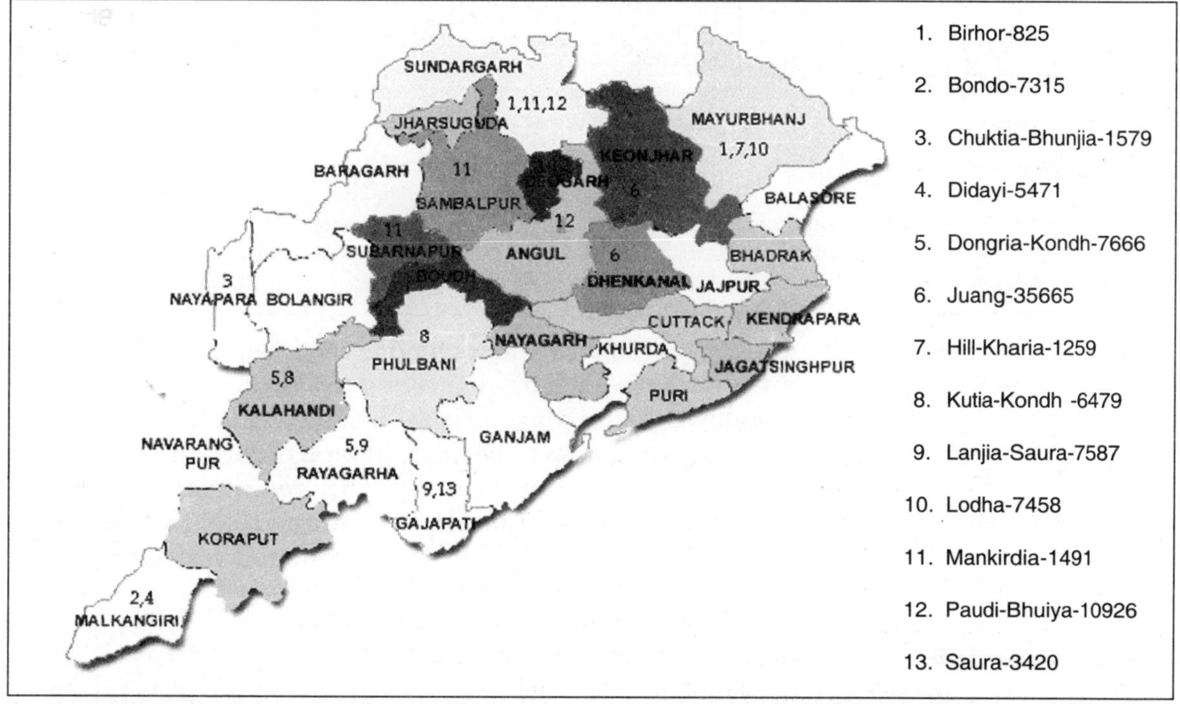

Fig. 6.2. Distribution Primitive Tribal Groups and their Population in different Districts of Orissa

There are 17 Micro-projects covering parts of 20 blocks and 12 districts striving continuously for the all-round development of 13 PTG having population of 59,710. Birhor is only the PTG for whom no separate Micro-project has been established, however, their development is being carried out through the integrated tribal development agency. The list of Micro-projects established over a period for development of PTG in the state is shown in Table 6.2.

Table 6.2. List of Micro-projects Established for Development of Primitive Tribal Groups in Orissa

No.	District	ITDA covered	Blocks covered	Micro-project	Established
1.	Angul	Non-I.T.D.A Area	Pallahara	PBDA, Jamardihi	10.03.1978
2.	Deogarh		Barkote	PBDA, Rugudakudar	01.05.1993
3.	Ganjam		Patrapur	TDA, Tumba	20.05.1978
4.	Nuapada		Komna	CBDA, Sunabeda	30.09.1994
5.	Sundegarh	Bonai	Lahunipada	PBDA, Khuntagaon	29.01.1979
6.	Malkangiri	Malkangiri	Khairput	BDA, Mudulipada	1976-1977
7	Malkangiri	Malkangiri -	Kudumuluguma, Khairput	DDA, Kudumuluguma	05.08.1986
8.	Rayagada	Gunupur	Bissamcuttack, Muniguda	DKDA, Chatikona	20.05.1978
9.	Rayagada	Rayagada	Kalyansinghpur	DKDA, Parsali	15.04.1988
10.	Rayagada	Gunupur	Gunupur	LSDA, Puttasingh	04.08.1984
11.	Gajapati	Parlakhemundi	Gumma	LSDA, Seranga	29.01.1979
12.	Gajapati	Parlakhemundi	Mohana	SDA, Chandragiri	01.04.1978
13.	Phulbani	Balliguda	Tumudibandha	KKDA, Belghar	1978-1979
14.	Kalahandi	Th. Rampur	Lanjigarh	KKDA, Lanjigarh	13.08.1986
15.	Keonjhar	Keonjhar	Banspal	JDA, Gonasika	10.03.1978
16.	Mayurbhanj	Baripada	Suliapada, Moroda	LDA, Moroda	06.06.1985
17.	Mayurbhanj	Karanjia	Jashipur, Karanjia	KMDA, Jashipur	01.12.1986

ITDA: Integrated Tribal Development Agency, PBDA: Paudi Bhuyan Development Agency, TDA: Tumba Development Agency, CBDA: Chuktia Bhunjia Development Agency, BDA: Bonda Development Agency, DDA: Didayi Development Agency, DKDA: Dongria Kondh Development Agency, LSDA: Lanjia Soura Development Agency, SDA: Soura Development Agency, KKDA: Kutia Kondh Development Agency, JDA: Juang Development Agency, LDA: Lodha Development Agency, KMDA: Hill-Kharia Mankirdia Development Agency.

Since PTG constitute the most vulnerable segments among ST, adequate information is not documented in terms of the progress achieved through developmental programs. Paucity of data on vital aspects makes difficult for prioritize the areas of development and making policy for formulating the PTG road map to be brought on par with the rest of the countrymen in the light of the research into their predicament. The present paper describes the prevailing status in highlighting the stressful situations required attention based on field experiences amongst Dongria Kondh PTG from the Niyamgiri hill terrains of Rayagada.

Dongria Kondhs

The Dongria Kondh (DK) is one of the most ancient tribes mentioned in Hindu myths and classics, notably the Puranas. The name signifies that a primitive community of hill-dwelling (dongar means high hill land) people. The Dongria Kondh call themselves Jharnia meaning those who live by the Jharana (streams) confined to Niyamgiri hill tracts covering the blocks of Kalyansighpur, Bissamcuttack and Muniguda in Rayagada district. Besides Orissa, they are found distributed in Andhra Pradesh. The immediate two neighbours of DK are Kutia and Desia Kondhs. Kutia Kondhs are hill dwellers live of Phulbani and Kalahandi districts while Desia Kondh are plain dwellers.

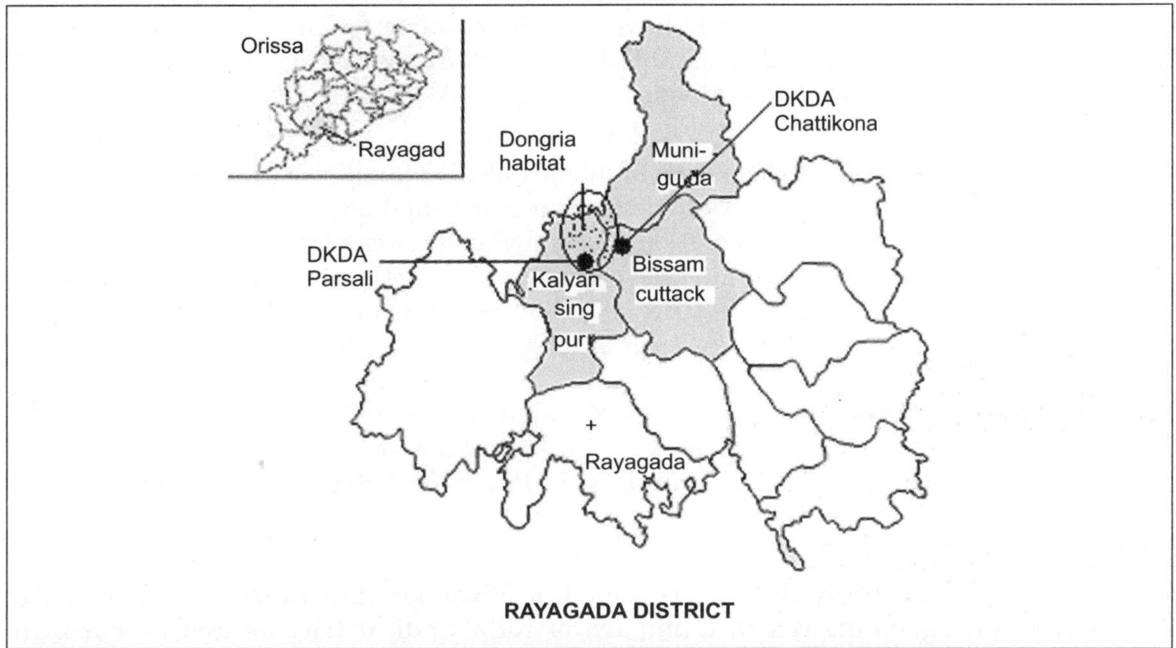

Demography	Dongria Kondh Development Agency	
District	Rayagada	Rayagada
Block	Bissamcuttack	Kalyansighpur
Micro-project area	Chattikona	Parsali
Total area km²	115.0	50.35
Elevation (ft)	1000-5000	1000-5000
Area shifting cultivation km²	3887.14	1079.00
Households shifting cultivation %	98.9 (545)	99.8 (1251)
Swidden land per HH	3.11	1.98
Revenue Block covered	Bissamcuttack/Muniguda	Kalyansighpur
Villages/hamlets	62 (8 unhabited)	49 (9 unhabited)
Total households	1284	551
Inhabitants Scheduled tribe	Dongria Kondh PTG	Dongria Kondh PTG
Co-inhabitants Scheduled caste	Domb	Domb
Population Scheduled tribe PTG	5874	2375
Sex ratio(1000 males)	1316	1385
Literacy (%)	12.82	9.26
Male	23.05	18.37
Female	4.82	2.68

Fig. 6.3. Dongria Kondh Development Agencies in Rayagada District

According to Thurston (1909), the number of Kondh sub-groups are fifty-eight, whereas Patnaik (1982) divided into three groups; Kutia Kondh are those who are leading isolated life of poverty and indigence, Dongria Kondh are primitive skilled horticulturists and Desia Kondhs who left their hill habitation and have settled down in the plains. Nayak et al. (1990) classified the Kondhs into five sub-groups (Malia, Kutia, Dongria, Kuvi and Desia). They have their own dialect called '*kuvi*', which is of Dravidian linguistic ancestry (Gordon, 2005). Out of seventeen Micro-projects in the state, two Dongria Kondh Development Agency (DKDA) projects have been functioning for their development since 1980s; DKDA-Chattikona (Kurli established in 1978) covers Dongarian villages in Bissamcuttack and Muniguda blocks while DKDA-Parsali (1987) looking after Kalyansighpur block (Table 6.2 and Fig. 6.3).

Altogether, there are 120 villages and hamlets and 1813 families with a total population of over 10,000 in three blocks. Sex ratio (females per thousand males) measures the balance between males and females in population and imbalances affect the social, economic and community life in many ways (Desai, 1994). The sex ratio within country is reported to be slightly high among the tribals, it is 1012 and 1002 per 1000 males during 1981 and 1991 respectively (Census of India, 1991). According to 2001. Census, the sex ratio found low for the district of Rayagada (1028) and the state (972). The sex ratio of DK stands significantly higher at 1318 and1352 females per 1000 male population respectively for DKDA areas of Parsali and Chattikona (Fig. 6.3). However, the sex ratio found as low as 920 females per thousand males among the Kutia Kondh PTG of Phulbani district (Basu, 1990).

Habitat

The DK inhabit exclusively in the forest-clad of Niyamgiri hill ranges stretches from Theruvali of Rayagada district to Lanjigarh of Kalahandi district located over a high plateau ranging 2000-4970 feet above the sea level. Each Dongria Kondh village is situated in the centre chain of hills of Niamgiris, which are inaccessible, hidden in the folds of mountains majority devoid road and transport facilities (DKDA, 2001; 2004). Their settlements are sparsely distributed on the hilltops and valleys situated in isolation often cut off from the general mass of civilization (Das, 1977). Their settlements are arranged as a cluster of houses in two rows. In each row, the houses are contiguous in a linear fashion and the street is located between rows. Dongria settlements often lack permanency as the entire settlements are abandoned if a number of deaths take place in the same neighbourhood. Many of the Dongria villages have limited number of Domb scheduled caste households confined separately to a corner, who live symbiotically in acting messengers, weaver and cattle herders for the DK (Das, 1984). All Dombs are all landless (Fig. 6.3).

People

Dongrias consider themselves as the descendents of Niyam Raja, the legendry ancestral king. They are also known to be *Drilli Kuan* or *Dongarian Kuan,* the name derived from a male unique traditional dignified cloth, wrapped around waist tightly in a manner that two embroidered ends remain hanging, one 4-5 feet in front and the other two feet at the back (Krishan, 1979). Males grow long hair tie into a knot at their nape and always carry an axe on the shoulder and a knife is kept hanging from the waist belt using for offence and defense in the forest. The women wear a lower garment not long enough to hide their knee and cover the chest with a small band of cotton cloth tied at the back. All these garments are woven by neighboring schedule caste community. Their personal adornment are unique with each male and female member using hair clips on their head and often pierce their ears and love to wear as many earrings as they can. Women are fond of ornaments and beautify themselves traditionally with several hairpins, earrings neck-rings, hand-rings made up of brass, iron and hyndalium prepared by them and purchased from local markets. Body tattooing is practiced by both sexes (Bulliyya *et al.,* 2006).

Religious Beliefs

The Kondh sub-groups once infamous for their pernicious practice of human sacrifice and female infanticide (*Tokri parbo*), which replaced by meriah buffalo sacrifice (*Kondru parbo*) to appease their god/goddess to bring good luck, prosperity and land fertility (Boal, 1982). The Dongria have a religion very close to animism. The gods and goddesses are always attributed to various natural phenomena, objects, trees, animals, etc. They have a god or deity for everything and anything. Their life is full of rituals, sacrifices and magico-religious observances throughout the year to their benevolent and malevolent ancestors, aimed at ensuring personal security and happiness, community well-being and group solidarity (Aparajita, 1994).

The theological pantheon is the earth goddess (*Dharani Penu*) at the apex and *Niyam penu* (Niyamgiri Hill) is believed to be the creator of Dongrias. In addition, a large number of village deities, ancestral cults, household deities and spirits, for instance, in a house, there is a deity for back and front street, kitchen, living room, implements and so on and so forth (Pfeffer, 2005). Breach of any religious conduct by any member of the society invites the wrath of spirits in the form of lack of rainfall, soaking of streams, destruction of forest produce, and other natural calamities. Hence, the customary law, norms, taboos, and values are greatly adhered and enforced with high to heavy punishments, depending upon the seriousness of the crimes committed. For social control in the village and at Muttha level (regional), there are hereditary religious leaders like Jani (religious head), Mondal (secular head), Bejuni (sorcerer), Barik (messenger) who coordinate to hold meetings where the punishment is awarded along with appeasement procedure is followed with animal sacrifice. The punishment may be in cash or kind and may lead to strict restrictions from the community if not obeyed.

Family and Marriage

DK is an endogamous group and within them the clans are exogamous divided into several patrilineal clans (*kunda*) forming socio-cultural territorial organizations (*mutha*). These include Attaka, Bangesika, Bralika, Hikoka, Huika, Jakaka, Jakesika, Kadraka, Konjaka, Kotaka, Krusika, Kruska, Kulesika, Kunuka, Kurchika, Kusika, Mandika, Manika,

Manjika, Nundruka, Palaka, Pidisika, Pisika, Prasaka, Pusika, Saraka, Sikaka, Ulaka, Urlaka, Wadaka, Wandelka, Wangesika, Wardelika, Warleeka, Warlesika etc. The Dongria family is often nuclear, although extended families exist. Female members are considered assets because of their contribution inside and outside the household and women are equated with the male members in constructing a house to cultivation. Women do all the work for household ranging from fetching water from the distant streams, cooking, serving food to each member of the household to cultivating, harvesting and marketing of produce in the market. Due to this, the bride price is paid to her parents when a girl gets married which is a striking feature of the Dongrias. However, the family is patrilineal and patrilocal. Extended families are either mono- or polygynous (a group consisting of a man and two or more wives and their children or group formed by remarriage of a widow or widower having children by a former marriage), claimed to be social and economic prestige. By custom, marriage must cross clan boundaries (a form of incest taboo). The clan is exogamous, which means marriages are made outside the clan (yet still within the greater Dongoria population).

The Census data shows 23.54 per cent of families are polygynous. Woman is treated as an economic asset to the family and for the reason girl child is preferred over boy child (Routray, 1987). Further the prevailing marriage practices go in favor of girls. The parents earn money through bride price that is given by the groom's parent as part of the marriage deal. Girls fetch high bride price to their parents whereas boy's parents have to pay bride price to get them married. The girl's dormitory (*adasbeta*) is common practice for village exogamy (Patnaik and Mohanty, 2002). The girls sleep at night in the dormitory (*Daa Sala*) and learn social taboos, myths, legends, stories, riddles, proverbs amidst singing and dancing the whole night, thus learning everything that is expected from a potential wife and mother. As regards the acquisition of brides for marriage is the most widely prevalent practice through capture, in addition to other practices such as negotiations, elopement, purchase and services. With the passage of time negotiated type of marriage, which is considered prestigious, is being preferred more and payment of bride price is an inseparable part of marriage.

Literacy

As per 1991 Census, the literacy rate among ST (29.6 per cent) in Orissa is far below the ST literacy of the country (52.2 per cent). The female literacy rate is far lower (18.2 per cent) as compared to overall female literacy for the country (39.2 per cent). In Orissa, male literacy is 64.1 per cent, the tribal male literacy is only 28 per cent. The tribal female literacy rate is particularly low at 8.3 per cent compared to 45.5 per cent for the total female population. Literacy rates among the PTG are still low ranging 5.7-7.6 per cent in 1981; it was 2.5 per cent among female population. Literacy rate among the DK population is less than 10 per cent, particularly among females (2-3 per cent) as against the literacy for the district (total 36.1 per cent, male 48.2 per cent and female 24.6 per cent) (PFI, 2005). Ashram schools are residential schools established for tribal children from a cluster of habitations and three such schools have been established at convenient places of DK settlements (Kurli, Parsali, Khambesi) run by Department of Welfare, Govt. of Orissa, with all sorts of facilities like free food, free reading-writing materials and other basic requirements like sitting mat, uniform, blankets, beds etc., Despite enrollment, attendance and achievement of students are far from satisfactory. The DK children tend to drop out from schools and assist their parents in domestic and agricultural activities (Kanungo, 2004). A linguistic survey conducted in four districts including Rayagada explored the possibility of execution of folklore in primary education for tribal primer *Kuvi*.

Economy

Orissa accounts for the largest area under shifting (*Podu*) cultivation in India, which an age-old practice being practiced in Eastern Ghats. About 5298 km^2 area is under *podu* cultivation and depend 1.5 lakh families of PTG annually (Dongaria Kondha, Kutia Kond, Lanjia Sara, Paraja, Godaba, Koya, Didayi, Bonda, and Paudi Bhuyan). They are called Dongria or dweller of "donger"(hill in Oriya) and love to settle in higher altitudes due to their economic demands. Their economies center round the dongar hill slopes for shifting cultivation, the abode of their deities and supernatural beings that provides them also with a metaphor for their worldview (Patro and Panda, 1994). Shifting cultivation or *Podu Chasa* as it is locally called, as part of an economic need retaining the most ancient system of agriculture dating back to the lower Neolithic period and primitive features of underdevelopment and cultural evolution. It is also known as field forest rotation or slash and burn agriculture. It is characterized as subsistence-oriented based mainly on collection of minor forest produce, hunting and, or a combination of hunting and collecting. The axe is the most important instrument for them and is used for multiple purposes including offence and defence and use of bows and arrows is still practise. The DK extensively practice the slash and burn (swidden) type of rotation cultivation. The hill slopes are clearly marked by areas under swidden cultivation. Plenty of jackfruits, orange and mango trees grow in the hills.

They are also able horticulturists along hill slopes and grow pineapple, banana, sago-pam (salap), citrus fruits, guava, papaya etc. Besides horticulture, they earn their livelihood through forests and animal husbandry (Sahoo, 1992). Rice, maize, ganja and ragi are main crops, besides various types of pulses (red gram and black gram), and oil seeds (kandul, masur, mung, chana, alsi (naizer), castor, mustard). The fruits of jamu, harida, bahada, amla, mahua, kusuma, kendu are of economic importance. Gathering of forest produce like siali creepers, kendu leaf, sal leaf, seeds of karanja (*Pongnamia glatera*) and mahua (*Madhuaka latifolia*) is made for daily domestic requirements (Dash et al., 2008). They raise livestock like goats, pigs and hens for meeting the demands of prostrations and for their own use on ritual occasions (Table 6.3).

Indebtedness

The DK in Niyamgiri area are at the level of indebtedness due to their poverty, disbeliefs and illiteracy. Often remain in debt to moneylenders in perpetuity that carried down to their descendants (Patnaik, 1988). Their principal source of debt is the mainland moneylenders (*kumuties*) and neighbourhood Dombs. Dongrias drink liquor very often prepared from mahua, sago palm juice and date palm juice. Their drinking habits, gifts and counter gifts and scarecity of food during lean periods compel to become indebted. They need money for payments of bride price, expensive marriage feasts, rituals, and magico-religious performances (Schnepel, 2001). Inter-clan feuds relating to property, hunting and marriage are impediment to the economic prosperity. The loan (*rina*) is taken either in cash or kind and the rate of interest (*Adi* or *Kantari*) is generally usurious (Arati and Sahoo 2004).

Table 6.3. Seasonal Collection of Minor Forest Produce of Dongria Kondhs of Rayagada

Season	Period	Major	Minor
Monsoon *(Barsa)*	Mid-June-mid-August	Mango, pine apple, Jackfruit, maize, banana	Siali leaves, Mahua fruit (tula)
Autumn *(Sharad)*	Mid-August-mid-October	Orange, zinger, banana	Siali leaves, custard apple, mushroom
Winter *(Hemanta)*	Mid-October-mid-December	Orange, ragi, turmeric, banana, brinjal	Siali leaves, castor, guava
Winter *(Sisira)*	Mid-December-mid-February	Rice, suan, ragi, turmeric, brinjal, beans, banana	Siali leaves, tamarind, green leaves,
Spring *(Vasanta)*	Mid-February-mid-April	Banana, black gram	Tamarind, red gram, castor seeds, m sticks, siali leaves, honey
Summer *(Grishma)*	Mid-April-mid-June	Mango, Jackfruit, Banana, tamarind	Siali leaves, Mahua flowers

With the development of horticultural orchards, there is a phenomenal increase of fruit production and spices (turmeric and ginger). However, the Dombs exploit them as the monopolizing trading community in taking the advantages of the symbiotic relationship. Because of high interest charged, they are unable to free themselves from debt and mortgage their plantations and orchids (Aparajita, 1994). In spite of debt legislation, the fraudulent and evasive practice of unscrupulous moneylending business continues that is hampering the effectiveness of the government and statutory credit agencies (Behera and Misra, 2005).

Food Security

Rayagada district is infamously known as the hunger pocket of Orissa. During 2001, the Kashipur block was under intense media, political and administrative attention for starvation deaths. The district is inhabited by the hill tribes, nearly 90 per cent of the population depends on agriculture but the land area is only 16 per cent, mostly with poor soil base and a large part faces drought with a wide seasonal variation in food consumption mainly in quality and quantity (Table 6.4). DK face acute shortage of food in the post-sowing monsoon period (July-September) and again around March when the *kharif* harvest has been exhausted. In such situations, consumption of mango kernels is the usual practice to compensate the staple food shortage. It is being used after a series of cleaning procedures to get rid of toxicity, which is added to the mandia preparation in place of rice.

Table 6.4. Seasonal Variation of Food Intake among Dongria Kondhs of Rayagada

Season	Period	Variation in foodstuffs
Monsoon *(Barsa)*	Mid-June - mid-August	Mandia, rice, mushrooms, salapa powder, ripe mango, jack fruit, amaranth saga, jack fruit seed, dry fish, few flesh foods
Autumn *(Sharad)*	Mid-August - mid-October	Mandia, salapa powder jau, rice, mango kernel, salapa juice, kandula dal, khesar dal, lentil, horse gram, baragudi, kating, simba, wild roots and tubers, drumstick leaves, pumpkin, fish, dry fish, pork, beef, buffalo fish, mutton, chicken
Winter *(Hemanta)*	Mid-October - mid-December	Mandia salapa powder jau, rice, salapa juice, guava, orange, kandula dal, khesar dal, lentil, horse gram, baragudi, kating, simba, wild roots and tubers, banana, potato, yam, drumstick leaves, pumpkin, fish, dry fish, flesh foods
Winter *(Sisira)*	Mid-December - mid-February	Mandia salapa powder jau, rice, wild millets, suan, kangu, kosala, bajara, janha, salapa juice, guava, orange, kandula dal, khesar dal, lentil, horse gram, baragudi, kating, simba, wild roots and tubers, banana, potato, yam, drumstick leaves, pumpkin, fish, dry fish, pork, beef, buffalo fish mutton, chicken
Spring *(Vasanta)*	Mid-February - mid-April	Mandia salapa powder jau, rice, wild millets, suan, kangu, kosala, bajara, janha, salapa juce, guava, orange, kandula dal, khesar dal, lentil, horse gram, baragudi, kating, simba, brinjal, ladies finger, burudi saga, wild roots and tubers, banana, potato, yam, drumstick leaves, pumpkin, fish, dry fish, pork, beef, buffalo fish, mutton, chicken
Summer *(Grishma)*	Mid-April - mid-June	Mandia salapa powder jau, rice, wild millets, suan, kangu, kosala, bajara, janha, salapa juce, guava, orange, kandula dal, khesar dal, lentil, horse gram, baragudi, kating, simba, wild roots and tubers, banana, potato, yam, drumstick leaves, pumpkin, fish, dry fish, flesh foods.

They were also taking local alternative non-food varieties like wild tubers, leaves, mushrooms, tamarind seed powder that contribute as rainy foods since generations as coping measures of food insecurity. Moreover, the powder from the pith of sago palm is being used commonly. In the past, they were able to cover most of the shortfall with foods gathered from the forests. Forest degradation and curtailed forest access has reduced the availability of natural foods on which they depended compelling to depend more on purchased foods to meet their minimum survival needs (Naik, 1989). Many households have become caught in a debt trap because of the precariousness of food security. This is the period Dongrias do most backbreaking labour in their dongar fields. Combination of half starvation and hard labour take heavy toll on their health.

Health Status

Although the National Health Policy (1983) accords high priority to extending organized services to those in the backward hilly tribal areas as well as to the detection and treatment of endemic diseases affecting tribals, yet they continue to be the vulnerable, mainly due to poor health and nutritional status (Bulliyya, 2005). Women and children are much vulnerable (Khan, 1993). The contributors to the increased disease risk include poverty and consequent undernutrition, poor environmental sanitation, poor hygiene and lack of safe drinking water leading to increased morbidity from water and vector-borne infections (Swain and Singh, 1990). None of these villages have electrification, sanitation or access to safe drinking water facilities. Lack of access to health care facilities that resulting in the increased severity and duration of illnesses, social barriers and taboos preventing them utilization of available healthcare services increase further vulnerability to specific endemic and communicable diseases (Dashora, 1995; Bara, 2004).

Orissa Health Strategy (2003) identified several public health problems in tribal areas, which include malaria, sexually transmitted diseases, nutritional, and genetic deficiencies (Chhotray, 2003; Balgir, 2005). The most common diseases detected among DK are parasitic infections, diarrhoea, dysentery, skin diseases, respiratory infections, whooping cough and measles (Bulliyya et al., 2006). Other diseases such as tuberculosis, leprosy and malaria are prevalent. Health facilities do not reach DK because the norms prescribed by the State Governments for establishing Primary Health Centres (PHC) and Health Sub-Centres are inappropriate for a dispersed population in small settlements in inaccessible areas (NFHS, 2000). The PHCs situated at K. Singpur, Bissamcuttack and Muniguda are quite inaccessible devoid of road and transport facility and often cut off en-routes with flowing canals and rivers. All these make difficult on the part of these social isolates in availing the medical facilities on regular basis (Swain, 1994). They employ traditional knowledge of the causes–cure of ailment, and consult their Disari, the medicine man, at times of need.

Nutritional Status

Malnutrition is fairly common amongst the PTG, especially young children and women debilitating their physical condition and lowering resistance to disease, leading at times even to behavioural impairment (Rao *et al.,* 1998). Dietary habits are practiced as per the subsistence accessibility. In general, rice and millets formed the bulk of dietaries of the DK Mandia gruel made out of boiling ragi powder and rice formed the main constituent of food and source of energy in the breakfast and lunch with or without a green chilli or dry fish. They take full meal of rice with a curry during night, however, a wide variation observed in day-to-day food intake both in terms of quality and quantity. The household intake of pulses, vegetables, fats/oils and sugar/jaggery are grossly deficient. Consumption of milk and milk products is taboo and they believe that milching the cow make suffer to the calf that in turn may lead to ill health of their children. The proportion of DK households consuming adequate amounts of both protein and calorie (P+ C+) accounted only 12 per cent, while about 60 per cent are consuming inadequate amounts of both protein and calorie (P- C-). The proportion of households consuming adequate protein but inadequate calorie (C- P+) is 11 per cent, and inadequate protein but adequate calorie (C+ P-) is 17 per cent indicating widespread protein inadequacy than calorie inadequacy. The nutritional status of preschool children (0-5 y) assessed according to weight-for-age (underweight), height-for-age (stunting) and weight-for-height (wasting) using standard classification. The proportion of children with underweight, stunting and wasting (<median-2SD) is 66 per cent, 63 per cent and 21 per cent respectively indicating growth retardation. Body weight of children (6-10 y) and adolescents (11-19 y) show that 60-80 per cent are malnourished (<85 per cent NCHS standard). Low body-mass index (BMI<18.5 kg/m^2) reflected in 55 per cent of adults as chronic energy deficiency. The proportion of over-weight (BMI> 25.0 kg/m^2) is negligible.

Micronutrient malnutrition particularly iron and iodine deficiencies are of public health significance in the DK (Sahu et al., 2005). Anaemia is widespread problem among preschool children, school-age children, adolescents, pregnant women and lactating mothers. Iron deficiency in terms of low ferritin levels is the contributing factor for anaemia. Iodine deficiency disorders are endemic in the Niyamgiri region. Goitre rate is 21 per cent in children, and their intake of iodine deficiency reflected in terms of low urinary iodine excretion. Nearly 10 per cent of households using salt having adequately iodine content of ≥15 ppm (Bulliyya et al., 2008). As most tribal women suffer from anaemia which lowers resistance to fatigue, affects their working capacity and increases susceptibility to disease particularly for those having closely-spaced frequent pregnancies (Khan, 1993). The nutritional status of tribal women directly influences their reproductive performances and the birth weight of their children, which is crucial to the infant's chances of survival, growth and development (Rasmussen, 2001).

Conclusion

The socio-economic and environmental milieu, in which the DK PTG located direct their precarious existence with lack of opportunity for improvement leading to food security and impairments of physical growth and development. Social isolation, poor communication, low literacy, exploitation and inadequate resources are the main concerns that need to be improved on priority basis. Knowledge on healthcare facilities, ongoing national health and nutritional programs and their optimum utilization should be promoted with measures for controlling communicable diseases and nutritional deficiencies. A multi-pronged intervention approach for sustainable livelihood coupled to improve their literacy levels leading to economic and social empowerment. There is an urgent need and the dire of the area for which they face continuous threats of eviction from their homes and lands. The existing infrastructure and welfare schemes are to be reinforced without compromise with targeted surveillance goals. To save the PTG, preparation of action plan for their survival, protection and development is required urgently for fulfilling basic needs and socio-economic update to meet the challenges of modernization.

REFERENCES

1. Aparajita U. 1994. *Culture and Development: Dongrias of Niyamgiri*. p. 304. New Delhi, Vedams eBooks, Inter India Publications.
2. Arati M, Sahoo T. 2004. A Comparative study of indebtedness among the Dongria Kondh and the Juang. *Adivasi*, 44 (1&2): 68-100.
3. Balgir RS. 2005. Detection of a rare blood group Bombay (Oh) phenotype among the Kutia Kondh primitive tribe of Orissa, *India. Int J Hum Genet*, 5(3): 193-198.
4. Bara F. 2004. Child rearing practices and socialization process among the Dongria Kondh. *Adibasi*, 44(1&2): 56-67.
5. Basu A. 1990. "Anthropological approach to tribal health" in *Tribal Demography and Development in North-East India*, Ed. by Ashish Bose, Tiplut Nagbri, Nikhlesh Kumar. pp.131-142, Delhi, B.R.Publishing Corporation.

6. Behera SK, Misra MK. Indigenous phytotherapy for genito-urinary diseases used by the Kandha tribe of Orissa, India. *Journal of Ethnopharmaology* 2005; 102:319-325.

7. Boal BM. 1982. *The Khonds: Human Sacrifice and Religious Change*. Warminister, Wilts, England, Aris and Phillips Ltd.

8. Bulliyya G., Dwibedi B, Mallick, G., Kar SK. 2006. Study on nutritional status of Dongria Kondh primitive tribe and Domb scheduled caste populations of Rayagada district. Bhubaneswar, RMRC Annual Report.

9. Bulliyya G. 2005. Health and nutrition profile of Orissa. *J Indian Public Admin.*, 13:300-311.

10. Bulliyya G. 2006. "Environment and health status of primitive Paudi Bhuiyan tribe in northeastern part of Orissa" in *Anthropology of Primitive Tribes of India*. ed. by P. Dash Sharma, pp.336-368. New Delhi, Serials Publication.

11. *Census of India*, 1991. Paper-1 of 1992: Final Population totals. Registrar General and Census Commissioner of India. New Delhi.

12. *Census of India*, 2001. Registrar General and Census Commissioner of India. New Delhi.

13. Chhotray GP. 2003. Health Status of Primitive tribes of Orissa. *ICMR Bulletin*, 33(10): 1-6.

14. Das PS. 1984 Ownership Pattern, Land Survey and Settlement and its Impact on the Dongria Kondh of Orissa. *Adivasi.* XXIII: 23-32.

15. Das S. 1997. Habitat and nutritional status of a Kondh village of Eastern Ghats, Orissa. *J Human Ecol*, 8: 13-19.

16. Dash PK, Sahoo S, Bal S. 2008. Ethnobotanical studies on orchids of Niyamgiri hill ranges, Orissa. *Ethnobotanical Leaflets*, 12:70-78.

17. Dashora R. 1995. Status of tribal girl child. *Soc Change*, 25(2-3): 207-216.

18. Desai S. 1994. *Gender Inequalities and Demographic Behavior*. India. New York: The Population Council, Inc.

19. DKDA. 2001. A Baseline Survey and Needs Assessment of the Dongria Kondh. Prospective Plan of Dongria Kondh Development Agency, Parsali. 1-46. Bhubaneswar, Government of Orissa, ST & SC Development Department.

20. DKDA. 2004. Dongria Kondh Development Agency, Chattikona, Rayagada. 1-46.

21. Gordon RG. 2005. *Ethnologue: Languages of the World*, Fifteenth edition. Dallas, Tex.: SIL International. Online version: http://www.ethnologue.com/

22. Government of India. 1984. Report of Working Group on Development of Scheduled Tribes during Seventh Plan (1985-90). New Delhi, Ministry of Home affairs.

23. Jena MK. 2002. *Forest Tribes of Orissa: Lifestyle and Social Conditions of Selected Orissan Tribes: The Dongaria Kondh*, pp. 258. New Delhi, D.K. Printworld.

24. Kanungo AK. 2004. Problems in educating tribal children: the Dongria Kondh experience. *AnthroGlobe Journal.* 22.

25. Khan AS. 1993. Genetic structure of Dongria Kondh of Koraput district of Orissa with special references to its impact of mortality and morbidity (unpublished Ph.D. thesis).

26. Krishan S. 1979. *The Kondhs of Orissa: An Anthropometric study*. New Delhi, Concept Publishing Company.

27. Naik PK. 1989. *Blood, Women and Territory. An Analysis of Clan Feuds of Dongria Kondhs*, pp.45. Delhi, Reliance Publishing House.

28. Nayak R. 1990. *The Kondhs: A Handbook for Development.* New Delhi, Indian Social Institute.
29. NFHS. 2000. Orissa (1998-99). *National Family Health Survey India*, pp.170-172. Mumbai, International Institute for Population Sciences.
30. Nityananda P. 2005. *Primitive Tribes of Orissa and their Development Strategies*, 1-304. New Delhi, D.K. Printworld.
31. Pandey GD. 2002. *Fertility and Family Planning in Primitive Tribes.* New Delhi, Serial Publications.
32. Patnaik N, Patnaik PSD. 1982. *The Kondh of Orissa: Their Socio-Cultural Life and Development*, pp.142-165. Bhubaneswar, Tribal and Harijan Research-cum-Training Institute.
33. Patnaik PSD, Mohanty BB. 1990. Dongria Kondh of Orissa- then and now. *Adivasi*, 30 (2&3): 28-41.
34. Patnaik S, Mohanty BB, Nayak PK. 2002. The Dongria youth dormitory: an agent of development. *Adibasi*, 1&2: 17-39.
35. Patnaik, PSD. 1988. Concept of debt among the Dongria Kondhs. *Adivasi*, 28 (2): 11-15
36. Patro SN, Panda GK. 1994. Eastern Ghat in Orissa: Environment. Bhubaneswar, Resources and Development, Orissa Environment Society.
37. Pfeffer G. 2005. The Meria Sacrifice and the Creation of Society. in *Tribal Society: Category and Ritual Exchange* (Contemporary Society: Tribal Studies Vol. 7). New Delhi: Concept.
38. PFI. 2005. *District Profiles of Orissa.* New Delhi, Population Foundation of India, 3-59.
39. Rao VG, Sugunan AP, Sehgal SC. 1998. Nutritional deficiency disorders and high mortality among children of the Great Andamanese tribe. *Natl Med J India.* 11(2): 65-8.
40. Rasmussen KM. 2001. Is there a causal relationship between iron deficiency or iron deficiency anemia and weight at birth, length of gestation and perinatal mortality? *J Nutr.*, 131:590S-603S.
41. Routray S. 1987. The status of women among Dongria Kondh. *Adibasi*, 27: 31-37.
42. Sahoo AC. 1992. Shifting cultivation to horticulture: a case study of Dongria Kondh Development Agency, Kurli, Chattikona. *Adibasi*, 32: 30-35.
43. Sahu T, Sahani NC, Satapathy DM, Behera TR. 2005. Prevalence of goitre in 6-12 year children of Kandhamal district in Orissa. *Indian J Com Med*, 30: 51-52.
44. Schnepel B. 2001. Kings and Rebel Kings: Rituals of Incorporation and Dissent in South Orissa. in *Jagannath Revisited: Studying Society, Religion and the State in Orissa*, ed. by H. Kulke and B. Schnepel, pp. 290-291. New Delhi, Manohar.
45. Singh KS.1994. *The Scheduled Tribes.* Vol. III. Delhi, Oxford University Press.
46. Swain S. 1994. Health, disease, and health seeking behaviour of tribal people in India. in *Tribal Health in India*, ed. by Salil Basu. New Delhi, Manak Publications Pvt Ltd.
47. Swain SSC, Singh JP. 1990. Morbidity status of the Kondha tribes of Phulbani (Orissa), in *Cultural and Environmental Dimensions on Health*, ed. by Buddhadeb Chaudhuri, New Delhi, Inter-India Publications.
48. Thurston E. 1909. *Castes and Tribes of Southern India.* Delhi, Cosmo Publications.

Women's Empowerment and Reproductive Health : Experience from Chapai Nawabganj District in Bangladesh

—Md. Mosiur Rahman

Abstract

This study investigate the various issues of empowerment and reproductive behavior of married women such as health status, decision making of reproductive behavior etc in some selected areas of Chapai Nawabganj district, using the information from 500 ever married women within the reproductive span (15-49 years). Findings reveal that women are found less concerned and deprived to take decision about their own health as well as their child health. The data shows that 55.0 per cent women received antenatal care during their last pregnancy but only 4.5 per cent has participated in decision-making about their antenatal care. At postnatal period, 51.65 per cent and 58.78 per cent women took treatment for themselves and their child respectively but only 5.14 per cent has participated in decision making about their postnatal care. The logistic analysis shows that respondent's current age, education, occupation, husband's education, per capita yearly income, assistance during delivery and decision for household affairs are mostly associated with antenatal caster seeking behavior of married women.

Introduction

The empowerment of women has been recognized through many international, regional and national conferences as a basic human right and also as imperative for national development, population stabilization and global well-being (Hakim A, S Salway and Z. Mumtaz, 2003). Reproductive and sexual health and rights are essential for the empowerment of women and to all quality of life issues concerning social, economic, political and cultural participation by women. Women's empowerment is the process by which unequal power relations are transformed and women gain greater equality with men (Haque R, 2005). At the government level, this includes the extension of all fundamental social, economic and political rights to women. On the individual level, this includes processes by which women gain inner power to express and define their rights and gain greater self-esteem and control over their own lives and personal and social relationship. Male participation and acceptance of changed roles are essential for women's empowerment (UNFPA, 2002).

Utilization of maternal healthcare depends not only on the availability of services but also on different other factors such as distance of healthcare facility; perception of women and their families regarding the need for care; social restrictions on freedom to movement; the opportunity cost of accessing healthcare; and the interaction between the client and the provider of formal healthcare system (IIPS, 2000). Also as a woman's social status and her healthcare intrinsically related, her low status often is the cause of poor access to essential healthcare (Report on Safe Motherhood Conference, 1987; Royston *et al.,* 1989).

Bangladesh is one of the developing countries in the world, the country suffered serious economic and demographic dislocations (Feyistan B and JB Casterine, 2000). Her population is about 14 million of which 48.6 per cent are female and 51.4 per cent are males (BBS, 2003). Now the sex ration is 100 : 103 that mean the half of the total population are women. But the gender inequality is so high and it is very high especially in the rural areas (Barkat A and M Murtaza, 2003). So now a day's women empowerment is a burning issue. Bangladesh society is known to be male-dominated. A married or unmarried woman is identified as the wife or daughter of a man in all social interactions. Most national policy-makers and programme managers involved with health service-delivery, including healthcare providers, employees in public and private sectors, community leaders, and Members of the Parliament, are male. Women's own decision regarding her reproductive health is mostly negligible and neglected in many developing countries. Thus, research that addresses the empowerment of women is seen as essential.

The aim of research in this area is to examine the impact of selected women's empowerment factors on the utilization of maternal healthcare.

Data and Methods

The data were collected from a field survey conducted in the district of Chapai Nawabganj of Bangladesh. These data were collected from both, rural and urban areas of Chapai Nawabganj district. Information was collected from 500 ever-married women by interview method, of them 250 were taken from rural areas and 250 from the urban areas respectively. Respondents were selected by purposive sampling method. For rural areas we had selected three villages under Baroghorian Union, and for urban areas we have selected Chapai Nawabganj thana of Chapai Nawabganj district. Data analytic methods envisaged in this paper are percentage distribution and logistic regression analysis.

Findings

Decision-making of Treatment for Women's General Illness

Decision-making is one of the direct indicators of women's empowerment and it leads to higher self-esteem. If women's decision-making power improves, their empowerment also increases. In Bangladesh, women are deprived to take decision for treatment in their general illness (Aziz KMS and C Maloney, 1985). But, like all other major indicators of women's empowerment, it should bring in mind that women would have control over the decision about her healthcare. Table 7.1 presents the percentage distribution of decision maker of treatment for general illness. The table indicates that the maximum, about 46.0 per cent of the respondent's treatment depend on their husband's decision. That is, husbands are the most dominant persons than that of their better half. The married women who are taking decision for treatment by itself uniquely are 17.80 per cent. Both, the respondents and their husbands about 36.0 per cent is the second highest percentage as decision maker of treatment for general illness. The decision makers including respondent's father, mother, brother etc. who are mainly for divorced or widowed namely other group has a tiny (0.5%) amount.

Table 7.1. Percentage Distribution of Decision Maker of Treatment for General Illness

Decision Maker	Percentage
Own	17.8
Husband	45.9
Both	35.8
Others	0.5
Total	**100.0**

Place of Treatment for Women's General Illness

Place of treatment plays an important role for the patients especially for a woman. Most people of Bangladesh are poor and less educated. They prefer the treatment place where they get treatment with a cheap cost and easily like as government hospital, village doctors etc (Majid M and *et. al.,* 2003). Though government hospitals have comparatively better treatment facilities, but in our country these types of facilities have no proper utilization. Village doctors have not enough training for quality treatment. Consequently poor and less educated people of our country are deprived from their treatment right. Table 7.2 presents

Table 7.2. Percentage Distribution of Respondent's Place of Treatment

Decision Maker	Percentage
Government Hospital	47.8
Clinic	21.7
Village Doctor	23.7
Others	6.8
Total	**100.0**

the percentage distribution of respondent's place of treatment for their general illness. The table 7.2 indicate that, the highest, about 48.0 per cent respondents go to the government hospital for treatment of their general illness. The remaining 21.7 per cent, 23.7 per cent and 6.8 per cent respondents go to clinic, village doctors and other places (Homio-doctors, Kobiraj etc.) respectively.

Impact of Empowerment on Utilization of Maternal Health Care

The two components of maternal care that is antenatal care and postnatal care are taken as dependent variable separately.

Women Empowerment and Antenatal Care

Antenatal care especially medical check-up during pregnancy is an umbrella term used to describe the medical procedures and pregnancy related care provided by doctor or a health worker in a medical facility or at home. The overall aim of antenatal care is to produce healthy mother and baby at the end of the pregnancy (Sundari Ravindran T.K, 2004). But there are no substantial unified criteria about what exactly constitutes antenatal care. There is a considerable variation in the content of antenatal care (Royston and Armstrong, 1989). Antenatal care has strong link with medical check-up during pregnancy, decision-making of medical check-up during pregnancy and assistance during pregnancy complications. Medical check-up during pregnancy is necessary for every pregnant woman. Women in Bangladesh still feel hesitation to take medical check-up during pregnancy. They also avoid it due to their poverty, lack of proper pregnancy knowledge, lack of awareness about pregnancy and lack of such medical center etc. But, now a day some NGOs associated with government are trying to give such types of facilities in a cheap and sometimes free of cost from various organizations like Maternity Center, Maternity Clinic and Urban Primary Health Care Center etc. From the table 7.3 we see that 33.3 per cent mother did not take any medical check-up during their antenatal period. But 54.4 per cent women are more conscious about medical check-up as well as antenatal care for the betterment of them and 12.3 per cent surveyed women had no need medical check-up because they did not conceive.

Decision-making of medical check-up during pregnancy is important indicator that ultimately leads empowerment of women. To increase empowerment of women in our patriarchal society, we should improve women's decision-making power. But they often feel shy about medical check-up as antenatal care during pregnancy. Almost all of them do not decide of their own about such type of needs. They take the decision from their closely related persons. Table 7.3 presents the percentage distribution of decision-maker for medical check up during pregnancy. From the table we see that among the women who had taken medical check-up during pregnancy, only 4.48 per cent had taken decision uniquely for medical check-up during pregnancy, which is very low compared with their counterparts (35.34 per cent).

Table 7.3. Percentage Distribution of Empowerment of Women and Antenatal Healthcare Check-up

Characteristics	Percentage
Medical Check-up	
Yes	54.4
No	33.3
Did not conceive	12.3
Decision Maker for medical check-up at the Time of Pregnancy	
Own	4.48
Husband	35.34
Both	58.08
Others	2.10
Assistance at Pregnancy Complications	
Expectation of Assistance	
Yes	79.48
No	20.52
Type of Assistance	
Husband	35.7
Mother-in-law	13.9
Health worker	46.1
Others	4.4
Respondent's knowledge about pregnant complicacy	
Severe headache	54.6
Convulsions	36.4
Vaginal bleeding during pregnancy	19.0
Fever more than three days	42.0
Bad smelling vaginal discharge	22.6
Other	1.2
Discussed with health professional about pregnancy related complications	
No	76.2
Yes	23.8

Pregnancy complications are very touching matter of women, because at pregnancy period, mental and physical depression do enforce on her mentality. Consequently she emerge assistance during this period from her close relatives such as husband, mother, mother-in-law, health worker etc. Table 7.3 presents the percentage distribution of respondents who expect assistance at pregnancy complications for the last birth. About 12 per cent of the total surveyed women did not conceive their pregnancy. So, among the conceive women, 79.48 per cent expect assistance at pregnancy complications and rest of them did not expect any assistance. Table 7.3 also shows the percentage distribution of type of assistance that is expected by women. From the table we see that, among the women who expect assistance at pregnancy complications, most of them (46.1%) expect health worker as assistance followed by their husband as assistance (35.7%). The remaining 13.9 per cent and 4.4 per cent expect their mother-in-law and others like mother, sister, sister-in-law etc. as assistance at pregnancy complications respectively. Pregnant women need to talk to health professional about their complications aroused during pregnancy, but from our study we find that only 23.8 per cent respondents talked to the health professional. Regarding pregnancy related complications most women have the knowledge about several headache followed by vaginal bleeding and convulsion.

Women Empowerment and Postnatal Care

A crucial component of safe motherhood is postnatal care. It is important for mother's treatment of complications arising from delivery, especially for birth that occurs at home. Postnatal check-up provides opportunities to assess and treat delivery complications and to counsel mothers on how to care for themselves and their newborns. Postnatal care is strongly associated with the treatment after delivery for mother and child and mother's decision-making of treatment after delivery. From table 7.4 we see that approximately 52 per cent women receive postnatal care check-up.

Delivery system is an important part of reproductive health. In general, delivery is commonly of two types such as normal and caesarean delivery. Caesarean delivery is more common among first births of urban women than that of rural (BDHS, 2004). Table 7.4 presents the percentage distribution for last birth by type of delivery. The findings show that, most of the deliveries are normal. About 90.0 per cent deliveries of surveyed women are normal and the rest are taking place by caesarean delivery.

This is also important for our study because it is related with women's empowerment. Table 7.4 elucidates the percentage distribution of decision-maker for treatment after delivery. From the table 7.4 we found that, about 18.0 per cent of the respondents did not produce child and/or did not take treatment after delivery. Among the respondents who took treatment after delivery for her own and/or their child, maximum, 55.38 per cent decision was own, which is very low compared with their counterparts, 36.64 per cent. Like mother, treatment of child after delivery is also important for our study. Table 7.4 presents the percentage distribution of respondents who took treatment for child after delivery. The findings shows that, about 12.0 per cent respondents did not produce child, so they have no need to take treatment for child. Among the child produced respondents, maximum (about 58.78 per cent) took treatment of their own after delivery. From our study we also find that 65.2 per cent respondents talked to husbands about her own health and the baby's health.

Table 7.4. Percentage Distribution of Decision-Maker for Postnatal Healthcare Check-up

Characteristics	Percentage
Receive Postnatal Care	
Yes	51.65
No	48.35
Types of Delivery	
Normal	90.27
Caesarean	9.73
Decision Maker for Types of Delivery	
Own	5.14
Husband	36.64
Both	55.38
Others	2.24
Child Treatment after Delivery	
Yes	58.78
No	41.22
Discussed with husband about her own health and the baby's health	
No	34.8
Yes	65.2

Factors Affecting of Respondent's Decision-making of Medical Check-up during Pregnancy

The examination of decision-making for medical check-up during pregnancy is an important phenomenon that effects women's empowerment. Different characteristics have demonstrated uniquely in the incidence of decision-making across reproductive health-cares such as decision-making of treatment for general illness and treatment after delivery, medical check up during pregnancy etc. Previously we explored the various important indicators of reproductive healthcare for women, but decision-making of medical check-up during pregnancy is the most important among them. This indicator may be influenced by some other indicators combined and independently. To examine the combined impact of the several variables to this indicator, the multivariate analysis has to be needed. For this circumstance, we apply logistic regression analysis to estimate the effects of some selected socio-economic, demographic and geographic factors on decision-making for medical check-up during pregnancy.

The logistic model is fitted by considering medical check up during pregnancy as the dependent variable which we dichotomized by assessing 1, if the respondents can participate in decision-making for medical check-up during pregnancy and 0 for otherwise. The explanatory variables considered in the model are respondent's current age, education, religion, place of residents, age at marriage, husband's education, household educational status (average years of schooling), per capita yearly income, type of family, and assistance at pregnancy complications, daily household expenditure, decision for household work and equal rights existing in the society.

From the results of the logistic regression analysis, it appears that current age is the most important factor affecting of decision-making for medical check-up during pregnancy among married women and it has strong significant association with medical check-up during pregnancy. From the study, we see that, women age group 40 and above years are 0.150 times less likely to go for medical check-up during pregnancy than the women who are at age group up to 19 years. So, we can say that married women aged at low level are much concourse than that of older for medical check-up during pregnancy. Education is also strong and positive effects on medical check-up during pregnancy for married women. The result shows that women with primary, secondary and higher education are 1.625, 3.282 and 35.867 times more likely to go for medical check up during pregnancy than the women who are illiterate (reference group) respectively. Husband's education has also strong and significant effects on medical check-up during pregnancy for married women.

The result shows that women's husband with primary, secondary and higher education are 1.941 times, 2.201 times and 1.829 times more likely to medical check-up during pregnancy than the women whose husband has no education (reference group) respectively. Per capita yearly income has also strong and positive significant on medical check-up during pregnancy for married women. The per capita yearly income of Tk. 30,000 and above are found to be 3.305 times more likely to take medical check-up. The result also shows that, women who have married at age group 20 and above years are 1.528 times more likely to go for medical check-up during pregnancy than the women who have married at age group up to 15 years as reference group. The results also elucidates that urban respondents are more likely to receive medical check-up than their rural counterparts. The result shows that, non-Muslim women are 1.692 times more likely to go for medical check-up during pregnancy than their Muslim counterpart (reference group).

Decision for household affairs is an important factor influencing the medical check-up during pregnancy for surveyed women and it has strong and positive significant impact. The result shows that, women who have decision-making power for household affairs are 2.667 times more likely to go for medical check-up during pregnancy than that having no such power. Expectation of assistance at pregnancy related complications has strong and positive significant effects on medical check-up during pregnancy for married women. The table 7.5 shows that, women who expect assistance at pregnancy related complications are 1.624 times more likely to go for medical check-up during pregnancy than those do not expect assistance. Control over daily household expenditure has insignificant impact on medical check-up during pregnancy for married women. The result shows that, women having control over daily household expenditure are 1.243 times more likely to go for medical check-up during pregnancy than that having no such facility (reference group). Equal right of male and female existing in the society has no significant effects on medical check-up during pregnancy. The result shows that women who agree to equal rights for male and females existing in the society are 1.183 times likely to go for medical check-up than that who does not agree.

Table 7.5. Logistic regression of Medical Check-up during pregnancy on some selected socio-demographic characteristics

Characteristics	Coefficient B	Significance Level	Odds Ratio
Place of Residence			
Rural (Ref)	—	—	1.000
Urban	0.244	0.327	1.277
Age of Respondent			
Up to 19 (Ref)	—	—	1.000
20 to 29	–0.739	0.093	0.478
30 to 39	–1.402	0.002	0.246
40 and above	–1.900	0.000	0.150
Respondent's Education			
Illiterate (Ref)	—	—	1.000
Primary	0.484	0.039	1.623***
Secondary	1.188	0.000	3.282***
Higher	3.580	0.000	35.867**
Husband's Education			
Illiterate (Ref)	—	—	1.000
Primary	0.663	0.006	1.941
Secondary	0.789	0.005	2.201
Higher	0.604	0.116	1.829**
Respondent's Occupation			
House wife (Ref)	—	—	1.000
Service (govt.)	–2.426	0.003	0.088
Service (non-govt.)	–1.241	0.040	0.289
Business	–1.116	0.061	0.328
Labor	0.587	0.549	1.798

Characteristics	Coefficient	Significance Level	Odds Ratio
Religion			
Islam (Ref)	—	—	1.000
Others	0.526	0.209	1.692
Household Educational Status (Average Year of Schooling)			
<5 (Ref)	—	—	1.000
5-10	–0.163	0.509	0.849
>10	0.449	0.326	1.567
Per Capita Income (Yearly)			
<15000 (Ref)	—	—	1.000
15000-30000	0.260	0.210	1.297**
>30000	1.195	0.013	3.305***
Age at Marriage			
Up to 15 (Ref)	—	—	1.000
15-20	–0.010	0.952	0.990
20 and above	0.424	0.263	1.528
Assistance at Pregnancy Complications			
No (Ref)	—	—	1.000
Yes	0.485	0.019	1.624
Daily Household Expenditure			
No (Ref)	—	—	1.000
Yes	0.217	0.222	1.243**
Decision for Household Affairs			
No (Ref)	—	—	1.000
Yes	0.981	0.000	0.2667**
Equal Rights Existing in Society			
No (Ref)	—	—	1.000
Yes	0.168	0.389	1.183*

Note: (Ref) = Reference category, Here ***, ** and * indicates p<.001 (highly significant), p<.01 (significant), and p<. 05 (less significant

Discussions and Policy Implications

Women empowerment and their reproductive behavior is much publicised concern among both the developed and developing nations and recently it has become a major topic of socio-economic and demographic research. Considering its importance, an attempt has been made in this study to investigate the various issues of empowerment and reproductive behavior of married women such as health status, decision-making of reproductive behavior etc in some selected areas of Chapai Nawabganj district. From the results, only 17.8 per cent of the respondents may take decision for the treatment of their general illness. For the last birth, about 55.0 per cent women received antenatal care and among them only 4.5 per cent is the self decision maker. Among the women who expect assistance at pregnancy complications, 46.1 per cent expect health worker corresponding 35.7 per cent expect their husband as assistance. At postnatal period, 51.65 per cent and 58.78 per cent women took treatment for themselves and their child after delivery respectively but among them only 5.14 per cent are decision-maker.

This indicates that most of the women are conscious about their healthcare for the betterment of them and their child but they are to wait for their husband's decision. On the other hand, this study also indicates that a large number of women terminate their pregnancy unsafely because they do not check-up in the period of pregnancy. In socio-economic and demographic impact on decision-making of medical check-up during pregnancy, the study shows that women who are relatively young are much conscious than that of their older counterparts for medical check-up during pregnancy. The study also shows that education has strong and positive significant impact on medical check-up at the time of pregnancy and as at the women's education level improves; their tendency for medical check-up also increases. Women's decision making for household affairs has also strong significant effect. The results elucidates that women who can make decision for household affairs are more likely to check-up at the time of pregnancy than those women who do not get such opportunities. Among other factors women's occupation, husband's education, per capita yearly income and assistance at pregnancy complications have also found significant effects on medical check-up during pregnancy.

Women's empowerment policy could be made on women's mobility, a limited role in household as well as society based decision-making, a limited control over all knowledge about their reproductive health. Considering this points, the study findings lead to the following policy implications.

- Inform and empower girls to delay pregnancy until they are physically and emotionally mature.
- Enable women to exercise their rights to control their own fertility and their right to make decision concerning reproduction, discrimination and violence.
- Improve the quality of reproductive health services and implement commitments to reducing the tragedy of maternal mortality.
- Increase gender equality and equal opportunities for women in all spheres of employment.
- Provide education and training that enable women to catch up and adapt to changing economic conditions.

- Improve communication between men and women on issues of sexuality and reproductive health and the understanding of their joint responsibilities so that they are equal partners in public and private life.

Conclusion

There is a more radical approach would aim at directly meeting women's "strategic gender needs" for greater influence over their own empowerment and reproductive behavior. Such an approach would involve action a multiple levels to increase women's access to resource of various types, through both strengthened informal rights and extended formal rights (legislation and state provision in women's interest).

REFERENCES

1. Aziz KMS and C Maloney (1985). *Life stages, gender and fertility in Bangladesh*, ICDDRB, Dhaka, Bangladesh.
2. *Bandgladesg Demographic and Health Survey (2004).* Niport, Mitra and Associates, Macro international Inc, USA.
3. Barkat A and M Murtaza (2003). "Adolescent's reproductive health in Bangladesh. Status, policies and programs and issues." Policy project report USAID Asia/Near east Bureau.
4. Feyistan B and JB casterline (2000). Fertility preferences and contraceptive change in developing countries: *International family planning perspectives* 26(3): 100-109.
5. Hakim A, S Salway and Z Mumtaz (2003). Women's autonomy and uptake contraception in Pakistan. *Asia-Pacific population Journal*, Vol. 18, No.1, March 2003
6. Haque R (2005). An article on women employment. Published on *Nari Mancha*, The daily prothom alo, October, 2005.
7. International Institute for Population Sciences (2000). "National family health survey, 1998-99", International institute for population sciences, Mumbai, India.
8. Report on the Safe Motherhood Conference (1987). Preventing the tragedy of Maternal Death. A report on the International safe motherhood conference, Nairobi, Kenya.
9. Royston E et al, (1989). The status of women and maternal mortality. In preventing maternal deaths, Ed, Erica Royston and Sue Armstrong, WHO.
10. Sundari Ravindran T.K, (2004). Zeroing in on gender discrimination. Cover story in health action.
11. UNFPA (2002). Women's empowerment and reproductive Health.Links throughout the lifecycle, published as part of UNFPA's advocacy booklet series, March 2002.

Interactive Effect of Self-concept, Level of Aspiration, Student Activism Institutional Environment and Social Motivation on Scholastic Achievement of Scheduled Tribes Students

—S.K. Lakhera and N.P. Uniyal

Abstract

The present investigation was conducted in the newly created state Uttrakhand. The territory of this state lying in the northern India is inhabited by a small numbers (approximate 4%) of hilly tribes (Bhotiya and Jaunsari) who speak their one single dialect. Bhotia people live in three district, Chamoli, Uttrakashi and Pithoragarh, whereas Jaunsari lived in very remote area of Chaukrauta block of Dehradun districts.

This study focused on the co-relationship between self-concept, level of aspiration, students activism, institutional environment and social motivation on scholastic achievement of ST students studying in higher education institutions of H.N.B. Garhwal University, Srinagar, Garhwal. By using multistage stratified random sampling technique a sample of 71 high and low achiever ST students, were selected to higher education institutions. Self-Concept Scale (Deo, 1985), Institutional Environment Description Questionnaire (I.E.DQ.) and Inventory of Social Motivation for Academic Achievement (ISMAA), Kukreti & Uniyal (1999), Educational Aspiration Scale Saxena (1984), and Students Activism Scale Uniyal (1992) all standardized tools was used to collect information regarding all above variables for scholastic achievement. Result of the study revealed that intellectual, social and aesthetic self-concept, institutional environment. Student activism, level of aspiration and motivation from family neighbours, friend and school caste a positive impact on the scholastic achievement of ST students.

Introduction

Scholastic achievement is the indicator of knowledge ability and skill acquired by the students in school subject at particular standard of education (Uniyal, 1999). In this modern competitive age it becomes indispensable to acquire better grades or to score high marks for it is regarded as a key to success. Not only this, but there are many professional institution which provide admission to the students on the basis of his/her performance in the entrance test while other institutes follow the criteria to admit the students at the performance shown by them in the course they have passed. There may be many factors which influence scholastic achievement of students. As it has been proved by various researchers, Rogers (1961) pointed out that much of the child's academic behaviour is influenced by his self-perception. According Ford (1992) motivation is one of the most significant factors, that effects human behaviour. Each and every action of man is guided by motivation in one or the other way. Motivation is the internal force, which excites an individual to act, stimulates the individual to work in certain direction (Kukreti et al. 2005). Stevenson and Baker (1987) found that the children of upper strata show better performance due to greater interest of their father and mother in their academic performance. Dessai (1979), studied the relationship between classroom environment, pupil's motivation and academic achievement. The researcher reported that the classroom environment was positively related with pupil's motivation and their academic achievement. Bindyadhar (2006), conclude that the tribal are not only socially disadvantaged, economically deprived and geographically cut off but also psychologically alienated. Hope (1930), Gradner (1940) found a positive relationship between achievement and level of aspiration. Shivappa (1980) found that educational aspiration was significantly positively correlated with academic achievement of rural and urban students.

Pathak (1975), in his study "students unrest and faculty examination system" indicated that students unrest significantly correlate with academic performance. Vidyarthy (1972) and Upadhyaya (1975) also indicated that students activism was significantly correlated with the academic performance of students. Whereas, Lipeart (1966) revealed that students agitations does not make any affect in student academic performance.

Some researchers conducted investigation to find out the correlates of scholastic achievement. Srivastava (1995) revealed that, parents loving, disciplining, dominating, and protecting behaviour effects positively upon pupils academic achievement whereas, rejecting and punishing behaviour negatively affects academic achievement. Patel (1994) reported a positive correlation between school environment and scholastic performance of students. But Narang (1987) had conducted an investigation to find out students relation with teachers and principals and its impact on students academic achievement. The investigator revealed that the relationship with principals did not effect the student academic achievement. On the basis of above mentioned studies it can be concluded that there was not even a single study which compared high achiever and low achiever ST students, in respects to their self-concept, level of aspiration, student activism, institutional environment and social motivation. The present investigation was conducted to fill this gap and to explore the co-relationship between above mentioned variables and scholastic achievement of ST students studying in higher educational institutions.

Objectives

The study was conducted with the following objectives:

(*i*) To know the impact of self-concept of the ST students on their scholastic achievement.

(*ii*) To verify how far the level of aspiration influence their scholastic achievement of the ST students.

(*iii*) To investigate the effect of students activism on the scholastic achievement of ST students.

(*iv*) To study the co-relationship between institutional environment and scholastic achievement of ST students.

(*v*) To compare the level of social motivation of high achiever and low achiever ST students.

Hypothesis: There exists no significant difference between higher achiever and low achiever ST students, in relation to their self-concept, level of aspiration, student activism, institutional environment and social motivation for scholastic achievement.

Methodology

Population: The present investigation was conducted on the students studying in the different institution of H.N.B. Garhwal University Srinagar, Garhwal. Therefore all regular ST students whether studying in constitute colleges, affiliated and government colleges falling under the jurisdiction of H.N.B. Garhwal University, have been considered as the population of the study.

Sample and Sampling Technique

In the present study keeping in view the adequacy and representative quality of the sample. Multistage stratified random sampling technique was adopted at the initial stage of sampling out of all colleges of H.N.B. Garhwal University, 10 colleges were selected randomly at the second stage considering the sex wise, caste wise, and faculty wise representation of students, 900 students were selected randomly. At the third stage personal data schedule was distributed among these 900 students on the basis of academic records of previous three classes. At the fourth stage, the high achiever (above 60 percentage marks and low achiever below 45 percentage marks), 71 scheduled tribe (ST) students were selected as the final sample.

Tools

For collecting the required information about student academic records for the past three years, personal data schedule distributed and to collect the data regarding independent variables the following standardized tools was used:

(*a*) Self concept scale (Prativa Dev, 1984)
(*b*) Level of aspiration scale (Saxena, 1984)
(*c*) Student activism scale (Uniyal., 1992)
(*d*) Inventory of social motivation for academic achievement (Uniyal, 1999).
(*e*) Institutional Environment Description Questionnaire (Kukreti & Uniyal, 1999)

Statistical Treatment

We employ arithmetic mean (AM) standard deviation (SD) and to measure the significant difference between two means the 't' test.

Results and Discussion

After scoring the responses of the subjects, the raw data were analysed statically. Firstly, the mean and standard deviation (SD.) of self-concept, level of aspiration, student activism, institutional environment and social motivation of high achiever and low achiever students were found out and then 't' ratio were calculated. The results are shown in tables 8.1 to 8.5.

Table 8.1. Mean and S.D. scores of High Achiever and Low Achiever ST Students on Different Dimension of Self-Concept Scale.

Sl. No.	Dimension of Self Concept	High Achiever Students (N=32)		Low Achiever Students (N=39)		't' value	Level of significance (5% level)
		M	SD	M	SD		
1.	Intellectual	29.156	3.380	18.717	5.419	9.908*	Significant
2.	Emotional	2.625	5.040	2.461	7.479	0.127	NS
3.	Social	24.904	4.091	20.796	4.608	4.00*	Significant
4.	Character	55.218	7.330	54.769	5.455	0.287	NS
5.	Asthetic	15.843	3.070	9.948	3.755	7.277*	Significant
6.	Total self concept	127.748	15.682	106.934	19.276	5.016*	Significant

*Significant at 0.05 level of Significance.
NS—Not Significance.

The above table 8.1 shows that except emotional and character self-concept, the all dimensions of self-concept *i.e.,* intellectual, social, aesthetic as well as over all self-concept have a positive relationship with scholastic achievement of students. In all these dimensions of self-concept, the high achiever students scored significantly higher mean values than low achiever students (P=< 0.05). In respect to emotional and aesthetic self concept there was no significant difference between and high achiever and low achiever students.

Table 8.2. Statistically Analysis of Different Dimension of Educational Aspiration among High Achiever and Low Achiever ST Students, Studying in Higher Education Institution

Sl. No.	Dimension of Self-Concept	High Achiever Students (N=32)		Low Achiever Students (N=39)		't' value	Level of Significance (5% level)
		M	SD	M	SD		
1.	Idealistic	23.656	3.924	20.692	3.286	3.40*	Significant
2.	Realistic	20.812	3.477	18.075	3.240	3.46*	Significant
3.	Total level aspiration	44.468	7.278	30.717	7.501	3.26*	Significant

*Significant at 0.05 level of significance.

It is evident from table 8.2 that there exists a statistically significant difference between high achiever and low achiever S.T. students on all dimension of level of aspiration i.e. idealistic, realistic as well as total level of aspiration (t=3.40, 3.46, 3.26 respectively, P<0.01).

Table 8.3. Comparison of Mean Values of Student Activism among High Achiever and Low Achiever Tribal Students

Sl. No.	Dimension of Self Concept	High Achiever Students (N=32)		Low Achiever Students (N=39)		't' value	Level of Significance (5% level)
		M	SD	M	SD		
1.	Student Activism	15.875	4.398	18.796	3.030	3.15*	Significant

*Significant at 0.05 level of significance.

From the data displayed in table 8.3 it is clear that scholastic achievement was significantly influenced by student activism. This show that group of low achiever students have higher mean scores than their counterparts high achiever students (t=3.15, P<0.05).

Table 8.4. Means, SD, and 't' Ratio of Institutional Environment Scores of High Achiever and Low Achiever Tribal Students

Sl. No.	Dimension of Self-Concept	High Achiever Students (N=32)		Low Achiever Students (N=39)		't' value	Level of Significance (5% level)
		M	SD	M	SD		
1.	Academic Encouragement	42.87	9.25	37.05	10.14	2.56*	Significant
2.	Inter Personal Trust	46.68	5.97	41.15	7.06	3.57*	Significant
3.	Democracy and Freedom	27.56	2.89	20.74	3.50	8.98*	Significant
4.	Autocracy and Strictness	11.68	2.58	13.10	2.33	2.39	NS
5.	Discipline and Control	27.12	2.31	22.20	2.86	8.01*	Significant
6.	Hindrance	17.12	8.04	18.10	3.76	0.60	NS
7.	Physical Material	48.03	3.85	44.48	5.41	3.21*	Significant

* Significant at 0.05 level of Significance.
NS – Not Significance

An examination of table 8.4, indicate that in comparison to low achiever ST students, the high achiever ST students scored higher mean values on their academic encouragement, inter-personal trust, democracy and freedom, discipline and control and physical material dimensions. While on autocracy and strictness and hindrance environmental dimension, the low achiever ST students scored higher mean values than their counterpart high achiever ST students of the same group. On the other hand, statistically we can say that there is no significant difference in between high and low achiever students in relation to their autocracy and strictness and hindrance dimension of institutional environment (t=2.39, 0.60, P>0.05).

Table 8.5. Mean and S.D Scores of High Achiever and Low Achiever ST Students on Different Dimension of Inventory of Social Motivation for Academic Achievement (ISMMA)

Sl. No.	Dimension of Self Concept	High Achiever Students (N=32)		Low Achiever Students (N=39)		't' value	Level of significance (5% level)
		M	SD	M	SD		
1.	Family Motivation	24.62	4.87	16.66	6.02	6.61*	Significant
2.	Friends Motivation	21.48	3.51	16.07	4.79	5.46*	Significant
3.	Relatives Motivation	24.31	2.75	19.05	4.12	6.41*	Significant
4.	Neighbours Motivation	25.68	3.19	18.00	3.27	9.98*	Significant
5.	Schools Motivation	24.78	3.19	18.71	5.51	5.79*	Significant
6.	Overall social motivation	121.59	12.49	88.51	4.26	13.2*	Significant

*Significant

In the statistics of table 8.5, indicate that as a whole, the high achiever ST students have significantly higher mean scores on all the dimension of social motivation than their counterparts low achiever ST students, because the obtained. 't' ratios were 6.16, 5.46, 6.41, 9.98, 5.79 and 13.2 respectively and all ratios are significant at 0.05 level of confidence.

Summary and Findings

Hypothesis formulated of the present study were partially accepted and partially rejected, because the results were found as below:

- When we compare the scholastic achievement of ST students with self-concept the high achiever students scored statistically higher mean values than low achiever students on intellectual, social, aesthetic as well as over all self-concept scale. But in the dimension of emotional and character the above comparing group were scored similar mean values.
- In case of level of aspiration, the high achiever ST students were found more significant mean scores than their counterpart of low achiever ST students.
- Student activism caste negative and significant impact on scholastic achievement of ST student.

- Autocracy, strictness and hindrance the dimension of institutional environment was no significant impact on scholastic achievement of ST students whereas, the high achiever ST students, were found to have significantly higher mean scores on academic encouragement, inter-personal trust, democracy and freedom, discipline and control and physical materials the dimension of institutional environment.
- High achiever ST students were found to have significantly higher mean scores on all the dimension of social motivation (family, friends, relatives, neighbours, schools and overall social motivation) than low achiever ST students.

Conclusion

On the basis of the result of the present study, it can be concluded that the high achiever ST students were high socially motivated and aspired with respect of low achiever ST students. The study also indicates that in comparison to high achiever ST students, the low achiever ST students received significantly low intellectual, social and aesthetic self-concept scores and low achiever ST students pay more activity role in their college life, than high achiever ST students. All these pieces of above information help investigators to draw a conclusion that there is close relationship between education and society. So the role of society and children aspiration can't be ignored to maintain the quality and status of education. In other words, in the development of educational achievement of learners, their positive self-concept and high level of aspiration with good institutional environment, low activation within institute and the behaviour of their classmate, relatives and educational institutions etc. are such social dimensions which can motive students to improve their academic performance. If school and home atmosphere is conducive, parents and teachers are alert and motive their children/students at every movement, there might be a positive influence on the over all scholastic achievement of ST students particular in this Himalayan region of Uttarakhand state of India.

REFERENCES

1. Deo, P., (1985), *Self-concept List* (SCL), National Psychological Co-operation, Agra.
2. Desai, S.D. (1979, *A Study of Classroom. Ethos, Pupils, Motivation and Academic Achievement*, Ph.D. Edu.msu.
3. Ford, M.E. (1992), *Motivating Humans: Goals, Emotions and Persona Agency Beliefs*, Newburg Park, C.A. sage.
4. Gardener, J.W. (1940). *The Use of Level of Aspiration.*
5. Hope, B.M. (1930), *Academic Performance and Personality Adjustment of Highly Intelligent College Students'* Genet. Psy. Monographs. 5, pp. 3-83.
6. Kukreti, B.R. and Uniyal, N.P. (1999), *Inventory of Social Motivation for Academic Achievement*, Edu. Deptt. H.N.B. Garhwal University, Srinagar Garhwal.
7. Kukreti, B.R., Saxena M.K and Gihar S. (2005). *Job-motivation Factors of Efficient and Inefficient Teachers and Quality Control in Teacher Training Programme*, Staff and Educational Development International, May, 2004.

8. Lipeart, S.M. (1966), Student Politics in Under Developed Countries, *Comparative Education Review*, 10, 2, p. 132.

9. Narang, R.H. (1987), A Comparative Study of the Socio-Economic and Home Factors, Affecting the Academic Achievement of Boy's and Girls (10 and 11 years) in the Urban and Rural Areas. Ph.D. Edu. Bom. Univ.

10. Patel, K.P. (1994), Organizational Climate in Higher Secondary School. *The Progress of Edu.*, Vol. LLLXVII No. 6, p. 144. January.

11. Pathak, A. (1975), Student Unrest, *Journal of Sociology*, Vol. VII.

12. Rogers, Carl. R. (1961). *On becoming a Person : A Therapistic view of Psychotherapy*, Boston: Houghton Mifflin. Co.

13. Saxena, S.K. (1984), Manual for "Educational Aspiration Scale". Published by Agra Psychological Research Cell". Belanganj Agra.

14. Shivappa, D. (1980), Factors Affecting the Academic Achievement of High School Pupils, Ph.D. Edu. Kar. Univ.

15. Srivastava, R.K. (1995). Effect of the Parent-Child Relationship Perception upon the Academic Achievement of Vth Class pupils, *Praachi Journal of Psycho-Cultural Dimension*, Vol II (1-2) pp. 27-32.

16. Stevenson, D.L. and Baker, D.P. (1987). The family School Relation and the Child's School Performance, *Child Development*, 58, pp. 1348-135.

17. Uniyal, B.P. (1992), Student Activism and Students Performance. D.Phil Thesis. H.N.B.G.U.

18. Uniyal, N.P. (1999), Interactive Effects of Self-Concept, Students Activism on Scholastic Achievement of Degree Students, Unpublished Ph.D. Thesis H.N.B.G.U.

19. Upadhyaya, D. (1975), A Study of Student Unrest in the Colleges of Eastern U.P., *International Journal of Psychology,* Vol. 4, No. 17.

Socio-demographic Characteristics of Female Migrants and Determinants of Female Migration

—Md. Rafiqul Islam & Md. Nure Alam Siddiqi

Abstract

In Bangladesh, approximately 50 per cent populations are women. This large portion of population is now participating in the overall development process and for this reason the study about female migration is quite important and imperative. The purpose of this study is to observe the socio-demographic characteristics of female migrants and determinants of female migration. For this, data was collected from Bogra Pourusova of Bogra district, Bangladesh by purposive sampling technique. Chi-square test is used to identify the association between causes of migration and some selected socio-demographic characteristics. It is seen that age at marriage, educational qualification, occupation, religious characteristics, marital status, type of family and type of migration of female migrants are highly associated with causes of migration. Moreover, logistic regression is employed to recognize the influence of some socio-demographic variables on causes of migration. Logistic analysis showed that age at marriage, occupation, religion, marital status, type of family (before migration), type of migration significantly effect on causes of migration of female migrants.

Introduction

Background of the Study

Migration is an integral part of human existence. It is an inevitable continuous process for human civilization. The pattern and source of migration is almost alike throughout the world. But, its applicability and effects are different from developed world to developing world. However, the recent speed of globalization has given new dimension to it. Both internal and international migration has great importance for a country. Internal migration is important almost everywhere and in some countries it is far greater than international migration. Internal migration has resumed greater importance as a component of people's livelihood strategies and in shaping the national economy. Internal migration involves men, women and children, and includes rural to rural, urban to rural, urban to urban and rural to urban flows. The trends of internal migration, particularly, rural to urban are increasing day by day.

In Bangladesh, two-thirds of all migration from rural areas is to urban areas and it is increasing very rapidly (Afsar, 2003a). The BBS (Bangladesh Bureau of Statistics) showed that lifetime internal migration has increased significantly. The proportion of lifetime migrants doubled (from 3.4% to 7.4%) between 1974 and 1982, and reached to 10.2 per cent in 1991 (BBS, 1994). 40 per cent of male migrants were moved from rural to urban areas and 33.4 per cent from urban to urban areas. In contrast, more than 56 per cent of women were migrated from rural to rural areas and 28 per cent from rural to urban areas. These figures indicate the high prevalence of marital migration and intra-district marriage and their influence on rural-urban movement.

The propensity of migration is usually influenced by a combination of push-pull factors. The urban sector plays an important role in providing employment to the labor force. Basic elements for employment i.e. industry, formal and informal sectors are mainly situated in and around the urban centers all over the world. Urban centers are the main sources of innovation, technological programme and culture. This sector has always been acted 'Pull' factor for the in-migrants. For this rationale, every year a large number of rural working populations enter into the urban areas in search of jobs and enjoy some health, education and housing facilities in the cities. Again, some 'Push" factors like floods, fire, drought, earthquake or epidemic, loss of employment, political, religious reason for which people are obliged to migrate from one area to another.

Most of the migrants in Bangladesh are male and they migrate to cities and towns to support their families. People migrated to cities and towns because they are attracted by livelihood opportunities. But now women of different age groups and status are now start to migrate with different motive. The reasons for women's migration are complex and may include demographic, economic, non-economic and demographic factors. Most of the women in Bangladesh have to migrate after their marriage and go to the place where their husband lives. But, now in the present time, more and more women are migrating for work not just as accompanying spouses. This so-called "autonomous female migration" has increased because of a greater demand for female labor in certain services and industries and also because of growing social acceptance of women's economic independence and mobility. In fact, the feminization of migration is one of the principal recent changes of population movement (Deshinkar and Grimm, 2005).

Review of Literature of the Study

A number of studies have been carried out on migration. Some of the relevant literature in the context of the present study is reviewed in the following.

Islam et al. (2007) observed that people migrate to certain places due to economic reasons and migration can alter the lifestyle of individuals and families and to improve their social and economic status. Faruk et al. (2007) studied about the socio-economic conditions of female migrants, they observed that maximum migrants have migrated in the age range 20-34 and most of them were illiterate, most of them do not earn money and consequently depend on their husbands. They also observed that those women who were engaged in different profession have a great chance of migration compared to women who were house wives. Rahman et al. (2007) identified the education, monthly income, type of family and land property significantly effect on causes of migration.

Afsar (2005) identified that there is a strong positive and negative poverty-migration nexus. Poverty induces migration as much as migration contributes to the eradication of poverty. Kuhn (2005) investigated the determinants of rural-urban migration by adult males in Matlab Thana, Bangladesh, from 1983 to 1991 in which the family migration was especially focused. Afsar (2003a) observed that migration played an important role in reducing poverty. Afsar (2003b) also showed that all types of migration have recently increased significantly. She tried to relate internal migration with development process in Bangladesh. Siddiqui (2003) identified that migration is an important livelihood strategy for poor people while ensuring that migrant workers receive maximum protection both at home and abroad. It describes the extent, nature and types of both short and long term international migration.

Elahi (1985) analyzed that perspectives of internal migration and historical background of urbanization in Bangladesh were elaborately discussed through socio-economic and demographic viewpoints. He also observed that rural-urban migration is widely held to be the chief cause of rapid growth of urban population in the most countries. Singh and Yadava (1981) revealed that outmigration of young male leads to decline in fertility at the place of origin. Yadava (1987) identified that the migration decision of an individual is influenced by marital status. It was reported that married persons usually migrate shorter distances in order to visit his family frequently. Hugo (1991) observed that across the less developing countries (LDCs) of Asia has been consisted acceleration of urbanization from rural to urban, an increase in the tempo of population redistribution from rural to urban areas since 1970s. He established that poorer and landless have a greater propensity of migration than richer and big landowners.

Importance of the Study

One ordinarily would not like to leave the place of birth, friends as well as kins unless that is absolutely necessary. Yet, people migrate from one place to another. Approximately 50 per cent populations of the country are women. This large portion of population are now participating in the overall development process of the country and for this reason the migration of female is increasing day by day. So, the importance of the study about migration is key importance in modern era. The importance emerges not only from the movement of people but also from its influence on the lives of individuals in addition to urban growth. Migration is bound to have an influence on population distribution thus resulting population redistribution within a country. So, migration changes the distribution of population both at the place of origin and the place of destination which affects the economic, social, demographic conditions of a country positively or negatively. Migration enhances the process of urbanization and it is inevitably linked to the process of economic development of a country.

In Bangladesh, the census data does not provide sufficient information to study the causes and consequences of migration and socio-economic and demographic characteristics of migrants. So, it is important to give concentration to micro-level studies based on sample surveys, which will help to study about different types of migration. It is essential to note that the characteristics of migrants are sufficient to explain the selectivity of migration because the decision of a person to migrate is largely dependent on his family background. The socio-economic characteristics of migrants can give some idea about which types of people involved in the process of migration. That is why, it is imperative to study the socio-economic characteristics of migrant households to get an idea about the influences and consequences of migration. This study provides a better understanding as why and when some females are obliged to participate in migration process while others not.

Objectives of this Study

Therefore, the fundamental aims and objectives of this study are addressed in the following:

(*i*) study the socio-demographic characteristics of female migrants, and

(*ii*) to identify the interaction effects of socio-demographic characteristics on causes of migration for female by applying logistic regression analysis, and to apply cross validation predictive power (CVPP) for verifying how much the model is valid.

Organization of this Study

This paper is organized as follows. Introduction is included in 1st section in which background of the study, review of literature of the study, importance of the study, objectives of this study and lastly organization of this study. Data and data sources of this study are presented in section 2. Section 3 describes the methods and methodological issues in which bivariate and logistic analysis and model validation technique are discussed. Results and discussion are reported in section 4. Finally, section 5 concludes the conclusion of this paper.

Data and Data Source of this Study

In this study, a total number of 285 female respondents were questioned during survey period in 2007. The respondents were interviewed by some selected questions from Bogra Pourusova of Bogra district, Bangladesh by purposive sampling technique. Various socio-demographic variables were considered at the time of data collection. These socio-demographic variables were analyzed in this paper.

Methods and Methodological Issues

Bivariate and Logistic Analysis

Bivariate analysis is used to test the association between the categorical variables and causes of migration by applying Chi-square test in the present study.

The logistic regression analysis is one of the most important methods for the successful application not only in demography but also all disciplines of knowledge. This method is very useful for identifying various risk factors in case of qualitative outcome variables. Cox (1958) first developed linear logistic regression model. More recently, Lee (1980) and Fox (1984) have further developed the Cox's model. This model expresses a qualitative dependent variable as a function of several independent variables, both qualitative and quantitative (Fox, 1984). In logistic analysis, female migration due to marriage is treated as dependent variable. Let Y be female migration due to marriage that is a dichotomous dependent variable, which takes values 1 and 0, that is Y is classified in the following way:

$$Y = \begin{cases} 1, \text{ if causes of migration is marriage} \\ 0, \text{ otherwise (service, business, labor, environment etc.)} \end{cases}$$

It is noted that age of respondents, age at marriage, respondent's education, respondent's occupation, religion, marital status, type of family before migration and type of migration are considered as explanatory variables that is used in this model.

Model Validation Technique

For model validation, the cross validation predictive power (CVPP) denoted, ρ^2_{cv} is computed by $\rho^2_{cv} = 1 - \frac{(n-1)(n-2)(n+1)}{n(n-k-1)(n-k-2)}(1-R^2)$.

Where n is the number of classes, k is the number of regressors in the model, and R^2 is the coefficient of determination. The shrinkage coefficient of the model is equal to the absolute value of $\lambda = (\rho^2_{cv} - R^2)$, (Steven, 1996). Closer the value of λ tends to zero, then the prediction is better. Furthermore, the stability of R^2 of the model is equal to 1- shrinkage coefficient. It is noted that CVPP is also applied as model validation technique for exponential and polynomial model (Islam et al., 2003; Islam, 2005).

Results and Discussion

Frequency distribution and percentage of female migrants by some selected socio-demographic characteristics are demonstrated in Table 9.1.

Age is an important demographic factor in the analysis of migration. From the table 9.1, it is observed that, most of the respondents (17.5%) are in the age group 30-34 years and 16.5 per cent respondents belong to 35-39 years age group. It is found that lowest age group is 15-19 years and it is 1.8 per cent. Age at marriage of the female migrants is an important factor that influences the migration. In our country, migration due to marriage is a major cause of migration for female. Most of the females live with their husbands after their marriage and so she is obliged to change her place of origin, that is father's house, so, in case of migration age at marriage plays influential factors. In table 9.1, it is found that the age at marriage of the female migrants is high in the age group 15-19 and it is 48.4 per cent and only 2.1 per cent female's age at marriage is 30 years and over.

Table 9.1. Frequency and Percentage Distribution of Background Characteristics of Migrants for Female

	Background Characteristics	No. of migrants	Percentage (%)
(i)	**Age group (in years):**		
	15-19	5	1.8
	20-24	22	7.7
	25-29	39	13.7
	30-34	50	17.5
	35-39	47	16.5
	40-44	44	15.4
	45-49	35	12.3
	50-54	22	7.7
	55+	21	7.4
	Total	285	100.0
(ii)	**Age at marriage (in years)**		
	10-14	54	18.9
	15-19	138	48.4
	20-24	68	23.9
	25-29	19	6.7
	30+	6	2.1
	Total	285	100.0
(iii)	**Marital status**		
	Married	272	95.4
	Widowed	9	3.2
	Others	4	1.4
	Total	285	100.0
(iv)	**Educational qualification**		
	Illiterate	25	8.8
	Primary	54	18.9
	Secondary	127	44.6
	H. Secondary	39	13.7
	Higher	40	14.0
	Total	285	100.0
(v)	**Type of family before migration:**		
	Unit	130	45.6
	Joint	155	54.4
	Total	285	100.0
	After migration		
	Unit	247	86.7
	Joint	38	13.3
	Total	285	100.0
(vi)	**Causes of migration**		
	Economic	7	2.5
	Marriage	183	64.2
	Service	49	17.2
	Business	6	2.1
	Labor	22	7.7
	Environment	17	6.0
	Others	1	0.3
	Total	285	100.0
(vii)	**Type of migration**		
	Urban to urban	103	36.1
	Rural to urban	182	63.9
	Total	285	100.0
(viii)	**Religion status**		
	Muslim	278	97.5
	Non-Muslim	7	2.5
	Total	285	100.0
(ix)	**Occupational status (before migration)**		
	Housewife	99	34.7
	Farmer	-	-
	Service	24	8.4
	Business	-	-
	Labor	2	.7
	Others	27	9.5
	No occupation	133	46.7
	Total	285	100.0
(x)	**Occupational status (after migration)**		
	Housewife	194	68.1
	Farmer	-	-
	Service	50	17.5
	Business	10	3.5
	Labor	24	8.4
	Others	7	2.5
	Total	285	100.0

Marital status plays an important role on migration. The migration decision of an individual is influenced by marital status. Generally, married female women are migrated to another place after their marriage. The table 9.1 shows that the female migrants 95.4 per cent, 3.2 per cent and 1.4 per cent are married, widowed and separated respectively. So, in this study most of the respondents are married.

Education is the key that unlocks the key to modernization, more clearly it can be said that education is the backbone of a nation. No nation can prosper without education. So education plays an important role in human life. Education is a very important factor in the analysis of migration. Several studies showed that migrants are usually more educated with respect to the place of origin and with respect to the place of destination. On the other hand, education is an important pull factor for which an individual takes decision to migrate from one place to another. The table 9.1 shows that most of the female migrants are secondary level educated and their percentage is 44.6 per cent. Among the female migrants 8.8 per cent are illiterate, 18.9 per cent are primary level educated, 13.7 per cent higher secondary level educated and 14.0 per cent have completed the graduation level.

From the table 9.1, it is observed that, 45.6 per cent female migrant were living with single family and 54.4 per cent female migrant were living with joint family before their migration but after migration, most of them (86.7 per cent) living with unit family.

People migrates from one place to another place for many causes, the causes of migration can be classified mainly as economic causes, demographic causes, social causes, political causes, education and cultural causes, geographical causes. In this study area, the causes of migration are classified into seven categories which are shown in Table 9.1. The table 9.1 represents that, among the female migrants most of the migrants are migrated to the present place due to marriage and their percentage is 64.2 per cent. The second cause of female migration is service and their percentage is 17.2 per cent.

The internal migration of a country may have the form rural to rural, rural to urban, urban to urban, urban to rural. As the study area is an urban area and in-migration is included in this study, so the types of migration are classified into two categories named rural to urban and urban to urban. The table 9.1 shows that maximum number of female migrants (63.9%) is migrated from rural area. Again, 36.1 per cent female migrants are migrated from urban area.

Very often religion acts as causes of migration. Most of the inhabitants in Bangladesh are Muslims. In this study, total respondents are classified into two categories namely Muslims and non-Muslims (including Hindu, Buddhist, Christian and others). From the table 9.1, it is observed that 97.5 per cent female migrants are Muslim and 2.5 per cent female migrants are non-Muslim.

Occupation is a very important factor in the analysis of migration. In every year, a large number of rural population migrated to urban area for better occupational status. Availability of job opportunity and medical facilities at the place destination plays a very important role in regard to the process of migration decision. On the other hand, pre-migration occupation also helps to understand the causes i.e. push factors behind migration.

Pre-migration occupation also helps to understand the causes of migration. The table 9.1 shows clearly that most of the migrants (68.1%) are housewives, 17.5 per cent of them are service holder, 8.4 per cent are engaged as labor and only 3.5 per cent engaged in business. It implies that although the housewives of our country are considered as unpaid family member, they do not go for earning as labor. The table 9.1 shows that most of the female migrants had no occupation before their migration and their percentage is 46.7 per cent, among them 34.75 per cent were housewives and only 0.7 per cent was engaged in labor.

The outcome of association between causes of migration due to marriage with some selected socio-demographic characteristics of female migrants is demonstrated in table 9.2. From this table 9.2, it is found that there is no significance association between current age of the respondents and causes of migration. But, it is seen that age at marriage, educational qualification, occupation, religious characteristics, marital status, type of family and type of migration of female migrants are highly significantly associated with causes of migration.

Table 9.2. Association between causes of migration and some selected socio-demographic variables for female migrants

Socio-demographic variables	Calculated value of χ^2 df, p	Tabulated value of χ^2	Significance at 5% level
Age group	χ^2_{cal}=4.194 df=2, p=0.123	χ^2_{tab}=5.991	Insignificant
Age at marriage	χ^2_{cal}=12.658 df=1, p=0.000	χ^2_{tab}=3.841	Significant
Educational qualification	χ^2_{cal}=7.703 df=2, p=0.021	χ^2_{tab}=5.991	Significant
Occupation	χ^2_{cal}=178.67 df=1, p=0.000	χ^2_{tab}=3.841	Significant
Religion	χ^2_{cal}=7.783 df=1, p=0.005	χ^2_{tab}=3.841	Significant
Marital status	χ^2_{cal}=14.131 df=1, p=0.000	χ^2_{tab}=3.841	Significant
Type of family before migration	χ^2_{cal}=16.703 df=1, p =0.000	χ^2_{tab}=3.841	Significant
Type of migration	χ^2_{cal}=52.375 df=1, p =0.000	χ^2_{tab}=3.841	Significant

The results of logistic regression model are demonstrated in table 9.3. It is observed that the effects of religious characteristics, present occupation of the female migrant, age at marriage, marital status, type of migration on the causes of migration due to marriage are statistically significant and other variables are statistical insignificant.

The regression coefficient for age group 20-24 years and for age group 25 and above years are –0.5136 and –0.5458 respectively. The odds ratio for these age groups are 0.006 and 0.004 respectively. This implies that the respondent's age group 20-24 years is 0.006 times and the age group 25 and above is 0.004 times lower risk for migration than the reference category (<20 years). The regression coefficient for the age at marriage is –1.806 and the odds ratio is 0.164 that means the risk of migration for age at marriage 18 and above is 0.164 lower than the age at marriage less than 18. It may be concluded that most of female are married less than 18 years.

The regression coefficient for service and others of the female migrants is found -3.814 and the odds ratio is 0.022 which implies that the female migrants who are engaged in different type of occupation were migrated due to marriage is 0.022 times lower than the house wife (reference category).

The regression coefficient for the Muslim female migrants is 4.251 and the odds ratio is 70.144, which implies that the Muslim female migrants have 70.144 times higher risk of marriage migration than the reference category of the non-Muslim female migrants. The regression coefficient for the female migrants who holds the marital status married is 2.251 and the odds ratio is 9.496, which implies that the married female migrants have 9.496 times high risk of marriage migration than the reference category, female migrants who are non-married.

The regression coefficient for the female migrants whose type of family before migration were joint is 0.566 and the odds ratio is 1.761, which implies that the female migrants whose type of family were joint has 1.761 times higher risk of marriage migration than the reference category that is female migrants whose type of family were unit before migration. The regression coefficient for the female migrants who were migrated from rural to urban is 1.109 and the odds ratio is 3.033, which indicates that the female migrants who are migrated from rural to urban area 3.033 times higher than the reference category, who are migrated from urban to urban area.

To test the adequacy of the logistic model, CVPP is applied here and its value is 0.569703 indicating that the model is more than 56 per cent stable. Moreover, the shrinkage of the model is = 0.028298. The stability for R^2 of this model is more than 97 per cent.

Conclusion and Recommendations

Although it is a traditional system that all the women have to migrate after their marriage, many women of Bangladesh now start to migrate from one place to anther for different motive and reasons. In Bangladesh, most of the female marriage occurs in the early age, as age increase the female migration due to marriage decrease. Educational qualification is an important factor that influences in making decision of migration, so educated female

Table 9.3. Logistic regression estimates for the effect on causes of migration with Socio-demographic variables

Socio-demographic variables	Co-efficient (β)	S.E of estimates	Significant	Odds ratio
Age of respondent				
<20 (R.C)	-	-	0.935	1.00
20-24	-0.5136	25.331	0.839	0.006
25 and above	-0.5458	25.311	0.829	0.004
Age at marriage				
<18 (R.C)	-	-	-	1.00
18 and above	-1.806	0.649	.005*	0.164
Educational qualification				
Illiterate (R.C)	-	-	0.174	1.00
Primary	1.771	1.193	0.138	5.874
Secondary and above	0.345	1.046	0.741	1.412
Occupation				
House wife (R.C)	-	-	-	1.00
Service and others	-3.814	0.816	0.000*	0.022
Religion				
Non Muslim (R.C)	-	-		1.00
Muslim	4.251	1.205	0.000*	70.144
Marital status				
Unmarried (R.C)	-	-	-	1.00
Married	2.251	1.163	0.053**	9.496
Type of family before migration				
Unit (R.C)	-	-	-	1.00
Joint	0.566	0.533	0.289	1.761
Type of migration				
Urban to urban (R.C)	-	-	-	1.00
Rural to urban	1.109	0.556	0.046**	3.033
Constant	1.471	25.385	0.954	4.356
Cox and Snell's R square =0.598				

•Significant at ρ <0.01, **Significant at ρ<0.05, Note: R.C means reference category.

actively takes part in the migratory process than lower educated female. Migration has a very deep impact on breaking the traditional social system. Now a day's people migrate to cities and towns and interested to living with single family, as a result joint family system is going to be decrease. In logistic analysis, it is identified that age at marriage, occupation, religion, marital status, type of family (before migration), type of migration significantly effect on causes of migration of female migrants.

Migration is no doubt inevitably linked to the process of overall development of a country and for this reason, to increase the women's participation in development process by migration, the following recommendations are suggested in this report:

(*i*) Promote gender equality and improve the status of women. Also promote equal rights of women and men in all spheres of development.

(*ii*) Increase women's participation in decision-making both at national and local levels.

(*iii*) Increase women's participation in the public and private sector of employment.

REFERENCES

1. Afsar, R. (2005). "Internal Migration And Pro-Poor Policy, Country" Paper, Bangladesh, Paper Prepared for Regional Conference on Migration and Development in Asia, Sponsored by the Department for International Development, UK., Lanzhou China, 14-16 March.
2. Afsar, R. (2003a). "Dynamics of Poverty, Development and Population Mobility: The Bangladesh Case," Paper Prepared for Ad Hoc Expert Group Meeting on Migration and Development, Organized by Economic and Social Commission for Asia and the Pacific, Bangkok 27-29 August.
3. Asfar, R. (2003b). "Internal Migration and the Development Nexus: The Case of Bangladesh," Paper Presented at the Regional Conference on Migration and Pro-Poor Policy Choices in Asia, Organized by the DFID, Sonargaon Hotel, Dhaka, Bangladesh, 22-24 June.
4. BBS. (1994). Bangladesh Population Census 1991, National Volume, Bureau of Statistics, Ministry of Planning, Government of Bangladesh, Dhaka.
5. Cox, D. R. (1958), The Regression Analysis of Binary Sequences (with discussion), *J. R. Stat. Soc.*, Vol. 20, pp. 215-242.
6. Deshingkar, P. and S. Grimm (2005). "Internal Migration and Development: A Global Perspective," Paper Prepared for International Organization for Migration (IOM).
7. Elahi, K. M. (1985). "Internal Migration Perspective of Bangladesh: Proceeding of the Second National Seminar," Bangladesh Population Association, Dhaka.
8. Faruk, A. O., M. R. Islam and M. M. Rahman (2007). Socio-economics Characteristics of the Female Married Migrants: A Case Study of Katakhali Pourusova of Rajshahi District in Bangladesh, *Middle East J. of Nursing*, Vol. 1, No. 3, pp. 6-9, June, 2007.
9. Fox, J. (1984), *Linear Statistical Models and Related Methods*, Wiley and Sons, New York.
10. Hugo, G. J. (1991). "Rural-Urban Migration, Economic Development and Social Change: Some Important Issues," Paper Presented in the Workshop on the Urbanization and Urban Poor, Dhaka, Bangladesh Institute of Development Studies, 27-29.
11. Islam, R., A.O. Faruk, M.G. Mostofa and M. E. Haque (2007). Living Standards of Migrants: A Study of Katakhali Pourusova in Rajshahi District, Bangladesh, *Middle East Journal of Family Medicine.*

12. Islam, M. R., M. N. Islam, M. A. Ali, and M. G. Mostofa (2003). "Construction of Male Life Table from Female Widowed Information of Bangladesh," *International Journal of Statistical Sciences*, Dept. of Statistics,University of Rajshahi, Bangladesh, Vol. 2, 2003, pp. 69-82.

13. Islam, Md. Rafiqul (2005). "Construction of Female Life Table from Male Widowed Information of Bangladesh," *Pakistan Journal of Statistics*, Vol. 21(3), pp. 275- 284.

14. Kuhn, R. (2005). The Determinants of Family and Individual Migration: A Case Study of Rural Bangladesh, A Working Paper Prepared for Research Program on Population Processes, Institute of Behavioral Science, University of Colorado, Boulder.

15. Lee, E. T. (1980). *Statistical Methods for Survival Data Analysis*, Lifetime Learning Publications, Beltmont, California.

16. Rahman, M., M.R. Islam and M. Rahman (2007). "Causes and Consequences of In-Migration at Rajshahi City Corporation, Bangladesh," *Journal of Engineering and Applied Sciences.* Vol 2(2): 305-308.

17. Siddiqui, T. (2003). "Migration as a Livelihood Strategy of the Poor: The Bangladesh Case," Paper Prepared for and Presented at the Regional Conference on Migration, Development and Pro-Poor Policy Choices in Asia. The Conference was Jointly Organized by the Refugee and Migratory Movements Research Unit, Bangladesh and The Department for International Development, UK, 22–24 June 2003, Dhaka, Bangladesh.

18. Stevens, J. (1996). *Applied Multivariate Statistics for the Social Sciences*, Third Edition, Lawrence Erlbaum Associates, Inc., Publishers, New Jersey.

19. Singh, S. N. and K. N. S. Yadava (1981). On Some Characteristics of Rural Out-migration in Eastern Uttar Pradesh, *Society and Culture*, Vol. 12(1), 33-46.

20. Yadava, K. N. S. (1987). "Volume and Pattern of Rural-Urban Migration in India," Seminar Paper Presented in the Department of Demography, Australian National University, Canbera.

Property Rights for Managing Natural Resources in India : Lessons from International Experiences

—K. Damodaran

Abstract

In India, population growth, economic development and industrialization have resulted in overuse/misuse of natural resources. Of late, environmentalist and policy-makers have realized the fact and suggested the community to manage the resources sustainably. But, the degradation of resources continues still because of the unchanged human behaviour. On the other, government has failed to control the depletion of natural resources due to ill-defined common property rights. However, the government has not taken any measures to strengthen the existing property rights institutions, whereas developed nations around the world have realized the inadequacies in managing the natural resources and has shifted the responsibility towards the community, i.e. through Collective Action. The present paper reviews the experiences of the developed countries. This discussion would ensure some ideas to rephrase our standards in managing natural resources, which may tie-up our society towards Sustainable Development.

Introduction

At present, the subject Environmental Management has attracted much concern of Environmentalist and policy-makers at global level. This is not due to the uniqueness of the Natural Resources rather because of the scarcity and degradation of natural resources. However, the commons have better understanding about the management and scarcity of natural resources. But, the knowledge of the commons did not do much in preserving the resources for the future generation. The question arises in this context, "Why the commons overuse and misuse the resources even having the knowledge about the management and scarcity of the resources?" For this, Environmentalist and Social Scientist respond that they are due to population pressure; poverty, ill-defined property rights, community and Government failure (see figure 10.1). However, the authors of the paper make stresses and justify that Property Rights is the prime factor for the degradation of natural resources. Since the ill-defined property rights are the major issue all over the world, it would be appropriate that we learn the dimensions of the Property Rights.

Property Rights

Property rights comprise the bundles of entitlements regarding resources use, and property rules and the rules under which those entitlements are exercised. Demsetz (1967), a major proponent of the property rights school says, “A primary function of property rights is that of guiding incentives to achieve a greater internalization of externalities”.

Dimensions of Property Rights

Property rights have many possible dimensions. However, the paper studies the four broad types of property regimes. They are: Private property, State property, Communal property and Open-access property.

Private property, assigns ownership to named individuals (including legal “individuals”, such as corporations), guaranteeing to those owners control of access and the right to a bundle of socially acceptable uses. It requires of the owners that they avoid specified uses, which are deemed socially unacceptable, such as fouling the water of streams. *Common Property* is owned by an identified group of people who have the right to exclude non-owners and the duty to maintain the property through constrain placed on. Citizens of a political unit who assign rule-making authority to a state agency own public property. The agency has the corresponding duty to ensure that rules promote social objectives. Citizens have the rights to use the resource within the established rules. *Open access*, has no ownership assigned, and is property open to all. Claims to resource are realized at the point of capture, and owners have no specified duty to maintain the resource or constrain use.

Property Rights and Natural Resources

The broad classifications of Natural Resources are Common Property Resources (CPRs) and Private Property Resources (PPRs). In India, as aforementioned, the rights of CPRs are open to all and it is combined with ill-defined property rights. However, PPRs are well defined and their management are better comparatively. Because of this, the CPRs have been exploited over the period (Figure 10.2). As mentioned in the introductory part, Poverty/ Population/ Community failure/Government failure cannot do much with the PPRs while; these can do much more in case of CPRs. Further, the populace were endowed with more the CPRs i.e. water and forest resources. In utilising the water resources, the commons extract more the ground water and also face problems in sharing the canal water for irrigation. In case of forest resources, the commons cut irrespective of green and dry which altogether leads to unsustainable development. The private property is concern; the owner of the property will not allow grabbing his resources, which is under his preview. Hence, Property rights act a major part in managing natural resource rather than the other.

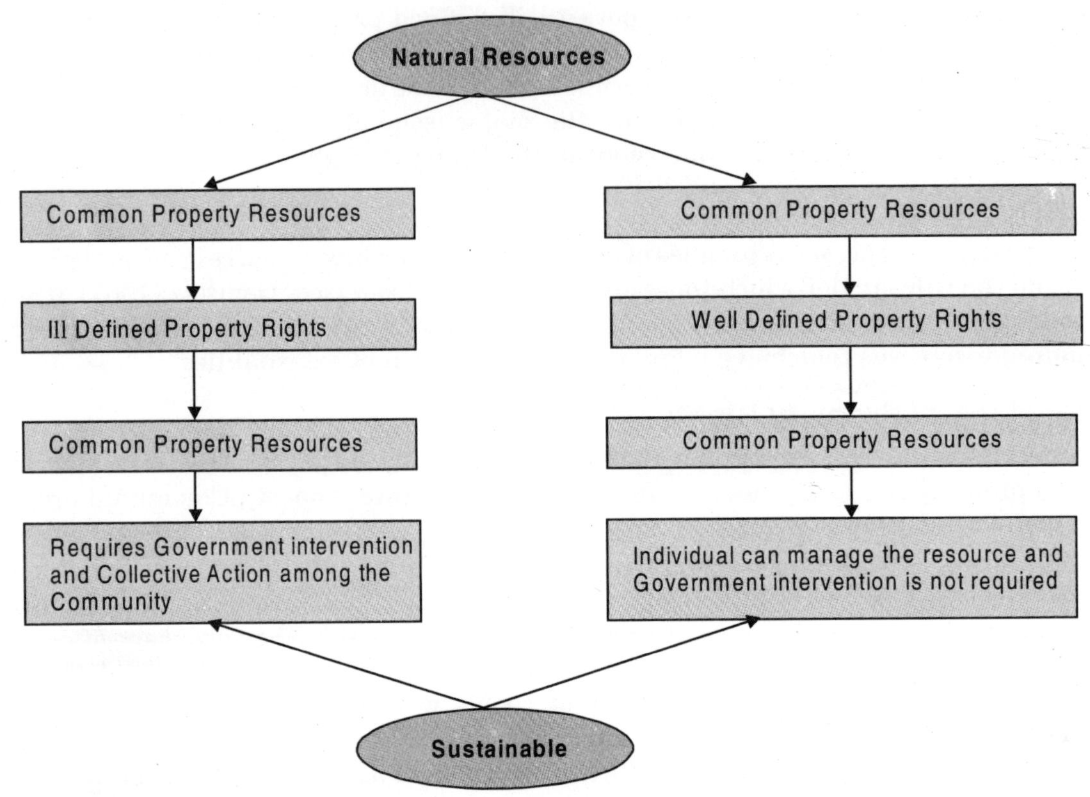

Fig. 10.2. Property Rights and Natural Resource Management

Government Failure

By keeping this, the Government planned to decentralise the rights of CPRs. As a result, in 1992, the 73rd and 74th constitutional amendments recognize the three-tier structure of the government by devolution of powers to local bodies, that is, panchayats in rural areas and municipalities in urban areas. The eleventh schedule contains environmental activities such as soil conservation, water management, social forestry and non-conventional energy that panchayats can undertake. The twelfth schedule lists activities such as water supply, public health and sanitation, solid waste management and environmental protection, which the municipalities can undertake. With these amendments these grass root-level institutions can facilitate greater participation by the people in local affairs, promote better planning and implementation of developmental and environmental programmes and be more responsive to the needs of the people. But, the State's inability to administer its management authority has made the environmentalist and socialist to think an alternative module. As an alternative, community based resource management were encouraged to operate with relatively little interfere of the Government.

Collective Action for Natural Resource Management

In developing countries, identifying the most effective community-level governance structure is a key issue because vulnerable populations are often unable to access services provided by higher levels of government, and hence rely on local communities for their provision (World Bank, 2000). There are many instances in natural resource management in which stable institutions of self-governance by the participants themselves emerge, and control access without resort to external government involvement (Ostrom, 1990). As the same, community participation in Natural Resource Management (NRM) has been engaging the attention of policymakers all over the world. Elinor Ostrom (1990) in her pioneering work on "Governing the Commons" had examined a wide variety of cases involving collective action by individuals using Common Pool Resources. Further, the government has to provide training, external financial support, credit facilities and forums to foster information among local communities, which may encourage the community to join in one hand to manage the resource beyond the generation.

International Experiences on Natural Resource Management

1. Devolving Rights of Water has Promoted Irrigation in Nepal

Farmer-managed irrigation schemes have a long tradition in Nepal, where farmers control 70 per cent of all irrigation. Nevertheless, the government had been heavily involved in developing new irrigation, with poor results. With a shift in approach, the government now promotes farmer management as a way to improve irrigation performance and to reduce the financial burden on the government of developing and operating irrigation systems.

The bank responded to the shift in emphasis by financing the irrigation, which was one of the line of credit pilot projects with resources totalling close to $20 million. The pilot project funds small and medium size surface and groundwater schemes that are owned, operated, and maintained by legally recognized water user associations. The association must request the investment, contribute to capital costs, and accept full responsibility for operations and management when construction is completed.

The results are impressive. In the first two years of operation, forty-three surface subprojects of the irrigation line of credit were completed out of sixty-one sub-projects processed and approved for implementation, an eighty-one tubewells were drilled. Altogether, these subprojects serve an area of some 3400 hectares and about 4500 households in eight districts. The project's success is due to the enthusiastic cooperation of farmers and the good dialogue between government officials and farmers. Having water user association take ownership and responsibility for oversight improved the quality of construction, adding a much-needed element of transparency in the use of government resources. Associations have created strong organization that achieved good cost recovery. They levied penalties on members who fail to abide by the rules. Many associations are too involved in the aspects of community development. Overall, the program improved the services and reduced cost.

2. Farmer's Cooperation Resulted in Changing Fallow Lands as Cultivable Lands in Sri Lanka

In the early 1980s the U.S. Agency of International Development funded the Gal Oya River. Institutional organizers were introduced into the system. Gaining the trust of the farmers, they began to organize larger groups of farmers along the distribution channels. These groups discussed their problems and communicated with the government irrigation department staff. This process has greatly improved communications between farmers and government officials. Conflict among farmers has declined substantially, and the improved system provides more water for farmers at the tail-end of the system. Careful to separate their organizations from party politics, the farmers have also eased ethnic tensions. In one area cooperating farmer's cleared a canal allowing 1000 hectares to be cultivated in the dry season, which had previously been left fallow. This benefited more than 300 families. The activities demonstration, participation, flexibility, and consensus were the key to the project success.

3. Water User Association in Responding Market Demand in Tunisia

Water User Associations (WUAs) have existed in Tunisia for most of this century, with the French colonial government introducing their legal basis in 1913. The government of Tunisia reaffirmed the legal status of the associations by legislation enacted in 1975 and in 1987. During the 1970s, however, the government became increasingly involved in developing irrigation. Recognizing the financial burden and inefficiency of this situation, in the mid-1980s the government began to strengthen WUAs and to allow more involvement by the private sector. The bank supported this change through three irrigation projects and two agricultural sector adjustment loans.

The most success has come in the south, where associations now control practically all tubewell irrigation schemes, ranging in size from 50 to 200 hectares. The association are responsible for all operation and management, including hiring the appropriate labour and paying for electricity. The associations are well structured technically and financially. While they perform routine repairs, the government performs large repairs, receiving a small contribution from the associations. One notable achievement of involving user associations is that farmers have greater flexibility to respond to changes in market demand for different crops.

4. Farmers Association Won Award for doing best in San Benito

The San Benito communal irrigation system occupies 137 hectares of prime agricultural land. The farmers organized themselves into an Irrigators' Association (IA) as a condition set by the National Irrigation Authority (NIA) for granting irrigation related assistance. With the assistance of the Irrigation Community Organizer (ICO), the San Benito Irrigator's Association was registered on March 21, 1986. The majority of farmers have acquired the land (mainly through loans) and only fractions are renters. All members of the Irrigators' Association are also members of a bigger farmer's cooperative called San Benito Multi-Purpose Cooperative numbering rice farmers.

The Irrigation Association launched its first major rehabilitation of the system in October 1996 with a 50-year loan obtained from the National Irrigation Administration. In addition to this, farmers contributed their own resources amounting to 10 per cent of the financial costs of rehabilitation. Chargeable costs of this rehabilitation project amount were paid within eight years. An assigned leader collects payments from the farmers, issues an official receipt and remits the amount collected to the Association. In total, farmers pay P800/ha/year for amortization and ongoing operations and maintenance. So far, the Association has kept up with its amortization payments to NIA, and won awards for being one of the best Irrigation Associations.

5. Decentralizing Rights to Commons for Managing Forest in Laguna

Makiling Forest Reserve (MFR) is a multiple-use forest reserve of approximately 4,244 ha straddling the provinces of Laguna and Batangas. The reserve is situated on Mount Makiling, ranging between 400 m above sea level and 20 m above sea level with slopes generally above 25 per cent. Today the reserve is administered by the College of Forestry, University of Philippines at Los Baños (UPLB-CF). The purpose of MFR has been to serve as a training and research laboratory for forestry studies.

The Government has shifted the management of forest to the University is due to government's low tolerance for *kaingeros* (slash and burn farmers), settlers, and illegal collectors. In the early 1970s, the university tried to evict those residing in the reserve. Although many moved and resettled, later on many moved back. Having lived in the reserve for decades (in many cases from before it was declared a reserve), the families feel they had a right to the land. As a result, contested claims to the land arose between the university and the forest residents. In the mid-1980s, however, a more tolerant approach towards established farmers and settlers was adopted in the hope of balancing UPLB's training aspirations with social justice imperatives set by the Aquino government. It was in this spirit that the university and the residents drafted a Memorandum of Understanding (MOU) specifying who has the right to live in the reserve. The list of residents is fixed in an effort to prevent migrants from adding to the population. In exchange for these rights, the resident farmers have agreed to protect the forest and create a buffer. The university has deputed community volunteers as forest guards along with forest guards who are employees of the university.

6. Community Involvement in Managing Forest Resources in Japan

Community forest use to supply indispensable inputs for farming and for rural life in isolated and largely self-sufficient communities located in mountainous areas in Japan Gunma prefecture, located 150 to 200 kilometres north of Tokyo. Grasses were extracted to produce green manure and compost for paddy fields and to feed horses, which were used for ploughing. Firewood was widely used as a major source of energy at home. In order to prevent overexploitation of these forest resources, strict management rules were implemented, such as the designation of date, time, place and amount of specific resources to be extracted each year. Collected firewood is usually divided equally at the end of the day and distributed equally to participating members, as in the contemporary management of hill forest in Nepal. This practice discourages the excessive extraction of firewood. The use of tools, such as saws, was also strictly regulated. In addition, collective work was organised, particularly for burning portions of forests to facilitate to re-grow of feeding grasses. The similarity of management rules between copse forests in pre-war Japan and contemporary hill forests in Nepal is striking.

Conclusion

In the light of the above, the authors conclude throught some selective cases that collective action is vital to manage the natural resources. These case studies reveal some concrete suggestions to the Governments at the regional level and suggest to them what to do and what not to do in achieving sustainable development. If the Collective Action is brought at community level, then the resources can be sustained beyond generations and also may pave way for sustainable resource and economic development.

REFERENCES

1. Anna Knox and Ruth S. Meinzen-Dick, (2001): "Collective Action, Property Rights and Devolution of Natural Resource Management: Exchange of Knowledge and Implications for Policy", Washington, IFPRI.
2. Brent M. Swallow, Ruth S. Meinzen-Dick, Lee Ann Jackson, Timothy O. Williams, and T. Anderson White (1997): "Multiple Functions of Common Property Regimes", EPTD workshop summary paper no. 5, Washington, IFPRI.
3. Coase, R. (1960): "The problem of social cost", *Journal of Law and Economics*, vol.3, pp.1-44.
4. Demsetz, H. (1967). "Toward a theory of property rights", *American Economic Review* 57: 347-59.
5. Hanna S. Susan. (1996): "*Property Rights, People and the Environment*", Washington: DC Island Press.
6. Meinzen-Dick Ruth, Anna Knox and Monica Di Gregorio (2003): "Co-Management Arrangements at the Makiling Forest Reserve" Washington: IFPRI.
7. Meinzen-Dick Ruth, Anna Knox and Monica Di Gregorio (2003): "Community-Based Coastal Resource Management in Anilao, Batangas" Washington: IFPRI.
8. Meinzen-Dick Ruth, Anna Knox and Monica Di Gregorio (2003): "San Benito Irrigators' Association and Multi-Purpose Cooperative Pila, Laguna" Washington: IFPRI.
9. Ostrom, Elinor. (1990): "*Governing The Commons: The Evolution of Institutions for Collective Action*", Cambridge: Cambridge University Press.
10. Reddy V. Ratna. (2000): "Sustainable Watershed Management: Institutional Approach", *Economic and Political Weekly*, September, pp. 3435-3444.
11. Swallow, Brent M., Dennis P. Garrity, and Meine Van Noordwijk (2001). "The Effects of Scales, Flows and Filters on Property Rights and Collective Action in Watershed Management" Capri Working Paper No. 16, Washington: IFPRI.
12. Thakur, R.S. (1984): "Herbage dynamics of some Natural and Modified Ecosystem of Shimla Hills", Project report quoted in Department of Environment, Government of India, Annual Progress Report, pp.37-44.
13. UNEP (1995): "*An Environmental Guide for the Community*", Hong Kong: Colorcraft Publications.

Empowered Knowledge and Underpowered Ethics: Need of Sharing Ethics for Eco-Friendship

—Mohammad Nasser Modoodi and M.H. Rahmani Doust

Abstract

Today, man enjoys more knowledge as well as more power than ever. In earlier eras, his knowledge was perfectly balanced with his ethics and the old ethical systems were making his power harmonized with the environment. But after the industrial revolution, from one side his knowledge's power tremendously has increased, and from the other side, the ethical systems almost remained at the same old level. So man has a huge and uncontrolled power and the mentioned balance has entirely been disordered. To rebalance of current situation, we should utilize our old experiences. Control of empowered knowledge needs the same level of empowered ethics. One of the functional ways to achieve a powerful ethics is to share the whole ethical systems around the world to empower the individual ethical systems. This may empower man's ethics and rebalance the new empowered knowledge in order to being again eco-friendship attitude for sustainable future today.

Key words: Empowered knowledge, underpowered knowledge, ethical systems, share of ethics, eco-friendship.

Introduction

When we survey the position of the world's population during the last few centuries, we find that it had more quantitative growth than ever before. Enjoying the help of their novel knowledge, now-a-days, human beings are able to remove hampers of this growth and control the growth rate. The extension of man scientific abilities has influenced his surroundings.

Once being part of his environment in ancient time, man is placed in such a situation that he can impose his will on everything. The long coexistence between man and nature has eventually been resulted in some ethical systems, which from one hand were appreciating to man's power and on the other hand were controlling his desires.

Each of these has a distinct feature of its own, but all of them aimed practically to guarantee the physical and mental health of their devotees in that indefinite world. Gradually, these ethical systems started to interpret the world to improve the life quality. The environment is one of the most common issues considered by them. Nobody is able to find out any ethics or codes of conduct in which environmental components (such as the sun, the earth, and water) are not respected. Even you can not encounter any commands against plants, animals, or any non-living objects there. All this is discussed under the following headings:

A Fundamental Question, Charged Knowledge and Non-Charged Ethics, Discussion, Global Eco-Friendship Ethics, Conclusion.

A Fundamental Question

The new world condition gives rise to number of questions such as whether the power originated from our new superior knowledge has ethically spoiled us, or the modern man is a creature with a low or non-ethical power?

There are enough evidences which do not prove this claim, and even reject it. Almost all developing countries are still following their old beliefs and their ethics influence the thoughts and decisions, both in social and political levels. Iran, India, Malaysia, Saudi Arabia, Egypt etc. are among these countries. In developed countries, on the other hand, although the power of old ethics has already been decreased, new, serious and strict rules have been replaced them. These modern ethics are only not against the old ethics but extremely confirm and guarantee them. Hence, it seems that the Modern man is not interested in being immoral or losing his old ethics. However, the question still is:

"What is the responsible for all man disordered behaviors and the present chaotic world?"

Charged Knowledge and Non-Charged Ethics

The old ethical systems enjoy an invisible intuitive dynamics without which they could not continuously keep existence after thousand of years. Such characteristic was called Idea by Plato, which is timeless and placeless. During the ancient era, man's knowledge gave him a limited power, so that his own ethics were enough empowered to control that particular amount of power. Incidentally there was a good balance between man's knowledge and his ethical power.

However, since the Renaissance Period, knowledge has been enormously grown. This massive growth of knowledge led to a disorder of the previous balance. This caused a sudden long jump for man in the world of science.

After industry revolution, the speed of knowledge accumulation improved very fast. This happened because of a public demand and will, and also focused attention on knowledge. Another important point was that all people of the world attempted to share their knowledge and scientific findings leading to a massive accumulation of knowledge for modern man. Today, knowledge is becoming more and more fat and this results in its charge and empowerment. But, while man was sharing and enriching his knowledge, he ignored another necessity which is responsible for his sustainable living ethics.

Discussion

It is probable that none of the world wide ethics alone can resist the new empowered and unique universal knowledge, and in the case of modern questions, they seem to be paralyzed to present reasonable solutions. The only problem is that; because the improvement of knowledge has lately been promoted, the old ethics are not able to balance suitably, at least in short span of time. It doesn't mean that we must retreat our new huge knowledge. In other words, we should improve our ethics to the same level achieved in knowledge.

Perhaps one of the best solutions to this inefficiency is to share the whole world ethics. To exposure the shared and enriched knowledge, we need the same shared and enriched ethics.

Global Eco-Friendship Ethics

Ethics, which is eternal, is the property of all people. Belonging to each race or country, nobody should hesitate that he/she is ethically an eco-friend. The common factor in all of the ethical systems is the belief of safeguarding of environment, which is acceptable and applicable by all.

Naturalism is a part of whole life of the Hindu population in India. Plants and animals are considered sacred by them. Nature worship in a form of belief that reinforces the view that all nature's creation has to be protected.

According to Vedas, God has provided a manual for mankind to maintains harmony in the world because human achievements are possible only when there is peace.

In Iran, two valuable assets highly respected by Zoroastrians are: the nature diversity and traditional knowledge. The Bible says that Christians around the world are bound to share God's love and every body must try to love the whole world. In Islam, any creature is eventually considered as a God's sign, so it should be completely respected by human beings.

Conclusion

A consideration of all these factors leads one to the inevitable conclusion that we should share our valuable ethics and meanwhile take care to safeguard our age-old spiritual values. Sharing of our own ethics with foreigners may appear painful in the beginning but will be like elixir in the end and finally leads towards well-regulated habits.

Scientific western patterns have successfully introduced public hygienic to India. India is introducing her peaceful nature philosophy to the world. Like that any country may share her best ethics and eco-friendship points with others.

A plenty of interpretative texts of the Vedas, the Koran, and the Bible are not only exactly the same on the surface but they originate from the same spring inwardly. These broad diversities add a potentiality to individual ethics resources as well as they draw people's attention as eco-friendly behavior. The environment education syllabus does not need to be invented or created. Fortunately, our wise ancestors have done it very well all around the world. The remaining things are how we can share and charge the syllabus to make a new balance against the new enriched knowledge. Enjoying the gift of a huge empowered knowledge, it seems we ought to share and change our ethics to rebalance not only our own living behaviors but also to live in a qualified co-existence level along with other creatures.

REFERENCES

1. Mohammad Nasser Modoodi, *Living Intelligently in the Intelligent Environment*, 2nd National Annual Conference on Environmental Education, Panjim, Goa, India, Aug. 2007: 33, pp & 49.
2. K.K. Misra, M.L.K. Murty. 2001. *Peoples and Environment In India*. Discovery Publishing House, New Delhi.
3. M. Sundarraj. 1997. *RG Vedic Studies*. International Society for the Investigation of Ancient Civilization, Chennai.
4. N. Ravi. 1999. *The Hindu Speakers on Religious Values*. Kasturi & sons Ltd. Chennai.
5. R. Rajagopalan. 2006. *Environmental Studies, From Crisis to Cure*. Oxford University Press, New Delhi.
6. Sanjay Perkash Sharma. 2003. *Hinduism Religion, Rituals, Fairs and Festivals*. RBSA Publishers.
7. *The living Bible, New Testament Paraphrased*. Tyndale House Publishers, New Delhi, 1976.
8. http://www.cnvc.org.
9. http://www. wellnessgoods.com.

Realisation of Rights and Entitlements of the National Rural Employment Guarantee Workers in Madhya Pradesh

—C. Subba Reddy

Introduction and Problem Formation

The National Rural Employment Guarantee Act (NREGA) was enacted in September, 2005 by the Union Government to provide guaranteed employment to the rural poor. Though there had been many schemes including Food for Work Programme, National Rural Employment Programme (NREP), Rural Landless Employment Guarantee Programme (RLEGP), Jawahar Rojgar Yojana (JRY), Sampoorna Grameen Rojgar Yojana (SGRY) etc., which were implemented hitherto towards this end, the present NREGA is all together different from the other schemes. The Rural Employment Guarantee Scheme (REGS) is based on rights based, community (wage seeker) centred, bottom to top approach. The state is legally bound to fulfill the demand of the wage seekers.

As per the NREGA the workers have been conferred with some rights and privileges and notable among them are: (1) The worker has the right to demand for unskilled work from state for 100 days per financial year, (2) The worker shall have the right to demand unemployment allowance from the state if state fails to provide him / her the work within fifteen days after submission of the application for work, (3) The state has to provide 100 days of work to the needy household which is willing to work, (4) Every worker who has participated in the work shall be entitled to receive wages not less than Rs. 60/- per day, (5) The wages payments should not be delayed beyond 15 days, (6) The workers are entitled to have basic work site facilities.

The NREGA calls for preparation of Rural Employment Guarantee Scheme (REGS) for each state keeping in view the main features of the act. Initially the Act was applicable to 200 backward districts in the country in 2005-06 and during 2006-07 it was extended to cover another 130 backward districts. The Scheme has been covering all the districts in rural India since 1st April, 2008. The scheme was launched by the Prime Minister, Dr. Manmohan Singh on February 2, 2006 at Bandlapalli village in Anantapur district of Andhra Pradesh.

The strength of the NREGS lies in the awareness of the wage seekers about their rights and entitlements as envisaged in the NREGA, transformation of the awareness in to enforcement of rights and effective utilization of these rights by the workers. In the above context the present study made an attempt to understand the performance of the state to make the workers realise the envisaged rights and entitlements of the workers through implementation of the NREGS. The present study was conducted in Madhya Pradesh by Poverty Learning Foundation–a private research organisation, in collaboration with National Institute of Rural Development (NIRD) as a part of nation wide survey on the instance of Ministry of Rural Development, New Delhi, to assess the performance of Rural Employment Guarantee Scheme (MPREGS) in terms of meeting the objectives of the NREGS.

Objectives of the Study

The specific objectives of the present study are:

1. To assess the awareness levels of the workers on the provisions of NREGS, including guaranteed working days, application procedure, unemployment allowance, time taken for the payment, Social Audit, Village Monitoring Committees (VMCs), etc. in Madhya Pradesh;
2. To elicit the level of materialisation of the envisaged rights/entitlements of the workers as per the NREGA by implementation of MPREGS.

Methodology

The study was conducted in twelve Gram Panchayats of twelve blocks in six districts. The districts were selected based on a set of both performance and development criteria pertaining to the district(s). In fact, this homework was done by NIRD itself and has given the list of six districts. Two blocks representing extreme levels of performance of the scheme (both high and low) were randomly drawn from each district and one Gram Panchayat was randomly drawn from the total number of gram panchayats in the selected block. The district and block authorities were consulted in selection of blocks and panchayats.

The study covered 547 wage seekers who participated in the REGS works during the financial year 2006–07. 50 workers were randomly selected from each village. However, the number fell short by 53 due to the non-availability of the selected workers in the village during the collection of data. The table 12.1 gives details about the area of the study and the sample workers.

The data were collected by interviewing all the selected workers on various issues. The Focus Group Discussions (FGDs) were also conducted in all the 12 gram panchayats with the village community including workers to substantiate the data collected from the individual workers.

Table 12.1. Sample coverage across districts

District	No. of workers	Percentage
Betul	100	18.3
Chaatarpur	99	18.0
Seoni	96	17.6
Shivapuri	93	17.0
Tikamgarh	68	12.4
Umaria	91	16.6
Total	**547**	**100**

The entire paper is divided into two sections. Section 1 presents the socio-economic characteristics including the caste group, age, income levels, occupation, etc., of the workers who reaped the benefits of the scheme by participating in the REGS. Section 2 is devoted to portray data analysis with respect to awareness levels of the workers on the rights and entitlements of the workers on the provisions of REGS such as knowledge about the 100 days guarantee of employment, submission of the application for seeking work, claiming the unemployment allowance, participation in the Gram Sabha for selection of the works and social audit, and the actual performance of the scheme in transforming the rights of the workers in to reality.

Section I : Composition of the Sample of Study

I. (*a*) Gender of the workers: It was noticed that out of 547 households 921 workers participated in the REGS' works (multiple workers from single household). The male participation is higher than that of female. The over all percentage of male and female population are 56.3 and 42.7 respectively.

I. (*b*) Age of the workers: The data shows that a majority of the workers (56%) hails from the age group of 15–35 years followed by the age group of 36-60 years. Old people (61 years and above) were also part of the workers group, accounting for 2.6 per cent.

I. (*c*) Caste-group of the workers: Schedule tribe emerges as the dominant group with 55 per cent of the workers in the total sample, followed by OBCs (27%), SCs (18%) and the OC (0.5%).

I. (*d*) Landholding status: The analysis reveals that in the overall sample of 547 families, one-third is found to be landless and one-half are marginal farmers. Small farmers account for 12 per cent. or one out of every eight workers.

I. (*e*) Occupational distribution of the workers' families: The occupational analysis of the workers shows that the non-agricultural labour form the largest chunk (42%) in the sample, followed by ag. labour (32 per cent) and cultivators (26%). The presence of artisans in the sample is hardly half per cent.

I. (*f*) Annual income of the workers' families: A majority of the workers (41%) hail from the income group of Rs. 5000–10000 followed by moderate income group (Rs. 10000 to 15000) is 24.4 per cent. The income levels of the workers are shown in table 12.2.

Table 12.2 . Distribution of the sample based on income

Income (Rs.)	No. of workers	Percentage
Up to 5000	89	16.3
5001 - 10000	227	41.5
10001 - 15000	133	24.3
15001 - 20000	53	9.7
20001 - 25000	34	6.2
25001 & above	11	2.0
Total	**547**	**100**

SECTION II: *Awareness and Utilization of Rights and Entitlements of the Workers*

II. (1) Awareness about the Provisions of NREGA

The study has attempted to assess the awareness levels of the workers about the various provisions of the Act including the minimum number of days of employment demanded by a household, the unemployment allowance in case the worker household is entitled if the government could not provide the work to him/her within the stipulated time (15 days), additional wages for travelling more than 5 kms to the work site, the time limit for payment of wages, etc., are some of the provisions have been selected and on which the workers were asked to respond whether they know about these provisions. The data show that the awareness levels of the workers on the provisions of REGS is abysmally low. Very few workers have a little idea about the issues like number of days of employment, the minimum wages, and the time taken for payment of wages. Particularly the issues like RTI, social audit and unemployment allowance were almost not known to the workers. The table 12.3 gives the details of the awareness levels of the participant workers about their entitlements on various provisions of the NREGA.

Thus it can be understood that the measures taken by the implementing agencies at GP level/block level are not sufficient enough to make the rural workers aware of the provisions of the NREGA. Therefore, a dire need is felt without losing any time further, the entire machinery needs to be geared up towards conducting awareness campaigns in the form of folklore, puppet shows, street plays, etc., in the rural areas. Both print and electronic media should also be extensively used so that the message on the entitlements will spread far and wide in the rural areas of the districts where the scheme is in operation.

Table 12.3. Awareness about NREGA components

No.	Component	Awareness of workers		Total
		Yes	No.	
1.	No. of days of employment (100)	48 (8.8)	499 (91.2	547
2.	Unemployment allowance	3 (0.5)	544 (99.5)	547
3.	Additional wages beyond 5 kms.	16 (2.9)	531 (97.1)	547
4.	Minimum wages	150 (27.4)	397 (72.6)	547
5.	Time limit for providing employment	28 (5.1)	519 (94.9)	547
6.	Time limit for wage payment	28 (5.1)	519 (94.9)	547
7.	About RTI	6 (1.1)	541 (98.9)	547
8.	Social audit	2 (0.4)	545 (99.6)	547

Note: (a) Figures in parentheses are percentages,
(b) Multiple entries have taken place.

II. (2) Awareness about the Process of Complaint

The awareness level about the process of complaints and the officers to whom the complaints should be submitted is at desperately low. Not more than even four per cent of the workers were aware of these problems. A majority of the workers do not know whom they should consult if the problems like non-issue of job cards, work is not shown in 15 days after the date of submission of the application, non-payment of the wages within 15 days etc., arise. The table 12.4 provides a clear picture about the awareness of the workers about the complaining process.

Table 12.4. Classification of workers based on the awareness of complaining procedures.

No.	Component	Awareness of workers		Total
		Yes	No.	
1.	Job cards are not given	17 (3)	530 (97)	547
2.	Work is not given in 15 days	24 (4)	523 (96)	547
3.	Wages not paid in time	22 (4)	525 (96)	547

Note: Figures in parentheses are percentages

It is observed from table 12.4 that about 97 per cent of the workers were not aware of the complaining procedure. Though there are grievance redress cells at block and district levels, many people were not familiar with the procedures. This appalling scenario calls for conducting an awareness campaign through all possible means so as to make the rural population well aware of the process of lodging complaint and get their grievances redressed.

II. (3) Source of Information

Without an exception of any district, the workers got information about REGS from the gram panchayat. Officials and NGOs besides both print and electronic media also played a role according to a few workers. As far as RTI and Social Audit are concerned, the few workers who reported to be aware indicated that they came to know from Gram Panchayat and officials besides NGOs.

II. (4) Application for Work

The NREGA indicates that 'Applications for work may be submitted in writing either to the Gram Panchayat or Programme Officer as may be specified in the scheme. The Gram Panchayat and Programme Officer, as the case may be, shall be bound to accept the valid applications and to issue a dated receipt to the applicant. Group applications may also be submitted.' (*The Gazette of India*, 2005, Schedule II) p. 14.

As the analysis reveals, slightly over half the workers were not aware of the requirement that they have to give an application for work. Seoni and Umaria, districts, registered the highest incidence (87 and 97 per cent respectively) of unawareness in respect of this dimension. Even as many as half of the workers did not submit their applications for seeking work. The table 12.5 gives the number of workers who were aware of submission of application and the actual workers who submitted applications for work.

Table 12.5. Awareness about giving application for work and actual submission

No.	Component	Awareness of workers			Total
		Yes	No.	NA	
1.	Awareness of submission of application	251 (46)	296 (54)	—	547
2.	Submission of application	278 (50)	221 (40)	48 (9)	547

Note: Figures in parenthesis represent percentages.

According to 50 per cent of the workers in the overall sample, application was given for seeking work. The overall observation and interaction with the workers in FGD highlights that the workers were not submitting their applications individually. It is noticed that the Sarpanches prepare the list of workers on his / her own discretion. This is usually done after the project is sanctioned.

II. (5) Employment Generation

As per the NREGA each household, which is willing and seeking work, must be provided with 100 days of guaranteed employment in a year. The Act says 'the state government shall in such rural areas in the state as may be notified by the central government provide to every household whose adult members volunteer to do unskilled manual work not less than one hundred days of such work in a financial year in accordance with the scheme made under this Act'. (*The Gazette of India, 2005*, chapter II, p. 3). However the empirical data reveals that majority of the families (92%) could not be provided with the maximum of 100 days of work. On an average each participating family was able to get employment from REGS for 42 days for the reference year (2006–07). The table 12.6 gives the details about the number of families got employment based on the classification of number of days.

Table 12.6. Distribution of households according to employment generation group-wise

Employment days	No. of households	Percentage
Up to 25	219	(40.0)
26 – 50	169	(30.9)
51 – 75	83	(15.2)
75 – 99	36	(6.6)
100 & above	40	(7.3)
Total	**547**	**100**

Note: The numbers in parentheses represent percentages.

The table 12.6 illustrates that only 40 families (7.3%) satisfied this requirement. In fact, 40 per cent (two-fifths) of the households studied could not get employment beyond 25 days and 31 per cent of the households got employment between 26 and 50 days. Further, one out of every 7 families could employment ranging between 51-75 days. It is further evident that 6.6 per cent or one out of every 15 households got employment in the range of 76-99 days.

The above results are almost confirming with the study conducted by National Consortium of Civil Society Organisations. 'All of this meant that of the 2.10 crore households who were employed under NREGA during its first year, only 0.22 crore received the full 100 days promised under the Act. The average employment per household was 43 days in 2006-07 and 35 days in 2007–08' (quoted in Ambasta, Vijay and Mihir, 2008).

II. (6) Employment Generation per Worker

As reported earlier, in all, 921 workers from 547 sample households participated in REGS and on an average each worker got employment for 25 days, moving in a range of 19 days (Tikamgarh and Umaria) and 30 days (Shivpuri). Not much of a variation is noticed in the average when the data are disaggregated caste-group-wise (OCs are excluded for the purpose of analysis as only three such households participated).

II. (7) Wage Earned

Given the wage rate of Rs. 63 per day (2006–07), the total wage earned by the participating family will essentially be a function of the number of days of employment the family got.

However, an attempt is made to have a look at the total wage a family earned through REGS. The analysis shows that on an average each family earned an amount of Rs. 2621 as wage and variations of a larger magnitude are noticed not only across districts but also across caste groups. Among six districts, Shivpuri emerges as the district with the largest wage amount of Rs. 3808 and on the other extreme, Umaria registered a figure of Rs. 1419.

II. (8) Minimum Wage

The Act says 'every person who has done the given work to him under the scheme shall be entitled to receive wages at the wage rate for each day of work, provided further that the wage rates specified from time to time under any such notification shall not be at the rate less than sixty rupees per day (*The Gazette of India, 2005*, chapter II, p. 3). When asked whether the sampled workers were paid the minimum wage, one out of eight workers replied in the negative and the magnitude is relatively in a larger measure in Tikamgarh, Seoni and Betul districts.

Table 12.7. Response of the workers over receiving of minimum wage

Response	Yes	No.	Total
No. of households	481 (88)	66 (12)	547 (100.0)

Note: The numbers in parentheses represent percentages.

Out of 66 workers nearly 50 per cent of them have got Rs. 2 less than the prescribed wage of Rs. 63, 17 per cent less than Rs. 3 and one-third less than Rs. 13.

II. (9) Distribution of Wages

The provision in the Act runs like 'in case of every employment under the scheme, there shall be no discrimination solely on the ground of gender and the provision of the equal remuneration Act, 1976 (25 of 1976) shall be complied with'. (Schedule-II, p. 16)

When asked how the wages were distributed among the group members, all workers said that there was equal distribution of wages. In the case of four workers, males were reported to have got more wages as compared to the female counterparts. Wages were paid only in the form of cash to the workers.

When asked whether they faced any problems in getting the wages, 34 (6.2%) of 547 workers reported they had to shell down some money in greasing the palms of those concerned with wage payment.

II. (10) Time Taken for Payment of Wages

As per the Act 'the disbursement of daily wages shall be made on a weekly basis or in any case not later than a fortnight after the date, on which such work was done, (*The Gazette of India, 2005*, chapter II, p. 3). In case the payment of wages is not made within the period specified under the scheme, the labourers shall be entitled to receive payment of compensation as per the provisions of the Payment of Wages Act, 1936 (4 of 1936) (*The Gazette of India, 2005*, Schedule-II, p. 16)

Only in 5 per cent of the cases was the wage paid beyond the stipulated period of 15 days, as per the information of the workers. While this was the scenario at the aggregate level, Shivpuri and Umaria registered cent per cent compliance and in Betul only in a lone case was the payment delayed. But in Chhatarpur, things appeared to be different–about 15 per cent reported delayed payments.

Table 12.8. Time taken to make the payment

Days	Upto 15 days	Above 15 days	Total
No. of households	521 (95)	26 (5)	547 (100)

Note: The numbers in parentheses represent percentages

The payment of wages was delayed due to delay in release of the amount. This has happened as some of the works were started much earlier than the release of the amount, just on the oral understanding of the officials concerned and the panchayat presidents. It is to be noticed that all these oral understandings followed the literal sanctions.

It was observed in National Consortium of Civil Society Organizations data in parts of Shivapuri district of Madhya Pradesh, delay of as much as two to three months in payment of wages have been reported. (quoted in Ambasta, *et al. ibid*).

II (11) Unemployment Allowances

The NREGA clearly spells that 'if an applicant for employment under the scheme is not provided such employment within fifteen days of receipt of his application seeking employment or from the date on which employment is sought in the case of an advanced application which ever is later he shall be entitled to a daily unemployment allowance in accordance with this section. It further says that if government fails to provide work to the job card holders the state has to provide unemployment allowance. "The unemployment allowance will be at least one-fourth of the minimum wages as per the REGS for the first 30 days and not less than half of the wage for the subsequent days" (*The Gazette of India, 2005*, chapter 3, p. 4). The study reveals that no unemployment allowance was paid in any of the study districts. However, state as a whole, the unemployment allowance was paid to 1574 workers to the tune of Rs. 4,75,000 in Barwani district.

II (12) Work within the Village

The Act says "As for as possible employment shall be provided within the radius of five kms. of the village, where the applicant reside at the time of applying. In case the employment is provided outside such radius, it must be provided within the block, and the labourers shall be provided ten per cent of the average wage rate as extra wages to meet additional transportation and living expenses" (*The Gazette of India, 2005*, chapter 6, schedule II, p. 15)

The field data show that out of 547 workers only 14 (2.6 per cent) were provided work out side their Gram Panchayat. (beyond 5 kms. and all these were paid additional 10 per cent of the wage to meet their travel expenses.

II. (13) Mandatory Facilities

As per the Act the facilities of safe drinking water, shade for children and period of rest, first aid box with adequate material for emergency treatment for minor injuries, and other health hazards connected with the work being performed shall be provided at the work site. In case the number of children below the age of six years accompanying the women working at any site are five or more, provisions shall be made to depute one of such women worker to look after such children. (*The Gazette of India, 2005*, schedule II, p. 16)

Though as per the officials and the implementing agencies all these facilities were provided at work sites, the data collected from the workers do not corroborate it. It is showing a negative scenario. Out of the four facilities that are expected to be made available at the work site, drinking water and first-aid box were provided at many work sites. The crèche and shades were provided at a limited places. The table 12.9 gives the responses of the workers.

Table 12.9. Response of the workers on the provision facilities at work sites.

No.	Facilities	Response		Total
		Yes	No.	
1.	First aid box	281 (51)	266 (49)	547
2.	Drinking water	426 (78)	121 (22)	547
3.	Crèche	120 (22)	427 (78)	547
4.	Shade	100 (18)	447 (82)	547

Note: The numbers in parentheses represent percentages

II (14) Muster Rolls

According to the Act muster rolls should be kept at work site for public scrutiny for ensuring transparency in implementation of the scheme. 'The gram panchayat shall make available all relevant documents including muster rolls, bill, vouchers, measurement books, copies of sanction orders and other connected books of accounts and papers to the gram sabha for the purpose of conducting social audit'. (*The Gazette of India, 2005*, ch. 4, p. 9). This facilitated the workers to know about the number of days he participated in the work and the corresponding wage etc. The data collected at individual worker level is shown in the table 12.10.

Table 12.10. Maintaining muster rolls at worksites

No.	Response	Yes	No	Don't know	Total
1.	Frequency	329 (60)	125 (23)	93 (17)	547

Note: The numbers in parentheses represent percentages

According to three-fifths of the workers (60%) muster rolls were kept at the work site. 23 per cent said that the implementing agency did not bother at all to meet this requirement. 93 (17%) workers exhibited ignorance about whether they were kept or not.

II (15) Awareness about the Works Sanctioned under REGS

The data analysis reveals that majority of the workers i.e 377 (70%) were not aware of the works sanctioned and implemented in the village under REGS. Only the rest (30%) expressed that they knew the works sanctioned in the village. This itself shows the less participation of the workers in selection of the works.

II (16) Participation of the Workers in Selection of Works and Social Audit

The NREGA made it a mandatory that the Gram Panchayat should conduct the Gram Sabha to facilitate the participation of the workers in selection of the works and express their view in social audit. '*Gram Sabha* shall conduct regular social audit of all the projects under the scheme taken up within the Gram Panchayat' (*The Gazette of India, 2005*, ch. 4, p. 9). The participation of the workers was highly expected.

Though the officials opined that the works were selected by massive participation of the workers in the village, the information collected from the individual workers on the participation of the workers in selection of the works and social audit gives a dismal scenario. It shows that there was a very less participation of the worker in the above two tasks. The table 12.11 gives details about the participation of the workers.

Table 12.11. Participation of the workers in selection of the works and social audit

No.	Problem	Participation of the workers			Total
		Yes	No	NA	
1.	Selection of the works	162 (30)	383 (70)	—	547
2.	Social audit	15 (3)	371 (68)	161 (29)	547

Note: The numbers in parentheses represent percentages

Ambasta, *et al.* (*ibid.*) mentioned about the people's participation in the planning of the works was very less. 'The general practice is that funds are first released by the DP and then activities are identified. In Shivpuri district, the focus continues to be on roads. The Gram sabha is not aware of the plans nor do people know that without their approval work can not start or be completed. In Tikamgarh district there are no annual working plans ratified by the Gram sabha. The plans are prepared by the CEO, block panchayat and GP secretary and forwarded for fund released to the DP".

As far the social audit is concerned all the partners of consortium report that "there is no real social audit process taking place in any location nor is there any system in place to do so. Provision for mandatory availability of muster rolls on work site is also not followed" Ambasta, *et al.* (*ibid.*)

II (17) Formation and Functioning of Village Monitoring Committee

As per the provisions, the works execution in the village should be monitored on regular basis. For this purpose, the VMCs should be formed and these VMCs should visit the field. The information given by the implementing agencies and other officials each and every work was thoroughly monitored. However the data provided by the individual workers who participated in the work did not corroborate the official information. As per the data provided 63 per cent of the workers expressed that the VMCs were constituted and functioning effectively. The rest of the workers opined that the VMCs were not constituted and they were not functioning at all. The table 12.12 gives the details.

Table 12.12. Formation and functioning of VMCs

No.	Issues	Opinion of the workers		Total
		Yes	No	
1.	Formation	344 (63)	203 (37)	547
2.	Functioning	341 (62)	206 (38)	547

Note: The numbers in parentheses represent percentages

The consortium report (*ibid.*) says in Shivepuri there was no social audit and vigilance committee at village level.

II (18) Workers Demand Services from GP and Officials

An attempt was made to understand whether the implementation of the NREGS did empower the workers to demand services from the local government and other government officials either in terms of providing works, services, information regarding the works, conduct of social audit etc. The ground scenario shows that a majority of the workers felt that there was no change in their condition with regard to demand more services from the government. Some of the workers even were not aware of the provisions of the workers and by using which they could demand services from official. The table 12.13 shows the pragmatic picture about the empowerment of the workers in demanding the services from government.

Table 12.13. Response of the workers in demanding service from officials and Gram Panchayat

No.	Issue	Opinion of the workers			Total
		Yes	No	NA	
1.	Demanding services from officials	11 (2)	338 (62)	198 (36)	547
2.	Demanding services from Gram Panchayat	40 (7)	318 (58)	189 (35)	547

Note: The numbers in parentheses represent percentages

II (19) Realisation of Worker about Right to Work

It was expected that participation in the REGS makes workers realize their right to demand work from the government. All the workers were asked to respond on this issue. The data analysis illustrate that though the workers did participate in the works carried out under REGS, they could not realize that it was their right to demand work. Only very few workers *i.e.,* 37 (7%) said that they realised their rights by participating in REGS works but they are not utilising it for demanding their work since the procedure of application and grievance redressal is a time consuming and complex one. A large majority of the workers *i.e.,* 510 (93%) did respond negatively that they were not still aware that they could demand their rights.

II (20) Information to People by Gram Panchayat

It was expected that the people in the villages would be informed about all the decisions of the Gram Panchayat after the enactment of NREGA, and Right To Information (RTI) Act. An attempt was made to test the hypothesis empirically in the studied area. The data collected from the individual workers show that the information about the decisions of the Panchayats were reaching to the people to some extent only. The table 12.14 shows the details of the data analysis.

Table 12.14. Classification of workers based on opinion on information to people

No.	Type of response	Large extent	Some extent	Not at all	Can't say	Total
1.	No. of households	42 (8)	272 (50)	62 (11)	171 (31)	547

Note: The numbers in parentheses represent percentages

II (21) Response of GP and Officials to the Needs of the People

It was felt, the implementation of NREGA would make the workers more aware of their rights and they would demand more services from the government. Ultimately it would make the local government particularly the Gram Panchayat and the government officials more responsive to the need of the people in general and workers in particular. However the data show that a majority of the workers opined that both the panchayat and the officials are not much responsive and achieving the objective is far from the goal. The details about the responsiveness of GP and officials to the needs of the worker are shown in table 12.15.

Table 12.15. Classification of the workers based on the perception over response of the GP and Officials

No.	Response	Large extent	Some extent	Not at all	Total
1.	Gram Panchayat	19 (4)	226 (41)	302 (55)	547 (100)
2.	Officials	9 (1)	168 (31)	370 (68)	547 (100)

Note: The numbers in parentheses represent percentages

Conclusions

The study shows that the awareness levels of the village community, the workers, the implementing agencies like Gram Panchayat, Block Level and District Level authorities is not up to the mark. There is a dire need to provide additional inputs like training to the officials at all levels *i.e.,* district, block and village level to give more orientation on various provisions of the NREGS. Though the training has already been given to them, still there is scope for further training on preparation of the perspective plan, shelf of the projects, creating more awareness to the local community on various provisions relating to the rights and entitlements of the worker, etc. The community participation in all the activities of the REGS, conducting of social audit etc., is to be further strengthened. Though there is scope for the lagged effect in creating awareness among the workers about the REGS, organizing the regular meetings in the village or at block levels and publishing a quarterly newsletter about REGS etc., are most useful in realising the rights and entitlements of the workers through the best implementation of the NREGS.

REFERENCES

1. Ambasta, Pramathesh, P.S. Vijay Shankar and Mihir Shah. (2008) "Two Years of NREGA: The Road Ahead", *Economic and Political Weekly*, Vol. XLIII, No. 8, February. 23 – 29, pp. 41-50.
2. *The Gazette of India (2005)* Registered No. DL – (N), 04/007/2003 -05, New Delhi, Ministry of Law and Justice.
3. Shah, Mihir (2004) "National Rural Employment Guarantee Act : A Historic Opportunity" *Economic and Political Weekly*, Vol. XXXIX, December 11 – 17, pp. 5287-90.

Going Beyond the Mask : The Present Trend of *Chhau* Dance among the Adolescent of Purulia

—Ashis Kumar Das

Introduction

The *Chhau* dance of Purulia district is a popular folk dance of Bengal. The *Chhau* dance, wearing a mask is usually performed by male dancers. There is no *Chhau* without mask. *Chhau* dance of Purulia has some characteristics of primitive ritualistic dance in its vigour, style and musical accompaniment a drum is used while performing. Earlier the dancers used to paint their face and body as per the requirement of the character (mostly mythological characters like Rama, Ravana, Ganesh etc.) and use of mask is a later development to make it more realistic and attractive.

Chhau dance was originally performed on the occasion of the tribal harvesting festival also known as the 'Sun festival' during the end of the month of *Chaitra* (March-April) in Bengali calendar. The festival continued for about one-and-a-half months till the next sowing season, which indicates it was interlinked with the social and economic life of the Bengal farmers. The situation has changed with the passing of time, as *Chhau* is now also performed during other festivals at different times of the year. *Chhau* mask dance is predominantly a Bhumij art. The majority of dancers are Bhumij, but Santal, Mahato, Scheduled Castes are also performing the art in different places.

The *Chhau* dance is epical in content, as it is based on various episodes of the Ramayana and the Mahabharata. Sometimes certain episodes of the Puranas are also used. At the end, generally, forces of evil are vanquished. No dais or raised platform is used; the dance, takes place on the ground around which, the spectators sit in a circle. The *Chhau* shows usually start around 10 at night and continue till after daybreak.

The use of the drum is an important part of *Chhau*. The dance opens with the beating of drums followed by an invocation to God Ganesha by a singer. As soon as the singer finishes the song, host of drummers and musicians step in again with the *dhol* and the *dhamsa* (indigenously made two faced percussion instrument and gigantic kettle drum played with sticks and fingers respectively) two traditional musical instruments used by the rural population in various parts of the country. The drummers themselves make tune on the *dhol* and the *dhamsa*. Along with the team of drummers the musical part, which is an integral prelude to the actual dance, is also vastly enriched by one or two musicians who play on an instrument, which is a unique improvisation of *Sheh-nai*, a variant of the flute. In fact the team of musicians by music and chanting of *bols-* (Beats) creates an inexplicably wonderful ambience prior to the dance. This is the time for the Lord Ganesha to appear on the dancing ground. He is followed in quick succession by other characters– gods, demons, animals and birds (2005: 112).

It is now very difficult to know what costumes the *Chhau* performers used when this particular dance-form came into being over two hundred years ago. The costumes used now are of various colours and designed *pyjamas* of deep green or yellow or red shade are worn by the artists who play the gods, while those, who play the demons (*asuras*) have on loose trousers of a deep black shade. Stripes of contrasting colours are used to make the costumes more attractive. The costumes for the upper part of the body are marked with various designs. Goddess Kali is a popular character in *Chhau* dance, and her costume is made of cloth of unrelieved black. Lord Kartik is another very popular character. Animals and birds are other characters that use the suitable masks and costumes to express their separate identities.

The masks used for *Chhau* in West Bengal are made in a village called Charida, located in Baghmundi area of Purulia district of West Bengal. Made of clay and paper, they are produced by a particular group of people who have been engaged in this business for generations (Sutradhara). These artisans, familiar with the details of the Indian epics, produce masks, which bear testimony to the high artistic skills they have achieved. As all the characters in the *Chhau* dance, are required to wear masks, it is impossible for the artists to show mood variations through facial expressions. Body movements, including movements of the peaks of the masks are used to illustrate different moods. The mask movements show anger, while shoulder and chest movements indicate joy, melancholy and courage etc. Jumping in the air is another movement which serves as a gesture of attack during the enactment of a war scene. Such jumpings (known as *ulfa*) are high hall-mark of acrobatic skill and physical prowess of the performers of *Chhau* dance.

The best *Chhau* dance groups or parties are located within Baghmundi P.S. They are the best because of their traditional vigorous and heroic style of performance. The other groups (Domordi-group, Birgram-group, Madla-group etc.) are more sophisticated and refined both in their themes and dance-styles. The Chorda-group of dancers is not only best performs of heroic *Pauranic* themes, but also are very much selective about such themes for their performance.

It has been well accepted in West Bengal and India that *Chhau* is one of the best folk dance and the dance groups of Purulia have been performing in various places of the world and are getting international reputation. To carry forward this age-old tradition of

Purulia, the adolescent should have great interest to learn and perform this dance and the government and various private dance schools should come forward to preserve this valuable art with respect. This paper will try to analyze the views of 130 SC/ST adolescent school going children of 11 blocks of Purulia district on their traditional *Chhau* dance and also interpret the impact of urbanization, and Vaisnavism on their age-old mask dance.

Field Area

As per 2001 census total population of the Purulia district is 25,35,516, out of which 89.93 per cent are residing in rural areas and 10.07 per cent in urban areas. About 51.18 per cent of the populations are males and 48.82 per cent are female. The percentage of Scheduled Caste and Scheduled Tribes are 18.29 per cent and 18.27 per cent. Total no of BPL families in rural areas of this district are 197381 (43.65%). Out of which SC families are 40645 (20.59%) and ST families are 47666 (24.15%). Total no. of BPL families in Purulia and Jhalda Municipality are 2573 (11.31%) and 571 (15.98%) respectively. Most of the family members have been associated with the cultivation, irrigation, small scale industry as day labourers.

The fieldwork has been carried out in eleven Blocks and one Municipality of Purulia district in November 2008, covering 13 villages and one municipal area to find out the trend of *Chhou* Dance among the adolescent of different communities. 130 children (93 Male and 37 Female) have been considered for focus group discussion and all the children have been identified through the NCLP (National Child Labour Project) schools whose main objectives to eliminate the child labour by ensuring education, health, nutrition and social awareness. Most of the children are from Santal, Bhumij and other Schedule Casts who are living in the interior villages and are following their age-old folk and traditional customs. These children are engaged in cultivation, grazing of cattle, collection of wood and fuel, household activities, and some girl children are looking after little siblings and are engaged in *Bidi* making.

Table 3.1

Community	No. of children
Santal	52
Bhumij	19
Mahato	9
Sabar	4
Scheduled Cast	39
Muslim	3
Cast	4
Total	**130**

The 130 adolescents are representing scheduled tribes like Santal, Bhumij, Mahato, Sabar, and scheduled castes like Karmakar, Hari, Rajwar, Teli, Bauri, Bene, Bhuinya etc. Seven children from Muslim and General Caste have also been taken to know their views about this mask dance.

Adolescents are persons between the age group of 10-19 years. The growth phases can be divided as early adolescence (10-13 years), middle adolescence (14-16 years) and late adolescence (17-19 years) (2005). The age of the sample group varies from 8 to 18 years and has covered three phases of the internationally accepted growth phases of adolescence. Most of the adolescents are 10 to 12 years old or representing middle adolescence (Table 13.2).

Table 3.2

Age Group	No. of children
8	3
9	19
10	34
11	30
12	26
13	8
14	1
15	2
16	3
17	1
18	3
Total	130

Observations

To the adolescents, *Chhau* dance is nothing but a mask dance. They are habituated to see the mask dance of several *Palas* or plays like *Mahishasur Badh, Shiv-Kali ,Genesh, Durga Parushuram, Chauba,* etc. but they prefer the play on fight of *Kartik* and *Ashur* the most. Beside this dance *Chhau* dancers act the *Palas* of Arjun-Kirat, Sakhi and various actions of birds and animals with respective masks and dresses.

This dance takes place during the *Gajan* and the festival on the occasion of *Shiva puja* during mid of May (*Jaishtha*), in the entire district of Purulia at night in the open field. Sometime they invite *Chhau* dance group from neighbouring villages within 2-3 km or from far or they perform by themselves in their own villages. But this dance cannot be seen in the year round except this season.

Twenty-nine adolescents out of 130 are able to perform this dance. *Agura Ulfa* (tumbling forwards), *Pachura Ulfa* (Tumbling backward) and taking a vault are the difficult poses among the many. Skillful dancers must be the master in tumbling or *Agura* and *Pachura Ulfa*. They have to utter the chant of *Lord Ganesha* fluently at the beginning of the dance. The *Chhau* dance group comprising of 25-30 people is master in different characters. At the same time each member is a master of a specific character. The dress and masks depending upon the *Palas* and character. But to acquire this skill needs hard work. Seven among the twenty-nine adolescents are able to perform *Agura Ulfa* and *Pachura Ulfa* skillfully. They belong to Barabajar, Joypur, Jhalda, and Ashara Blocks. They have learnt the dance by themselves or from the neighbouring villages. Some of them practice this in the morning and some in the evening. Even two of them practice on the bank of the river. Some of their friends gather at the bank of the river to see the dance but they do not practice and join at all. Some adolescents are interested to learn this traditional dance but they do not have the opportunity. There is a great risk of hand and leg injury in case of not taking the professional training from a master. So many children avoid practice by self. Except the 29 young people among 130 believe that this dance is unable to give them economical establishment and social respect. So they are not interested in the dance. Though few of them have joined dance group and perform but the number is very less. Most of the dancers stay in Purulia and perform but they are deprived of wealth and social respect. None consider them as an artist rather they are the victim of rude satire. The adolescents among who can dance, believe that this is a fact. They are learning the dance because they love it. One dancer can earn only Rs. 50-60 per day during fastival. Besides this dance is not performed throughout the year. So financially they suffer a lot. Seven adolescents dancers had been asked, whether they wanted to earn a living by joining government and private jobs after finishing education or by performing *Chhau* dance. They preferred the service or business instead of *Chhau* dance for social respect. To answer this question, Ganesh Karmakar (age 13) said 'if I join in any service I will be accepted in elite society and I will be able to earn social respect in my village and from my in-laws'.

These children have been given two options during group discussion. Suppose one organization is offering them desk work and other organization wants to engage them as *Chhau* dancers and both of them are offering 5000 per month for the service. Which organization they would prefer and why? Though both organizations are providing same amount, still all of them preferred the desk work as it provides social respect. According to them the villagers show more respect to the serviceman than the *Chhau* dancer. Then they have been asked which one they would like to choose if the *Chhau* dance provides 7000 per month, and service 5000 per month. This time also they preferred the service except *Chhau*. So, to them social position and reputation is much higher than financial security.

The villagers believe that girl children cannot perform *Ulfa;* hence they are not preferred for the dance. It is like a social taboo. The most of the members of a *Chhau* dance group are male and they perform their skill in different villages in the evening, so it is difficult for a girl to join and perform *Chhau* with this type of group. Society will not permit a girl to perform in night with other male dancers in different villages. This lack of social security as a form of acceptance is a great hindrance to the girls who wants to learn *Chhau*.

Impact of Vaisnavism and Hindu Greater Culture

In many blocks and villages of Purulia (like Balarampur Block, Joypur Block) there is no existence of *Chhau* dance but they have *Kirtan* party. This *Kirtan* group consists of 10-15 singers. Chorus performance of *Kirtan* or the songs devoted to Lord Visnu with *Khol* or drum and other musical instruments for non-stop 24 hours during 2-3 nights. This non-stop 24 hours singing is called *Astoprohar Harinam Sankirtan*. It is believed that this *Harinam Sankirtan* will purified the environment and will help the villagers to ward off all the evil effects. Generally one devotee of a village hire a *Kirtan* group and other villagers join them for three days. At the end the *Kirtan* group is paid Rs 8000-10000 with refreshment. Persons from Scheduled Castes and Scheduled Tribe can join in this team but the leader must be a Bramhin. He takes the half of the income and divides the rest among the others. He also influences others to join in his *Kirtan* group. Many people come to enjoy this *Kirtan* and do so by sleepless night. Some of the devotees invite the group in their respective villages. Each member of a *Kirtan* group earns Rs. 5-7 thousands from 2-3 shows. Being influenced by the *Harinam Sankirtan* villagers have constructed *Hari Mandir* or *Hari* temples in several tribal villages and they are habituated in Kritran instead of their own traditional folk songs and dance.

The young generation is confused now. Many adolescent are registering themselves in *Kirtan* party after leaving their own traditional songs and dance practice because the acceptance of this party is more and so-called 'elite' Hindu Bramhins and Hindu religion are associated with this activities. Besides, *Kirtan* ensures more economical satisfaction including other refreshments and other facilities. *Kirtan* is being performed on the occasion of death, new born, and in other Hindu religious festivals.

In three Municipalities of Purulia district (Purulia Municipality, Raghunathpur Municipality and Jhalda Municipality) Hindi songs and Bengali Filmy songs are well accepted, as these are urban prone. Even some clubs invite singers, film actors, actresses from Kolkata and Mumbai to perform dance, songs. During the group discussion with 25 urban children it has been found that they do not have the skill of *Chhau* dancer and some of them have not even seen any *Chhau* dance in their life.

Case Study

Name: Abinash Mahato, Age 11 years, Male.

Village : Vaddi (Mukundupur)

Block : Joypur.

The previous name of Mukundupur was Vaddi. The potters of Scheduled caste communities made the group of *Chhau* and they performed in villages. Abinash's father performed in that group and Abinash had been with the *Chhau* dance from his childhood.

He knows all steps of *Ulfa* as he was practicing with the group. A *Hari Mandir* was constructed and a *Kirtan* party has started their performance in the village three years ago. The group has now become popular after performing in several villages and has started earning a lot with the leadership of local Brahmin. The father of Abinash joined in that group leaving *Chhau* dance. Gradually the *Chhau* group disappeared. Now his father earns well. Abinash also does not practice *Chhau* dance anymore. His *Chhau* masks are the victim of rust, now. Now Abinash sings *Kirtan* well and does not want to perform *Chhau* dance in future. He wants to do service in future after receiving education. At the same time he wants to perform *Kirtan* if time permits, with his father because both money and social respect are crucial.

Conclusion

The *Chhau* dance or the age-old mask dance may be well appreciated in the elite society of West Bengal, India and around the world, but it has no such acceptance at the grass root level young generation of Purulia. Behind the mask the *Chhau* dance has been affected badly by the impact of Vaisnavism, Hindu religious culture. The impact of urbanization is another reason, which is influencing the young generation to take over the lifestyle of urban society by leaving their traditional age-old culture. No inputs on this art of dance are being provided in the primary school and other government and private schools as co-curricular activities. Hence young generation are indifferent and believes that *Chhau* dance has no respect and acceptance rather it is the culture of lower caste. Being a oral tradition it has been felt that many important parts of this dance have been changed or abolished, and if it is not preserved and nurtured many of the art form and *mudras* (performing style) will be eliminated gradually in the course of time.

REFERENCES

1. **Bhattacharyya, Asutosh** 2005. (4th Edition). *Folk Lore of Bengal.* (in Bengali) National Book Trust India, New Delhi, 2005.
2. ***Empowered Adolescents***; Ministry of Youth Affairs and Sports Government of India.
3. Indialine.com/travel/westbengal
4. www.purulia.gov.in

Development of Social Policy Strategies: An Anthropological Prospective

—Lev Yakobson

The majority of people are dissatisfied with the situation in the social sphere. Support of the authorities, maintenance of democracy and development of market economy largely depend on whether it will be possible to come up with a social strategy which would be a suitable basis for consolidating the Russian society. It does not imply populist promises which have been made by various parties of the opposition. The government must pursue an open and responsible social policy. On the face of it there is almost no alternative to populism when according to the National Centre for Public Opinion Survey (VTsIOM) about 60 per cent of people assess their situation as poor and or very poor and only 4 per cent as good.

In these circumstances abstractions implying that social policy is to be focussed basically on the most needy minority are hardly appropriate. Still less constructive are abstract appeals to re-establish e.g. the average real wages of 1991 (i.e. to raise the current level by almost three times) and at the same time prevent unemployment and sharply reduce inequality; as well as abstract references to West European systems of social guarantees which are based upon incomparably higher per capita GRP. A social strategy should first of all be specific and appropriate here and now. The government, unlike the opposition, cannot speak for "all the good things". The objective is not to compile an exhaustive list of urgent problems, instead, it is to define the key ones and determine inter-related approaches to their solution. The range of available social policy measures is relatively narrow and is well. known. Realistic dilemmas include the following:

- Should nominal guarantees in cases when the state at large or a specific section of the budget system is unable to reliably fund them be retained or cancelled;
- Should drafting of new laws governing social policies be based on optimistic assumptions of economic growth or on the "guaranteed zero-growth minimum plus improvement bonus" principle;

- Should labour market regulation be focused on ensuring maximum employment or on improving the situation of those who already have jobs;
- Should there be incentives for job search or should the unemployed habitual standards of living be supported;
- Should efficiency of public services be sacrificed to their equal distribution;
- Should priority be given to direct leveling of living standards including geographically, or to dynamic improvements for all the social groups except the wealthiest ones ("equal acceleration at different speed"). While defining the general direction of development one cannot avoid making a choice; another question is how radical should the policy be under specific choices.

It is not realistic to quickly fill the gap between the desirable and the available. It is realistic and necessary to involve all strata of the population in the positive change process. This can only be achieved by targeting policies (actions rather than appeals) at the most important needs, ideas and abilities of social groups, communities etc., which is incompatible with stereotyped levelling of living standards and implies differentiation on the basis of a common strategy. Democratic nature of power implies that social policy priorities are driven by values and problems which are most urgent for people.

During 1990s discussions on social policy were as a rule conducted in the context of socialist and neo-liberal values. In practice this was matched by the following alternative: whether to maintain the inherited system of social protection or to knowingly dismantle many of its sections. Meanwhile, results of sociologic research indicate that neither values are able to become a basis for social peace in the current situation in Russia. Socialist values are largely associated with totalitarian past and confrontation, particularly redistribution of property; they are nor supported by the most active strata of the population. Liberal values are not strongly rooted in either public consciousness or public practice. The society is rather inclined to values associated with conservatism. It does not imply trying to maintain status quo or revive socialism, but rather a focus on "family" and "public" values, organic development solidarity, justice etc. which is part and parcel of encouraging personal initiative and aversion to social engineering.

These sentiments are natural when formation of a market economy is ahead of civil society development, i.e. market-related institutions are not properly reinforced by non-market self-organization institutions which would ensure protection of an individual and representation of his interests. As a result, there is a tendency to combine economic freedom with state patronage. In similar circumstances similar sentiments were prevailing in Western Europe; as in today's Russia, they were often associated with national peculiarities and had a nationalistic tint.

These sentiments are matched with a social policy which can be termed as "progressist paternalism" of Dizraeli of Bismarck kind. In brief, progressist "bourgeois" paternalism, unlike the socialist one, implies active interference of the state into opportunity-making and moderate involvement in distribution of welfare (revenues, housing etc.). Thus, socialist approach includes detailed uniform regulation of labour relations (which restricts employment or forces it to use "grey" schemes under a market economy), while a conservative one implies creating conditions for maximum number of potential employees and employers concluding contracts to their satisfaction. Obviously, these approaches have matching different systems of labour law, distribution of housing etc.

For socialists and liberals equality is a priority (of revenues for the former, of rights for the latter). A conservative approach prefers integrity and adequacy. Under it, generally speaking, the aim is not to ensure maximum equality of a Dagestan peasant, Novosibirsk worker and Moscow entrepreneur, but rather to help each of them successfully fulfil their roles in life on the basis of their own rather than artificially enforced ideas of what is proper. This by no means eliminates concerns over consolidation of the society and social mobility, primarily through education.

Integral elements of a conservative strategy are fearless recognition and overall accounting of social heterogeneity without its mandatory safeguarding. During intensive public changes a conservative policy can and should be pro-active. But it cannot be built on the basis of a priori schemes and formal comparisons (for instance, national indicators of revenues distribution, cross-country and cross-regional comparisons in terms of cash revenues etc.). Qualitative comparisons are only meaningful for these purposes in the context of specific way of living.

From this point of view, it is more appropriate to compare social realities in Russia to the ones in Byelorussia or the Ukraine than to the ones in the US or Sweden. This is not a reason to give up efforts in the social sphere but is meaningful for their reasonable distribution. Concreteness of the conservative approach implies special attention to details, repetitive process of strategy development and amendment. The proposed thesis are an attempt to revel some of its features.

Speaking of the three inter-related aspects of social problems–poverty, inequality, instability–there are reasons to believe that for most people instability is currently the most significant factor. The significance of poverty as such is comparable to instability for older age groups, disabled, a large portion of people living in depressed regions etc.

This is confirmed, inter alia, by materials of a recent survey performed by the Public Opinion Fund. For all the groups surveyed unemployment and proper government were priorities, while primarily elderly and low-income people were concerned over pensions and benefits, most of all in large cities where there are opportunities to adapt through subsidiary plots of land etc. Objectively the poverty problem is very acute. Cash revenues of 43.8 mn people are below living wage (this is 29.9% of people vs. 23.8% in 1998 and 20.8% in 1997). Average newly-assigned pension is 70 per cent of the pensioner's living wage (in 1998 it was 114.7%). The structure of food consumption is unsatisfactory for millions of people.

However, those who are directly facing this problem do not always think that there is no alternative to budgetary/distributional increase of their revenues to match the living wage. They are more interested in stabilization of employment, timely payment of current wages and pensions, more opportunities to get extra work-related revenues including in kind. In brief, people are being more realistic than populist politicians.

This by no means justifies neglect of the poverty problem. At the same time, strategic choice should be aiming at reliability of guarantees, even if at the cost of their amount in a number of cases. Consolidation of the state including more effective co-operation of branches of power, federal, regional and local authorities, can help break the vicious circle of declared uninsured guarantees and their actual breach. Stability of social policies is obviously only attainable through clear fixing of realistically feasible level of social support for needy groups, unconditional guarantee that their situation is not going to deteriorate and gradually raising this level as far as it is economically viable. In most cases consistency, irreversibility and universality of positive changes is more important at the moment than their rate, and the latter is more important than the final benchmark.

To the extent possible, fixing of guarantees should precede their rationalization on the basis of target groups. We will have to temporarily fix, or rather openly recognise, existence of inequality, primarily territorial. The difference in indicators of living standards, for instance, the ratio of average wage and social payments to living wage, average term of unemployment, real per capita healthcare and education expenditures etc., is enormous by subjects of the Russian Federation and even more–by sub-regional territories. Production of GRP is very unevenly distributed across the country (its per capita level in 5 regions is over 1.5 times higher than Russia's average, and in 11 regions it does not reach 0.5 of the average). Forced leveling implies, on the one hand, intensive re-distribution incompatible with production stimulation, on the other hand, neglecting interests and needs of people living in relatively well-off territories in terms of formal indicators.

For example, formally speaking issues of employment and healthcare are generally solved better in larger cities than elsewhere, but surveys conducted there indicate a high degree of concern over the state of labour market and access to medical services. Standards and way of living in the regions including ways of adapting to factors causing poverty inevitably reflect territorial peculiarities. Thus, the same amount of pension has different values for a rural family in the North Caucasus and an urban family in the Central Russia. It is vital to counteract further growth of inequality including between regions, and work on leveling of living conditions for all strata of population. However it is not an abstract "inequality in general" that is important, rather, peculiarities of inequality in contemporary Russia.

During early 1990s, there was a dramatic growth of income differentiation (in 1991-1993 Gini coefficient went up 1.5 times). Later during certain periods inequality of cash revenues went down to a certain extent, in other periods, specifically after the 1998 crisis, it went up but on the whole the distribution model remains stable (thus, Gini coefficient for 1999 and 1993 is almost the same). Both the model itself and its rejection by the society have become habitual.

However, it is not differentiation of revenues as such that is rejected, but rather unequal access to their sources which is rightly related to the actual depth of inequality. Without accepting "getting rich through connections" people largely approve of differentiation if it is due to differences in abilities, individual efforts, willingness to take risk etc. For example, in a survey in Perm Region only 21 per cent of respondents believed that entrepreneurs' revenues were unfairly high, while 40 per cent of respondents gave this valuation to revenues of state bodies' staff, and 34 per cent to revenues of directors of large enterprises; only 1.5 per cent of respondents thought the same of revenues earned by cultural, art and cinema workers.

A strategy of pro-active economic opportunity-making and ensuring equal access to these opportunities could get more public support than mechanical leveling of revenues and, unlike the latter, would directly contribute to economic growth. Under this policy incentives created by the state are capable of playing at least the same role as guarantees. From the point of view of opportunity-making labour market policies are top priority. Its key features in today's Russia are rigidity and dramatic segmentation. Not only territories (the difference between ratios of the number of registered unemployed and number of vacancies varied regionwise by thousand times) but professional, age, gender and other groups are clearly in unequal situation. High rate of hidden unemployment is combined with high rate of hidden employment. Maintaining balance at this market is largely ensured through forced leaves, overdue wages and various deviations of actual, including non-cash, remuneration from the official one.

Thus, the russian Statistic Agency estimated hidden (grey) wages in 1998 to be RR 319 bn or about 25 per cent of the reported ones. In these circumstances there is an objective need for differentiated influence on various territorial, industrial, professional and other markets. Specific sets of motives governing employees and employers at each market have to be taken into account. Thus, for employees having personal plots of land the amount of wages in some cases is less important than other benefits of official employment.

For aged employees maintenance of professional status often is the most important factor, especially if it is used to be prestigious one or two decades ago, while young employees are more targeted at maximising revenues etc. At the same time, general focus of employment policy should be defined as labour market consolidation, *i.e.* removal of its numerous internal barriers. It implies enhancing labour mobility, ensuring transparency of labour relations, openness of the market for fair competition (including minimising the role of personal connections), ousting its grey segments and unreliable incentives.

For this purpose wages should become a real and flexible market mechanism which distributes labour resources by ensuring their most complete and effective utilization. Accordingly, state interference in labour market pricing at this stage should be minimum. At the same time, employees should be helped if they need to find a new employer, change occupation and place of residence. This is an expression of the state's role in opportunity-making.

Only if one fails to find gainful employment including through significant but feasible changes in the way of living it would make sense to offer social assistance through unemployment benefits; eligibility to the benefit and its amount should depend on the family's financial position. Any other approach in the current situation will be adverse to economic modernisation. Labour market consolidation also implies reducing employers' redundancy costs which under current laws are one of the key barriers for growth of legal employment. In the long run, labour market consolidation is mostly dependent on elimination of structural disproportions.

The key role in resolving this strategic problem is to be played by the education system. It is currently more targeted at internal criteria of continuity and academic excellence rather than ensuring employment, broadening career opportunities for graduates, contributing to positive structural economic changes, effective utilization of budget funds, satisfaction of solvent demand of companies and families for education services etc. Disregard of society's specific demands caused serious disproportions in vocational training system including transformation of a number of higher educational institutions into centres for training prospective unemployed and at the same time insufficient attention paid to primary and secondary vocational training as well as skills development system.

Training skilled workers and medium-level professionals is critical not only for dramatic improvement of the situation at the labour market and industrial growth but also for the formation of a large modern middle class as a basis of social stability (due to excessive number of certain professionals higher education in this country will not be able to guarantee high earnings in the near future). By ensuring high quality of primary and secondary vocational training, one can create a channel for social mobility which would be more adequate to current conditions and accessible for families from different strata and groups.

At the same time, it is important not to loose the advantages of the higher education system which is traditionally strong in Russia by focusing efforts primarily on supporting leading higher educational institutions and schools while changing training structure in favour of occupations guiding technological progress and demanded by the labour market.

In healthcare there is currently probably the largest *vs.* other spheres gap between nominal and real status of social policy institutions. Laws regulating provision of medical care are targeted at its assumed free character and general accessibility, compliance to standards of the most developed countries and use if most up-to-date technologies. At the same time, in terms of its actual recourse base Russian healthcare is comparable to developing countries, and not the more successful ones. Current per capita healthcare expenditures in Russia is several times lower than in the West, and differences in capital supply of the sector are still more significant. At the same time, structure of recourses and operations based on them are not rational.

The share of physicians in medical personnel is excessive. And less than a quarter of physicians provide primary care (while as a rule more than half do in West Europe). Surveys show that around a third of Russian physicians do not have the necessary information about modern methods of treatment. At the same time, the number of patients served by one physician is currently almost half of 1970 level. Two-thirds of medical and proventive services involve hospital stays (around one their in West Europe), average hospital stay is unwarrantably long.

Lack of relevant equipment in most medical institutions prevents them from using the most current medical technologies. Additionally, equipment is very unevenly distributed both across the country and between institutions in large cities. Elimination of differences requires investment of a scale which in foreseeable future will not be available in the consolidated budget and Mandatory Medical Insurance Fund. Bearing in mind the role of modern technologies in ensuring quality of medical care, their general accessibility (on the basis of quality) is not going to be achieved in the next few decades. In reality distribution of high quality services is to a large extent driven by two factors: users' social status and market forces. Additionally, the market of medical services is not sufficiently legalized and is therefore under-regulated.

According to a survey conducted in the framework of Boston University Project, direct user payments cover less than half of the total expenditures for medical care and medicines. In its turn, about half of payments are to purchase medicines (it has become typical for hospital patients to buy their medicines). Only around one-fourth of the remaining portion is "grey market" payments (probably, relevant amount were undervalued by respondents because from the law point of view it means bribes, and not only being bribed but also bribing is a crime). The rest is open payments to medical institutions for services which generally should have been provided free of charge.

However, because users' payments, including official ones, are interpreted by the laws at best as temporary and marginal, there are virtually no attempts to bring some degree of order in terms of their efficiency and fairness. In particular, there almost no differentiation of payments on the basis of patients' financial situation. The ultimate obstacle is the concept of full and equal access to medical care for the entire population on which current legislation is based. Due to economic restrictions, this concept is certainly non-workable, thus causing inadequacy of healthcare regulation. At the same time, equating fairness to equal access is a barrier to a more just targeted distribution of mid range services.

Healthcare needs a transition from equal access concept to a relative equality concept. There is no workable policy which would ensure independence of high quality medical services consumption from patients (or their employers, relatives etc.) Solvency. However, this inequality can and should be compensated by Preferential State funding of medical services for the low-income people. For this purpose, it is necessary to fully legalize the system of additional payments in healthcare and to allocate a portion of the budget and MMI funds to cover additional payments required for obtaining services of general technological level by low-income people. As to services with technological characteristics (and respective costs) materially exceeding general level, their distribution should be made via a transparent and regulated market.

To enhance efficiency of education, healthcare and other sectors of the social and cultural complex it is necessary to significantly reform their organisational and economic mechanism. Key features of the current mechanism were designed for practically full state funding and were targeted mainly at ensuring control over distribution of public funds and services. This is matched, on the one hand, by restricted rights of institutions, on the other hand, by extremely weak regulation of market relations.

Such a mechanism has specific requirements to both the budget and social homogeneity. It can work only if average income groups were generally satisfied with the supply of public services and did not try to influence their producers through solvent demand (openly or semi-legally). To some extent these conditions are practicable in a highly developed welfare state which has never existed in Russia; equal access to education and healthcare during the Soviet period was a fiction which is confirmed by the analysis of departmental and territorial distribution of social and cultural resources. Currently a non-civilised, predominantly grey market has spontaneously been shaped in the social and cultural sphere, where a consumers is unprotected and the state is not properly fulfilling either its regulatory or fiscal function. At the same time, elements of the social and cultural sphere in some cases started to be more flexible in reacting to consumer demand.

However, as the state is passive and ineffectively spends funds "for network maintenance" instead of playing the role of the strongest agent in an actually emerged market, the demand mainly reflect interests of the most solvent families and companies. The private consumer demand is inevitable. The aim is not to make it grey but rather to make maximum use of it for developing social and cultural sphere and ensure more targeted spending of public funds for the benefit of the disadvantaged. It is necessary to improve state funding of education and healthcare. But in foreseeable future it is impossible to achieve a situation which was the basis for designing the purely distributory mechanisms.

An alternative could be a model which is not directly targeted at distribution but primarily at high efficiency of services production and on this basis—their broad accessibility. Under this model an organisation offering services is an independent entity which can design its own strategy in response to incentives offered. Therefore, state and municipal funding should become an incentive focusing producers at both effective operations and socially preferable distribution of services. State funding should be performed predominantly in the form of orders placed on a competitive basis. This is an example of switching form direct distribution of funds to creation of economic opportunities.

State (federal and regional) and municipal orders can be combined in the framework of one institution and be complemented by orders from companies, individuals etc. As a result there could be a standard, effective and transparent mechanism for formation and use of budgetary and extra budgetary funds in the sphere of social and cultural services. The actual inequality of social and cultural servicing including by territories will not be immediately eliminated. However, elementary pre-requisites for influencing it by legal methods, namely transparency and legality of the object of influence itself. State's participation in the market of social and cultural services should not be limited to the role of the main source of demand. This market needs regulation including state control of the quality of services. In the field of pensions, social payments, housing and utilities it is viable to make policies more specific on the basis of targeted guarantees and incentives in the broad sense.

This approach is in principle characteristic of the reforms implemented in the last few years, but it was not always used consistently and adequately. Thus, social guarantees should in most cases be targeted at families (households) living in specific regional, urban or rural conditions, rather than at an abstract individual. This is to some extent taken into account for the purposes of defining social housing standards as well as criteria for payment of social benefits to people having children.

Generally speaking, the same principle is provided for in the Federal law "On state social support". However, it makes sense to gradually spread this principle to other types of social payments (pensions, unemployment benefits), on the other hand, it should be implemented on the basis of a more detailed analysis of social and economic context. For example, the objective of reforms of housing and utilities sector can only be achieved if federal standards are changed taking into account dynamics of people's cash revenues. Additionally, specific accounting of the context implies territorial differentiation of shape and timing of the reforms. For example, only through targeted differentiation the actual discrimination of residents of some regions in terms of the cost of housing services and utilities can be eliminated. Thus, the ratio of the maximum cost of housing services and utilities and revenues in Moscow is 3.7 times lower than Russia's average, in Aginsky Buryatsky Autonomous District – 4.4 times higher than the average.

Average values do not reveal stratification by the level of revenues in all regions without exceptions including the ones with the highest revenues. In Moscow subsidies are offered to residents who cannot pay for social living space standards in the amount adequate to federal standards of maximum cost of housing services and utilities and permissible share of expenses for these purposes. At the same time, in regions similar to Aginsky Buryatsky Autonomous District absolute number of residents are unable to pay for the social standards of housing space under the model currently selected.

On the whole, regional character of social policy should be one of the key features of a strategy for the next decade. It should be borne in mind that given broad differentiation of territorial communities' living standards direct uniform rationing of certain parameters at the federal level is not an unquestionable achievement. People who are in most need of social support (vs. opportunities and incentives) are mostly part of local communities. Strictly speaking the issue is not to ensure that all the unemployed, disabled or pensioners have the same living standards, but rather make sure that living standards of each of them is comparable those of working neighbors.

Discussion of specific ways to implement this principle is only possible in the context of reforming inter-budgetary relations. There is no simple way to reform them, i.e. because at the moment asymmetric and unregulated inter-budgetary relations are disguising the general imbalance of the state's social liabilities and extended budget potential. The state's inability to fulfill its functions is incompatible with clear and transparent distribution of resources and liabilities between its elements. The situation when each element can re-direct public's claims to other elements makes it possible to avoid responsibilities in the short and sometime medium term.

A kind of a "social non-payment" mechanism currently implicitly present in the Russian version of budgetary federalism ensures spontaneous adaptation of social policy institutions to macro-economic restrictions. In this respect analogy to usual non-payments is suitable; they ensured "mating" of mutually unmatched micro- and macro-processes. In both cases incentives for economic activity are severely damaged, and in case of "social non-payments" federal unity is disrupted in the long run. The actual amounts of funding of many social policy areas significantly vary across the country. The situation in healthcare, e.g. is typical.

Per capita public healthcare expenditure in Moscow was 2.3 times higher than Russia's average, while in Daghestan it was three times below the average. Inter alia, there are large differences between neighboring regions (e.g. Lipetsk region's per capita healthcare spending was 1.4 times more than Voronezh region's). Revenues from mandatory medical insurance were even more varied. Sub-regional differences are often a lot higher than regional ones.

Active efforts to mitigate the historical differences including those which would comply with the requirements of the current laws, would result in a material intensification of inter-regional re-distribution. In the situation when economic growth trend is not yet stable and tends to be sporadic, intensification of re-distribution is hardly allowable. Therefore, at the moment there is practically no alternative to openly recognizing of the existing inequality and such a reform of social laws and inter-budget relations which would properly take into account that it will be impossible to eliminate this inequality in the near future.

It appears that the objective of the reform for the near future is to focus efforts on resolving three types of specific problem and leave aside the abstract issue of reducing territorial inequality. Firstly, it is necessary to prevent uncontrolled intensification of social differentiation during uneven economic growth. Secondly, it is necessary to encourage activities of regional and municipal governments aimed at independent settlement of social problems. Thirdly, the inter-budget flows should, to a greater extent, be aimed at funding programmes, staged, not automatically renewed and targeted at either eliminating specific social and political risks or at supporting specific positive trends of social development.

While determining forms and methods of spcial policy it is not permissible, as emphasised above, to ignore specific status of the civil society. This status greatly restricts the range of practicable options. At the same time, supporting development of a civil society as such is an integral element of social policy. In the long term this element is the most promising one, however, relevant changes are likely to take a long time.

Due to Russia's historical peculiarities civil society's control over the State has never been effective. Civil society was growing stronger at the turn of the 19th century but the process was interrupted by force. In the following decades citizens' attempts at autonomous self-organisation were suppressed and persecuted. The pressure was only removed just over a decade ago. Moreover, legal prerequisites for the development of public associations and other non-governmental non-commercial organisations, charities etc. were created. However, these changes can be characterised as necessary but insufficient for the formations of a mature civil society.

Various groups of Russian people were prepared to self-organisation to varying degrees. This readiness was most strongly demonstrated by the business community and representatives of the middle class in larger cities. The majority of viable non-governmental non-commercial organisation are concentrated in these cities. At the same time, the business community tends to be targeted at solving its own most urgent problems, rather than at contributing to resolving more broad issues related to the society at large. Russian middle class is relatively small.

Many of the most reputable non-commercial organisations are relying on foreign sources of funding. For a considerable share of people public organisations are still associated with either pseudo-independent Soviet style structures or with organisations which are explicitly or implicitly aimed at political struggle. To put it differently, public structures are too often assumed to be involved in the State's activities. The desire to participate in re-distribution of its resources often prevails over the intention to independently look for and use other means to reach social objectives. Self-organisation and mutual assistance as such are common in forms characteristic of traditional family and friendly relations. Another urgent problem is related to many cases financial abuse by non-state non-commercial organisations. Many of them have actually commercialized their activities, some are criminal. Forms of non-commercial organisations are sometimes used by profitable businesses to avoid taxation.

Therefore, there is a trend to reduce tax benefits for the non-commercial sector. In its turn, this trend does not encourage development of non-commercial organisations, including respectable ones. Thus, it was not enough to just eliminate barriers to effective self-organisation of people. As a result, in foreseeable future the State will have to assume the social functions? Which in a more mature society could be fulfilled with less involvement of public bodies. This makes targeted efforts to support autonomous self-organisation of people even more urgent.

It includes, *e.g.* using non-public non-commercial structures (including state-funded) for servicing old and disabled people, providing subsidies and reduced-rate loans to various consumer co-operatives etc., tax benefits for companies and individuals for voluntary medical and social insurance as well as charity. However, all of this is justified only in conjunction with reviewing legislation on non-public non-commercial organisations. The requirements to them should be much more specific, thus allowing to be more accurate in discriminating between profit-making businesses and non-commercial activities.

Priority social policy measures should be aimed at

- Improving federal and regional laws on the basis of an analysis of its compliance to both resources of relevant elements of the budget system and priorities defined by people during sociological surveys;
- Removing provisions restricting employment in legal sectors from labour laws while retaining work safety requirements;
- Switching to funding of social and cultural organisations predominantly through purchasing services offered to the population;
- Making stages of the social reforms more specific taking into account territorial peculiarities of income formation and utilisation;
- Enhancing incentives, through tax and other benefits, for charity, voluntary medical and social insurance and other forms of self-organisation for the purposes of solving social issues.

Ethnicity in Modern Sociocultural Network : A Case of Rajshahi City in Bangladesh

—Md. Mustafa Kamal Akand

Abstract

The present paper discusses the livelihood strategy of a few groups of ethnic minorities such as Santals, Paharia, Oraon and Mahili in course of urbanization process and at the situation of socio-economic crises and insecurities derived mainly from their entitlement, identity and ethnicity. Ethnic divisions are traditionally maintained by the efforts of their members as part of a social interaction and for a long period of time ethnicity persists among them as a product of inherent process, which favors ethnic solidarity. But identity never remains as a static icon to the minorities after taking harbor in urban areas; rather there emerge a bargaining or negotiating identity in order to adapt to the urban complexity. Therefore, individuals sometimes identify themselves ethnically; or at sometimes they are obliged to identify themselves in terms of religion, nationality, class, occupation and other forms. Among the other magnitude of rolling identity, conversion to Christianity is regarded to be more favorable to the ethnic migrants as to face the crises of economic and social unpleasantness during their urban existence. This paper examines the nature, potentialities and specialty of ethnic identity under the influence of Christianity and rapid urbanization process and their encompassing socio-economic complexity in Bangladesh.

Background of the Study

Bangladesh is commonly portrayed as the native soil of the Bengalee nation having only one language, a unilateral cultural tradition and a common historical heritage. Yet a significant number of small ethnic and indigenous communities have been living here from the time immemorial. These ethnic communities have their own languages and very distinct crystal-cultural traditions of their own and similarly from their very existence in the Bangladesh territory, these ethnic groups recognize them as different from the Bengalis though most of them now speak in Bangla and it is used as a second language of these communities. Although they use Bangla as their second language but in various consideration ethnic groups are different from the mainstream Bengali people with their differential ethnicity, social structures, cultural institutions and traditionality. These ethnic peoples are concerned to restore their own ethnic boundaries, ethnicity, cultural heritage and identity based common world-view. At the same time Bengalis are also serene to maintain this notion of 'otherness' (Schendel: 1998, Karim: 2000). At present, more or less, 1.2 million ethnic people have been living in this country as minor groups (GPRB: 1991).

From the historical viewpoint, most of the ethnic communities in present Bangladesh are not the original inhabitants of Bengal and the majority of them have migrated from different parts of this subcontinent and from its adjoining hilly regions of Arakan. They are known to be descended from different linguistic groups in different stages of the early historical period. Some descended from the Munda, coming from the east, perhaps during one to four millennia B.C., and the Dravidian from the west, just prior to the time of the Indus Civilization.

Majority of them came from Indo-Aryans, who had migrated into the country from the west beginning about 1700 or 1500 B.C., and mixed with indigenous groups of various 'racial' stocks like *Kols, Sabara, Pulinda, Handi, Patni, Dom* and *Chandals*. These ancient local people were of two categories, such as Hindu and non-Hindu (*Mlecchas*) (Maloney: 1984, Sultana: 2002). Another dominant group, the Tibeto-Burmese came from the east over the past one and a half thousand years and settled mainly in the Chittagong hill tracts.

The Barind region is predominantly inhabited by the ethnic minorities like Santals, Oraon, Paharia, Mundas, Mahili, Ho, Rajbanshis and Kots or Kochas (Ali: 1998). A few numbers of other ethnic sub-groups or substrata such as Kol, Pahan, Malos, Mahatos, Bhuiya, Ganjhu, Kukamar, Kurmi, Paliya, Gorrats and Tures are to be found in different parts of Barind area. A small number of scheduled sub-castes having the Bengal aboriginal origin and Indo-Aryan or 'Sadri' speaking groups like *Sabara, Namashudra, Jaliya Kaibarta, Bhuimali* and *Bede* also live in Barind tracts (Maloney: 1984, Karim: 2000, Chowdhury, A: 1998, Ali: 1998).

In regard to the socio-cultural manifestation, the Santals, Paharia, Oraon, Mahili and Mundas are the integrated part of rural and peripheral localities and all of these groups are essentially agriculturalists in profession. Some of them are traditionally engaged in making bamboo crafts (Mahili), artisan, tradesmen (Rajbanshi) and service (Kots or Kochas) groups too. From the very beginning of their migration to Bangladesh territory, they started to rely heavily on advanced horticulture and finally became peasantized.

They principally maintained their livelihood by exploiting natural environment with the help of traditional technology, manual labor, simple and reciprocal economic pattern as well as simple social and political structure. Every ethnic group has a particular mythical explanation of their origin, traditional religious beliefs on supernatural powers and relevant ritual practices. Before their conversion to Christianity, religious beliefs of these groups were animistic and nature-worshipping but at the same time they acknowledge *Thakur* as their creator and religious practices are more inclined to Hinduism (Maloney: 1984).

It is evident that at the epoch of present day population movement and rapid urbanization in our country, towns and cities are attracting a great number of rural people to migrate to the urban areas. Dissatisfaction with the prevalent rural livelihood also acts as major push factor to take the decision to move. Existing surveys and study results show that all types of migration from rural to urban have increased significantly and the growth of urbanization in our country has been increased due to rural-urban migration. In fact, rural-urban migration is the major contributor along with other indexes in the ongoing urbanization process of Bangladesh.

Therefore, towns and cities are becoming the ultimate choice of habitation and people are literarily rushing to the big cities and towns of the country. Similarly, the city of Rajshahi has emerged as a key place of destination for rural migrants coming from different adjacent districts of northern Bangladesh. Keeping pace with the majority Bengali population, the rural ethnic groups also responding to the urbanization process in the contemporary demographic movement and several ethnic migrants such as Santals, Paharia, Oraon, Mahili and Rajbanshi, those who were sometimes the inhabitants of the rural areas of Rajshahi, Dinajpur, Rangpur, Pabna, Bogra and other agrarian districts of northern Bangladesh, are coming consistently to the city of Rajshahi in search of better life. As these migrants are belonging to a distinct cultural tradition, they dreadfully referred their city residences as foreign land and look upon their native villages as their true homes. A modern city life is a strange cultural organism to them and in many considerations; complex urban cultural setting is not conducive to their traditionality and simplicity. Ethnic identity, ethnicity, different life-styles and mannerisms frequently brand them as strangers to the city. Therefore, identity and traditionality fall in the state of jeopardy in the process of modernity and complexity of pluralistic urban society.

The present paper deals with the identity problems of ethnic communities those who are residing in the city area of Rajshahi municipality in northern Bangladesh. It focuses principally on the crisis of identity and potentialities of ethnicity among some groups of marginalized ethnic minorities under the influence of modernity, contemporary trend of Christianization process and the impact of complex urban socio-culture.

Methodology

The present paper is an outcome of the data collected from five cluster settlements of the ethnic migrants located in Dingadoba area under Rajpara Metropolitan Thana of Rajshahi city in northern Bangladesh. Dingadoba is popularly known for the ethnic congregation and majority of the ethnic migrants in the city are concentrated in that area. A total number of 878 migrated ethnic populations with different ethnic background have been coherently residing in 183 household units. Participant observation was the principal method of data collection and ethnographic interview was conducted covering fifty household heads of different ethnic groups. A good number of FGDs have been organized to unfold the study problems and key informants technique was also employed to gather information as well as to cross check the collected materials.

Ethnicity and Economic Relation

The ethnic communities of Rajshahi city, in general, are historically positioned at the bottom of the economic strata of the country and marginalization, pauperization and poverty are the residual characteristic feature of these ethnic communities. Prior to the reasons of ethnic migration to the city, among others, economic reason therefore appears to be the imperative one and majority of them have migrated to the city in search of employment (Karim: 2000, Akand: 2004). From the anthropological point of view, the relationship between ethnicity and the access to economic resources is the basic criteria of analyzing the potentialities of any cultural manifestations.

During the situation of drastic economic crises and its fluctuation, the forms of ethnicity multiply and the social distance/exclusion between groups generally increases. Therefore, ethnicity cannot serves as an integrating function and new power relations, solidarity and binding values are gradually established (Chazan: 1986). Ethnic communities in the study area face the similar problem and it is evident that the question of identity becomes most important in negotiating the economic crises and unemployment difficulties of the urban economy.

The persistent discrimination and ethnic disqualification from the dominant population always force the ethnic minorities to rotate their traditional lifestyle as ethnic culture is usually not regarded to be an asset rather a barrier of attaining dignified job in urban economy. For instance, no ethnic labor, male or female, boys and girls, is allowed to work in hotels, restaurants and food supplying shops or even in a tea stall of the city because of the stereotype that the Santals, Paharia, Oraon, Mahili are 'dirty' and 'polluted' community as the ethnic migrants have come of a scheduled sub-caste background whom should not be allowed to work in food-making or supplying factories, restaurants, shops or other permanent jobs though the ethnic migrants have already left their identity of schedule sub-castes and took the Christianity. But they are still dismantled by the notion of untouchability. Ethnicity itself plays as a barrier to self-employment and small business also. The majority people show reluctant to hire a labor or a rickshaw/van pulled by the ethnic labor judging their alcoholic habit.

On the other hand, ethnicity brings some advantage! to gain access to some certain 'disguise' service sector of urban economy like sweeper, cleaner, spraymen, nursemaids, gardeners and the like. The poor migrants male and female perform these tasks in different offices, educational institutes, hospitals and clinics in the city.

Conversion to Christianity also made them excluded from various manual labor domains mostly available in the households, farms or factories owned by the majority Muslim entrepreneurs. For example, the ethnic women are not allowed to work as maidservant in the Muslim households though the city dwellers are deficient of finding adequate maidservants for their household operations.

Their labor is totally disregarded in the urban economy and ethnic women labor is remained unused. Similarly, only a limited Christianized ethnic persons have been employed as servicemen like office-clerk, peon, watchmen, *mali* (gardener), nursemaid and the like in the missionary offices, hospitals and clinics, educational institutes and other organizations particularly operated by the Christian collaborative NGOs but the majority of ethnic poor remain unemployed and fall in a tremendous economic crisis. Therefore, ethnicity and traditional identity becomes mostly in a 'state of hiding' in order to cope with the persistent economic crises and poverty.

Identity and Marriage Rules

The ethnic communities in the surrounding countryside were sometimes the part of traditional peasant society and their social organizations paradoxically functioned as per their livelihood strategy. Traditionally in the near past, the ethnic groups practiced a typical agrarian family organization principally extended in nature and as a basic social unit; the family usually consisted of husband, wife, married and unmarried children and their offspring. Joint families with grown-up married sons were also practiced more or less in larger quantity. Household, therefore were enlarged in nature and economic activities were performed at utmost totality. Gradually, traditional extended family unit lost its dominance due to change in several socio-economic relations like land tenure system, modernization and influence urbanization and extended paws of market economy (Ali: 1998, Gomes: 1988, Vidyarthi: 1976, Troisi: 2000).

Regarding the rules of marriage, the Santals, Oraon, Mahili and Munda are well known for their traditional ethnic endogamy and clan exogamy. Each of the these ethnic group is sub-divided into some patronymic clans and according to their marriage rules, it is strictly forbidden for any person to marry within his or her own clan. In their rural setting, they retain their long-practiced marriage rules of taking no brides or grooms ignoring clan or ethnic rules. Cousin marriage (cross and parallel) is still prohibited.

After taking harbor in urban areas, marriage rules among all the minorities have been drastically changed and the retention of clan or ethnic rules has been totally disappearing. Inter-ethnic marriage or marriage between Bengalee and ethnic adults are allowed. There are several cases of marrying outsiders in the study area and the rules of clan or ethnic boundaries have nothing to say about the union between two persons. For instance, Anthony Bishwas, a Paharia ethnic male has married to a non-ethnic Bengalee Christian woman, Shushila Gomes, Gabriel Hansda, a Santals male married to a Mahili woman, Catherina Hebrom and Samuel Toppo, an Oraon man married to a Paharia woman name Dipalee Bishwas and many such cases are to be found among the migrants. Marriage between different ethnic male and female is possible in the urban areas and only Christianity is considered as the solo criteria of marriage whoever he or she bears an identity of ethnic or Bengalee origin.

Marriage rules have been significantly Christianized through the imposition of new meaning of the union. Modern Christian laws and customs has invigorated marriage rules.

Some preconditions have incorporated in the marriage arena such as compulsory marriage training for the adolescents, definite age attainment, registration of marriage with the Church and prohibition of divorce or co-wives etc. The elaborated participation of Christian churches and missionaries in matrimonial affairs has made the marriage union more ascertain and stable.

Christianity, the Umbrella Identity

Under the influence of modernity and complex urban cultural plurality, the traditional individual ethnic identity of the Santals, Paharia, Oraon and Mahili are gradually becoming obsolete and latent. From the study field, it has been obvious that two major causes are functioning behind this process of rotating identity.

Firstly, ethnic peoples are not well organized on the basis of common ideological and historical unity referring to ancient language, religion or political process among themselves that usually appears as a strong force of maintaining ethnic identity. Rather each group is segregated and habituated to a distinct way of life, language and world-view. Moreover, interpretation of their history and ideologies is also ambiguous and gloomy due to lack of modern education among them. Ethnic people also have no organized exertion to invigorate their traditional ethnicity though social identity becomes more important in the moment when it seems threatened.

Secondly, contemporary Christianization process under the rubric of modernity and rationality is mightily influencing the ethnic minorities by which a large number of ethnic people are changing their ethnic identity and the economic viability of change is so crucial to them (Roosens: 1989). Material support in the forms of cash incentives, education, health services, shelter and various development programs from the Christian missionaries and their ally organizations directly stimulate to change their traditional identity. Ethnic people have the single option to survive and enthusiastically consider the identity of Christianity as more secured and viable one to fight the economic crises.

Conclusion

The traditional ethnic minorities of the Rajshahi city are encountering a strong stimulation to alter their traditional livelihood and ethnicity in order to cope with the complexity of urban culture, its encompassing economic difficulties and modernity. Because of the marginalized socio-economic position, the ethnic minorities face the problem of adaptation to the unfamiliar urban life from their very first day of urbanity and consequently they are forced to replace their age long ethnic identity. Ethnicity and traditional socio-cultural manifestations of the ethnic minorities limit the scope of access to the economic resources and traditional ethnic identity makes them almost secluded from the mainstream urban socio-cultural network. Therefore, a clear transformation in ethnic identity is obvious among them and Christianity has become the unaccompanied choice of identity to negotiate the ongoing pace of modernity.

NOTES

1. Ethnic group is largely biologically self-perpetuating, shares fundamental cultural values, realized in overt unity in cultural forms and has a membership which identifies itself and identified by others. Ethnic or tribe is a cultural system in itself and usually tends to confined geographical territory. While ethnic sub-group or sub-strata is regarded to be a part culture and have not any confined geographical territory. They naturally stemmed from a certain ethnic group with nearly unchanged values and ideas and spread over a territory with varying ecologic circumstances and the later groups never be considered as same by their former group, though these sub-groups are occupying basic ethnic cultural traits for a long period of time (Narroll: 1964, Barth: 1969). In Indian civilization, these groups are known as polluted sub-castes (Maloney: 1984, McNee: 1976).

REFERENCES

1. Akand, M.K., 2004. "Folk Culture and Adaptation to the City: A Case Study of the Paharia in Rajshahi" *Asian Folklore Studies',* Institute of Anthropology, Nanzan University, Japan, Vol. 64, No. 1, July, 2005.
2. Ali, A, 1998. *Santals of Bangladesh*. Dhaka : Institute of Social Research and Applied Anthropology.
3. Barth, F., 1969. *Ethnic Groups and Boundaries: The Social Organization of Cultural Difference*, London: Allen and Unwin.
4. Chazan, N., 1986. "Ethnicity in Economic Crisis: Development Strategies and Patterns of Ethnicity in Africa." In D.L. Thompson, (ed) *Ethnicity, Politics and Development,* Colorado: Lynne Rienner, 137-158.
5. Chowdhury, A. (ed), 1998. "The Ethnic Communities of Barind Tract." University of Dhaka Department of Anthropology, Unpublished.
6. Dalton, E.T., 1872. *Descriptive Ethnology of Bengal*. Calcutta: Office of the Superintendent of Government Printing, West Bengal.
7. Das, A.K. *et al,* 1966. *Hand Book on Scheduled Castes and Scheduled Tribes*. Calcutta: Government of West Bengal.
8. Datta M.N., 1955. *The Santal: A Study in Culture Change*. Calcutta: Manager of Publications, Government of India Press.
9. Eriksen, T.H., 1993. *Ethnicity and Nationalism: Anthropological Perspectives*, London: Pluto Press.
10. Gomes, S.G., 1988. *The Paharias: A Glimpse of the Tribal Life in Northern Bangladesh*. Dhaka: Caritas, Bangladesh.
11. GPRB, 2001. Population Census National Report (Provisional).
12. Hunter, W.W., 1876. Statistical Account of Bengal: Vol. VIII and IX, London: Trubner & Co.
13. Karim, A.H.M.Z., 2000. 'The Occupational Diversities of the Santals and their Socio-economic Adaptability in a Periurban Environmental Situation of Rajshahi in Bangladesh: An Anthropological Exploration,' Paper presented at the Annual Conference of the Indian Anthropological Society, Shantiniketan, India.
14. Maloney, T. C., 1984. "Tribes of Bangladesh and Synthesis of Bengali Culture." In M.S Qureshi (ed), *Tribal Cultures in Bangladesh*, University of Rajshahi: Institute of Bangladesh Studies.
15. O' Malley, L. S. S., 1910. Bengal District Gazetteer, Vol. 22 *Santal Parganas*, Calcutta: Bengal Secretariat Book Depot.

16. Roosens, E.E., 1989. *Creating Identity*, London: Sage Schendel, W.V. and Ball, E. (eds), 1998, *Banglar Bahujati: Bangali Chara Onnannyo Jatir Prosanga*, Delhi: International Center for Bengal Studies (ICBS).
17. Sultana, A., 2002. 'Santal Sangskritite Khristo-dharmer Provab: Rajshahi Zellar Panchti Gramer Upor Acti Nritattik Gobeshana', Institute of Bangladesh Studies (IBS), University of Rajshahi, Unpublished Ph.D. Dissertation.
18. Thompson, D.L. (ed) 1986. *Ethnicity, Politics and Development,* Colorado: Lynne Rienner Publishers.
19. Triosi, J., 2000. *Tribal Religion: Religious Beliefs and Practices among Santals*, New Delhi : Monohar Book Service.
20. Vidyarthi, L.P., 1976. *Tribal Culture of India,* New Delhi: Concept Publishing Co.

Clinical Nutritional Status of Indian Girls in Deprived and Disadvantaged Communities: A Special Reference to Select Macro-and Micro-Nutrients

—A.B. Srilatha, A.B. Subhashini and G. Nagamani

Abstract

Rural India has 49 per cent of girls in the age group of 10 to 19 years. Gender discrimination, poverty, poor food intakes, traditional customs and illiteracy affects the normal growth and development, nutritional status and health of the girls. It results in adverse consequences in girl's life during motherhood and future of her child. To assess clinical nutritional and micronutrient status profiles, a sample of 362 girls from six rural communities (n=120) including scheduled castes (harizan n=90) and tribes (n=152) were examined. Heights, weights, food intakes and serum micronutrient status was assessed using standard anthropometric, diet survey and biochemical methods.

Findings indicate that all the girls studied are far below the ICMR and NCHS standards for heights and weights. Rural girls are better than tribal and harizan girls. Harizan girls are worst affected. Food intakes of the girls in all the three communities are far below the ICMR Recommendations. The Schedule Caste and Tribal girls showed significantly deficit intakes for calories, protein, iron and calcium than their rural counterparts. Serum micronutrient profile reveals a very low values in comparison to expected normal values for serum iron, zinc, calcium and vitamin A. Significantly low values are recorded for serum protein and albumin. The findings suggest that there is an urgent need for nutrition intervention and education programmes for rural and other socially deprived adolescent girls to support the growth and safeguard the mother-child lifecycle.

Introduction

India is a land of different castes and religions. In rural areas, most of the girls are illiterates and 4 per cent of girls between 15 to 19 years were already married. Girls between the age range of 10-19 years contribute to 11 per cent of our total population. The adverse situation of children specially the girls in the SAARC region is largely caused by ignorance, poverty, prejudices, gender bias, cultural practices and poverty manifesting themselves in low birth weight, malnutrition, ill health, growth retardation, slow learning, low productivity, low earning capacity and unemployment. Therefore the consequences are faced by infants and the children.

This picture is very grim and pathetic in deprived and disadvantaged rural, scheduled caste (harizan) and Tribal (girizan communities. The girl infant born in these poor communities is weak, stunted and illiterate. Thus, the majority of girls in poor deprived and under-privileged sections of societies suffer from anaemia, chronic energy deficiency, protein energy malnutrition, vitamin A and calcium deficiency with poor statures. Despite the nation wide focus on socially deprived communities, the studies on these deprived female populations are much limited and sparse. In view of the facts stated above, the present community-based study was conducted to assess physical and clinical nutritional status of Indian girls from different socially deprived communities and also to draw comparative status profiles of girls on physical growth, nutrient intakes, clinical and serum macro-and micro-nutrient parameters.

Methods

The study was conducted in the Chittoor district of Andhra Pradesh during the period of November 2005 to October 2006. From the study area following random sampling technique, the sample of 362 girls, 10 to 18 year are drawn from rural areas, scheduled caste and tribal communities covering 4 different mandal areas of chittoor district. The tribal communities covered are Sugalis, Chenchu, Malla and Enadies. The girls are distributed into three different age groups viz., 10 to 12 years, 13 to 15 years and 16 to 18 years, respectively. A group of 120 rural girls, 40 each, covering 3 age groups, 90 scheduled caste girls, 30 each in three age groups, 152 tribal girls i.e 51, 51 and 50, respectively in three different age groups are studied. All the subjects were from low socio-economic group.

Physical Anthropometry

To assess nutritional status, anthropometric data on weights and heights, standard equipment like detector scales (INC, New York, USA), Calibrated UNICEF, platform beam balance was used to record weights to the nearest of 0.1 kg. Standing height was measured to the nearest of 0.5 cm using anthropometric rod and the data was compared with heights and weights of Indian Council of Medical Research and National Centre for Health Statistics for assessing the nutritional status of girls.

Nutrient Intake

Data on the nutrient intake of each girl was collected for three alternate days in a week by 24 hours Recall method and one day weighment method. The raw amount of food consumed by the girl was estimated and subsequently, the nutrient intake was calculated. The intakes of energy, protein, calcium, iron and vitamin A iron of each girl was calculated based on the nutritive value of Indian foods of Indian Council of Medical Research, National Institute of Nutrition (NIN), Hyderabad. And compared with recommended dietary allowances (RDA) suggested by the ICMR for different age groups were used to assess the adequacy of nutrient intakes by the study subjects.

Clinical Survey

The prevalence of different nutritional deficiencies were assessed by using a clinical survey schedule designed as per the classified list of signs for various nutritional deficiencies given by Jelliffe (1966).

Biochemical Estimations

Biochemical analysis was carried out by collecting blood from the subjects and serum was used for analysis of macro (haemoglobin, protein and albumin), and micro nutrients (calcium, iron, zinc and vitamin A). Cyan methaemoglobin method (Dacie and Lewis, 1975) was employed for estimation of haemoglobin in the blood. Serum proteins and albumin were estimated by Biuret method (Raghuramulu et al., 1983). Immediate analysis is carried out for vitamin A estimation by using antimony trichloride method based on carrprice reaction. Serum zinc was assessed using standard procedure in Atomic Absorption Spectrophotometre. Dipyridyl method (Ramsay, 1954, 1958) was followed to estimate serum iron content of the blood. Calcium was estimated by Colourimetric method.

Results and Discussion

The present study was undertaken in three deprived and disadvantaged communities of Chittoor district. The period 14-18 years of active growth for girls. The data in Table 16.1 reemphasizes the anthropometric features of girls studied from three different communities on heights and weights and compared with ICMR and NCHS standards. *t' values were calculated for the differences on heights and weights between the three age groups of girls coming from three different communities. All the girls from three communities are far below the ICMR as well as NCHS standards. Rural girls are better than scheduled castes and tribal girls. The scheduled caste girls are found to be inferior and weigh significantly less than that of rural and Tribal girls. The differences between the heights and weights of the girls from three communities are significant ($P<0.01$) at 1 per cent level.

Table 16.1. Mean Heights and Weights of Rural Indian Girls—A Comparison between Three Deprived Communities

Age	ICMR Standard	NCHS Standard	Height (cms)			ICMR Standard	NCHS Standard	Weight (cms)		
			Rural (n=120)	Rural Harizan (n=90)	Girizan (n = 152)			Rural (n=120)	Rural Harizan (n=90)	Girizan (n=152)
10-12Y	144.96	147.80*	136.45**	122.62**	130.73**	37.91	39.07	32.21**	19.81**	30.42*
13 - 15 Y	154.82	160.70	142.29**	135.76**	139.92*	46.70	51.59	40.25**	31.72**	39.13**
16-18Y	155.90	163.25	150.00**	140.52S*	150.60 **	49.90	56.55	43.43**	39.41**	42.20**

Note: Significant at *5% Level **1% Level NS—Non-Significant

Table 16.2 presents the data on clinical nutritional status of girls the clinical survey revealed that most of the girls showed clinical signs and symptoms manifested by nutritional deficiencies such as calcium deficiency, vitamin A, zinc deficiency and iron deficiency anaemia. It is obvious that out of 362 girls, 30 girls were normal *i.e.,* they did not show any signs of nutritional deficiencies. The least affected group showing these symptoms is 10-12 years of age group. About 20 per cent of the subjects are showing signs and symptoms of vitamin–A deficiency among rural harizan girls and 2.5 per cent among rural and girizan girl subjects.

Table 16.2. Presents the Data on Clinical Status of Girls from 3 Deprived Communities for Micro Nutrient Deficiencies

Micronutrient deficiencies	Rural (n-120)		Rural Harizan (n-90)		Tribal (n-152)	
	No.	%	No.	%	No.	%
Calcium	2	1.7	12	7.5	14	21.28
Iron	85	70.7	90	100	50	52.5
Vitamin A	18	15	36	40	50	32.7
Zinc	36	30	50	55.6	40	23.1

Table 16.3 refers the mean dietary nutrient intakes of girls from three different communities. From the data, it was explicit that food intakes of girls in all the three communities are significantly below the ICMR recommendations. The Scheduled Caste harizan and girizan girls had deficit intakes for calories, protein, iron, calcium and vitamin A than their rural counterparts.

Table 16.3. Mean Nutrient Intakes of Rural Indian Girls—A Comparison between Three Deprived Communities

Nutrients	RDA	10-12 y			RDA	13-15Y			RDA	16 - 18 Y		
		R	RH	G		R	RH	G		R	RH	G
1. Energy (K.cal)	1970	1445.2	1419.98**	1065.73**	2060	1620	15K1.9**	1551.87**	2060	1950.85	1460.5**	1917.13**
2. Protein (gin)	57	31.25	28.2**	20.0**	65	42.78	30.3**	25.60*	63	40.53	30.6**	35.43*
3. Iron (mg)	19	16.5	12.21**	10.59**	28	23.5	15.34**	14.34**	30	24.5	20.10**	15.50*
4. Calcium (g)	600	320	250**	310**	600	390	340**	320**	600	430	314**	330**
5. Vitamin -A	600	411	311**	306**	600	497	448*	458*	600	448	406*	405*

Note: Significant at *–5% level, **–1% level, NS–Non-significant

It is observed that irrespective of the ethnicity of the family environment, both rural-harizan and girizan girls are not consuming required amounts of nutrients. The per cent deficits are significantly more for protein, energy, iron, calcium and vitamin A. Among the three ethnic groups rural harizan girls are consuming very deficit intakes for all nutrients than rural and tribal girls.

Table 16.4. Mean Serum Profiles of Rural Girls for Select Macro- and Micro-Nutrient Levels— A Comparison between Three Deprived Communities

Nutrients	Normal Values	10-12 Y			1.3- 15 Y			16-18 Y		
		R	RH	G	R	RH	G	R	RH	G
1. Haemoglobin	12 g/dl	8.58	8.23**	8.90	8.9	8.6*	9.0	8.94	8.94	9.1
2. Protein	7.2 g/dl	5.46	4.95^{NS}	4.75	5.81	4.28^{NS}	5.93	5.25	5.25	5.65
3. Albumin	4.75 g/dl	3.47	2.37*	2.475	2.90	2.52	3.89	3.50	3.70	3.94
4. Vitamin-A	1 15 μg/ml	40	34**	42	49	40**	42	39	39**	49*
5. Iron	112 μg /100ml	37.05	33.05^{NS}	33.05	35.30	30.01^{NS}	42.2	39.01	39.01	40.9
6. Zinc	50-12 μg /ml	75.2	69.05*	63.5	77.4	70.2*	75.2	69.8	69.8	69.2
7. Calcium	9 mg/100 ml	3.38	2.45^{NS}	3.28	3.09	2.85^{NS}	3.01	2.97	2.97	2.98

Note: Significant at *5% level **1% level NS—Non-Significant

REFERENCES

1. Anand, K. Kant, S., S.K. Kapoor, (1999), Nutritional Status of Adolescent School Children in *Rural Worth Indian Pediatrics*, Volume 36, august, 810-815.
2. Anita Saxena and Stanely J. Ulljasyek (2003), Seasonal food intake and nutrient distribution patterns among rural Rajput Children, Rajasthan, India, *The Ind. JL. Nutrition Dietic*, 40, 333.
3. Anonymous (1989), Growth of Affluent Indian girls during Adolescence. Nutrition Foundation of India, New Delhi, Scientific Report, 10: 24-40.
4. Ballabriga, A., (2000), Morphological and Physiological changes during growth an update, *European Journal of Clinical Nutrition*, 54, Supp., 51-56.
5. Basta, S. Karyadi D., Scrimbhan N.S. (1979), Iron deficiency anemia and the productivity of adult males in Indonesia, *Am. J. Chin. Nutrition*, 32. 916-925.
6. Benefice, E., Garmia, D. and G. Nadiya, (2004) Nutritional Status, growth and sleep habits among Senegalese adolescent girls, *European Journal of Clinical Nutrition*, 58, 292-301.
7. Bentley, M.E. and P.L. Griffiths (2003), The Burden of Anemia among Women in India. European *Journal of Clinical Nutrition*, 57, 52-60.
8. Gopalan, C. and Suminder Kaur, (1989) "*Women and Nutrition in India*" (ed. by C. Gopalan. NFI, Special Publication Series No. 5, 108-148.
9. Jelliffe, D.B. (1966), The assessment of nutritional status of the community. World health organisation, WHO Monograph Series No. 583.
10. "National Nutrition Monitoring Bureau, *Report of Survey* (1972-97), National Institute of Nutrition, ICMR, Hyderabad.

Ideological Dilution: Moving Sights on Anthropology of Childhood?

—Nanjunda D.C.

Abstract

Contemporary society clings to the notion that ideal Childhood is both necessary and attainable. There is an emerging scholarship on children and childhood, which attempts to ground explanations and interpretations in the contexts, communities and culture in which children are actually living. This body of work is descriptive rather than prescriptive where definition of childhood are normative; they grow out of the experiences in particular cultures or communities, for particular groups of children, in particular sets of circumstances. Neither is this scholarship a claim for cultural relativism, nor an attempt to turn a blind eye to the horror which children experiences all over the world.

A Prospective

As an anthropologist working on the ways that other sociologists have written about children and childhood, it can say about the gaps that exist in the discourse between educationalist, and sociologists and the way in which sociologists have focus on certain aspects of children's lives delegating other facets to other disinclines. In doing so, certain features of children's lives have fallen through the disciplinary gaps and examined under-theorized. This paper gives a picture how sociologists have understood children in the past, concept of childhood in the changing society, and the roles of children have played in ethnographic monographs and in anthropological theory, including a brief examination of more recent field of child centered anthropological and insights this has brought to the study of children. This paper concludes that not only there is space, and the provision of this space is not merely a token gesture, but their is a necessary to be inclusive of young people if the emerging knowledge we have of childhood is to be legitimate.

Culture and society are the centrally focused concepts of sociology and social anthropology. The specific study of childhood in sociology has a much-shorted history. Sociologists have long pointed out the economic significance of children, their role in legitimating marriages and the implied economic contracts at marriage, which assign children to one lineage or another. Man being the central concepts on whom the anthropological studies involve among, the major issues related to the childhood also is an important subject matter of anthropological studies. Many researches have shown that of the childhood issue and intensity of the problem is depended upon various social and cultural factors.

The last three decades have seen the emergence of a new discipline of childhood studies, made up of contributions from sociology, sociology and cultural studies, challenging previous studies of children based on paradigms from psychology and education. This new discipline has revolutionized the study of children and demanded that they be looked as important subjects in their own right. The last decade has seen an upsurge of interest in childhood studies and a reexamination of the ways in which children and their lives have been understood and analyzed within the social sciences. Sociology, anthroplogy and cultural studies, all now have thriving sub-disciplines which focus primarily on children and which have challenged the dominant paradigms that development psychology and education have traditionally brought to the study of children. As an anthropologist working on the ways that anthropologists have written about children.

In doing so, certain features of children's lives have fallen through the disciplinary gaps and remained under-theorized. Nowhere is this more obvious than in the theoretical interplay between studies of women and studies of children which have, at times, appeared mutually antagonistic which children being seen either as a problematic aspect of women's gender roles, or by those interested in child-centered research, as a distinct category of people often unconnected to their careers.

Childhood issue has drawn increasing international attention and condemnation since the 1970s. During the same period many international NGOs and agencies have begun to speak out against the inhuman conditions under which children work in many developing countries. The issue of child labour and childhood issue has generated renewed interest because of the new economic policies formulated in line with the structural adjustment programmes developing countries have adopted hoping to help them integrate into the global market economy.

This interest among economists and social scientists began during a transition period in which the incidence of childhood had been declining for more decades. One reason may be because there is an ongoing worldwide debate on poverty reduction among the vulnerable sections of the society, where a large proportion of working children is found. In the same way it is revealed that problems of children are viewed as a major hurdle to the overall development of an economy. It is also known that dependence on childhood minimizes the human capital accumulation, which is a prerequisite for development.

Childhood concept varies in different societies and largely depends on cultural practice. Few studies have shown that a childhood concept is largely influenced by the contract between children and the parents. Mergret Mead (1971) has opined that, "with childhood and human rights, the paradox is social construction verses relativism". However, Susan Bissell (1982) Write the 'childhood issue is a much more subtle one'. This concept of childhood grows out of the experiences in a particular culture or communities, for particular groups of children, in particular sets of circumstances. Neither are these views claim for cultural relativism, nor an attempt to turn a blind eye to the horrors which children experiences all over the globe. She continues that "the problem is how to articulate a standard, or divergent standards for the beginning of a moral and ethical reflection on cultural practices that takes into account but does not privilege our own cultural presuppositions".

In the third world countries interpretation of the childhood concept is largely based on the economic contribution of the children to the family. It is generally proved that family farming makes the greatest use of childhood in the context of unpaid family assistants. Blechred (1995) has observed that "it is not so much the child who is exploited by the common social system as the whole family". The factors like cultural, social and economic situation of the family obviously has repercussion on the child.

Weiner (1999) in his study has revealed that how economy, socialization and the role of parents like cultural objectives causes childhood. According to him " the values by which the activities of children are judged and the nature of socialization process, the process of socialization and the cultural objectives to which it responds, are clearly inter-dependent with the structural economics system within which socialization occurs". The nature of child's socialization is associated with the class position of his parents in case of India. The effect of prevailing domestic organisations, the system of kinship and marriage are also important points as these clearly influence the development of child actives through their sets of rights and obligations.

"independent effect of socio-cultural variables is the attribution of sex roles among children in a family system. Cultural factors have independent effects with respect to both family structures and sex roles. So the parents' perceive role of children as associated with the values attached to the children by their parents, with the image of future which is perceived by the parents" (Weiner:1999).

Carl em Rosen (2001) in his study has observed that gradual evaluation of child labour is due to class consequences. While writing on the existence of child labour in country like India he observed that child labour becomes visible after attaining the civilization. Immediately after the civilization, workers started to acquire skills in their respective professions and gradually it led to the formation of caste system in India. This caste system is responsible for the creation of have's and have-nots among the people (rich and poor). Due to this, a new working force has emerged not only in India but also in the world in general, that is the child labour and finally it affected on the their childhood periods.

Analyzing the effects of the caste system in India in the context of childhood. The upper class took more advantages of education, urbanisation and industrialization. Among the lower caste groups, because of their economic dependency upon the upper caste groups, bad childhood period is more prevalent among the children belongs to the weaker sections of the society.

Carre Oliver (2001) adds "that the compartmentalization of groups of people on the basis of a caste hierarchy with a well-defined traditional occupational role for each of the caste group has resulted in social inequalities".

Naidu (2002) endeavored to focus light on various social and cultural factors influencing the existence of childhood paradigm in India. He observed that "Childhood largely depends upon normative attitudes towards children in society, the culturally determined roles and functions of children, the values by which the activities of children are judged and the nature of socialization process. In industrialized countries, there is general disapproval of participation of school age children in the formal labour force." The participation of children in housework is approved, by parents at least. In many countries, participation in various types of economic activities from an early age of childhood is considered as an essential part of their socialization. The prevailing modes of domestic organisations and system of kinship and marriage also affect childhood.

What children must do is influenced by what the system of kinship considers the rights and obligations of children. In many places, the delegation of aspects of parental roles, and the institutionalized practice of fostering of children by non-parental kin, involve widespread transfers of the obligation to train and maintain children and the right to enjoy the services of the young. Such practices may involve an element of apprenticeship and specialist training.

It is also revealed that in a transitional society, the case of childhood is also regarded as an economic practice because of the persistence of tradition-bound occupations and occupational immobility. But this society is also not free from the influence of modern science and technology development existing in the modern world and the use of childhood period for economic activities is also regarded as a social evil. If this society has a democratic form of Government, the use of childhood as a social evil gets more currency there. Hence, the practice of childhood, exists simultaneously both as an economic practice and as a social evil in a transitional society. The use of childhood, in fact, regarded as a social evil because of the abuse of childhood on a large scale.

The use of childhood (labour) is a characteristic of transitional societies which enfold multi-class-based social stricture and a complexes of traditional and pre-capitalist production relation operating under the rein of the dominate bourgeois ideology and mode of exploitation. This also holds true in respect of Indian society wherein, multi-class social structures exist and a complex of traditional and pre-capitalist production relations are operative in an articulated capitalist mode of production and exploitation, despite its having a number of legislative and administrative measurements to curb the use and abuse of childhood period.

Moreover, various practices, saying cultural traits, are indeed not as ancient as it appears and are the results of socio-economic evolution. They have no "cultural" foundations since they result from economic strategies in a context of survival or wealth rising. The dowry issue in India illustrates perfectly this specificity. Marriage and the practice of dowry are strongly embedded in a rigid social context of norms and caste rules. At the same time, new economic and development opportunities have a considerable impact on social organisation in Indian society. The social status of a person is largely determined by his caste. Within a context of economic development, particularly in urban areas, the social status takes into account of several elements: caste, education, nature of the occupation, and income. Within such context, the identity, and therefore the social status, of an individual is not determined by rigid, hereditary factors such as community and caste affiliation, but by economic factors (income, education and occupation etc.).

In a well-developed urban areas, this leads to a bigger socio-economic heterogeneity within a given caste. So, a striking social change is operated across India and implies new strategies notably within the family which directly and indirectly plays a vital role in framing safe or unsafe childhood of the children of that family. The changes in social status play indeed a major role in the marriage institution, which is regarded as a mean to strike up family relations and to enhance social mobility.

Gender and Childhood

Discrimination of girl children in the specific period of childhood does exist in India and it is often studied only as a part of the overall pattern of discrimination against girls. As for as childhood is concerned, "what has been observed on the most on the subject matters is that the parameters are often defined in such a manner that discrimination is not even apparent". Thus, a large amount of works in which girl children are engaged do not even figure as child labour.

Studies have revealed that in Indian, girl children are engaged in running the household from a very early age, even before they are capable of wage earning activities. This includes collection of water, fuel and looking after the younger siblings. But, such activities are not considered to be child labour as these are part and parcel of their family activities. Even when the girls reach the older age group of nine and above, a significant portion of their time remains unaccounted because it is consumed by these activities. The first point that is often stressed in the case of girl children is that there role as childhood is one, which does not receive much attention (Sinha, 2000).

A second aspect that has received attention is the manner in which traditional and cultural factors play a major role in deciding the chilhood patterns of girl children in India. Among Indian communities, it is the male child who is expected to assume the dominant role in all traditional activities including festivals and religious occasions which results in an almost automatic discrimination of girls. This manifests itself in a number of ways, which have been documented in detail. Adverse sex ratio, female infanticide, deliberate neglect of girl children in the younger years, lower nutritional and educational status and even the nature of work performed by girls are some of the indicators which amply support the fact of discrimination of girl children in India.

Two main areas of research have elicited anthropologist's interest in case of childhood issue: the family context of work and relation among socialization, work and schooling. The growing number of publications of Sociology on childhood issue in the underdeveloped countries has raised a renewed interest in the family context of work. Child employment is mostly limited by the free-labour requirement of families that is satisfied by giving children unremunerated and lowly valued tasks (Cain, 1997). While servicing the immediate household is young children's mandatory task, poor children coming of age may also be sent to work as domestics and apprentices for wealthier kin.

There is a persistent belief, which finds its origin in the neo-classical approach, that schooling is the best antidote to childhood. Although to some extent schools and work can co-exist as separate arenas of childhood, schooling is changing the world orientation of both children and parents. This notion suggest that schooling increase the costs of child rearing while reducing children's inclination to perform mandatory task for the circle of kin (William, 2001).

The articulation of gender, age and kinship plays a cardinal role in the valuation of poor children's childhood period and is instrumental in explaining why some work is condemned as unsuitable and some is *lauded a salutary.* Hierarchies based on gender, age and kinship combine to define children's mandatory tasks as salutatory work and condemn paid work. Sociology has sought to explain the apparent inability of the market to avail itself more fully of the vast reservoir of cheep childhood by pointing out that the free labour requirements of poor families are satisfied by giving children lowly valued tasks. Employment is clearly not the only nor the most important way children's work is exploited: Child work contribution to the family are instrumented to its substance and to the production of goods that reach the market a prices far below their labour value. The moral assumption that "poor children's socialization should occur through the performance of non-magnetized work exclude this work to economic realm that included childhood; it is as much a part of children explications" (Nineuwenuys, 1996).

The argument of cultural specificities is often a wrong argument in the hands of the conservatives finding a special interest to maintain situation in the state. This argument is not relevant taken in a broad sense which would include all practices. In this sense, it is not an opposable argument to human rights and child's rights. It does not mean that it is necessary to deny any contextual specificity. But on one hand these contextual specificities are not necessarily cultural and can be led to change with context; on the other hand they have to be confronted to human rights and to child's rights to establish if they do not constitute a fundamental violation of these rights.

We cannot deny that cultural factors influence the place of a child in society. Each society considers differently a child; norms and traditions influence the perception of childhood. However, it is not a reason to justify the precocious working age of children in bringing the cultural argument. In several cases, economic considerations determine the childhood decision and not cultural factors. For proof, numbers of industrial countries have recently revised their legislations in a worrying way in reducing the minimum age to work.

It is the case of France that has just lowered the age of work for apprenticeship from14 years to 13 years. If this measure aims to favour the insertion of young persons in the professional life, we have to consider the negative repercussions of this policy. It reduces, for instance, the professional trajectories of the young persons by "formatting" them too much early.

The question is what is the best mean to reach the state of adulthood? The UN considers that schooling is the best way to attain good adulthood, which increases human capital and has a positive impact on growth and development of any society and culture. All the children must have the same childhood which consists in going to school and to endow their free time on leisure. It is necessary to acknowledge the apprenticeship as an intermediary form but it is also necessary to differentiate two aspects of the apprenticeship taken in the broad sense.

The first aspect is an effect of socialisation. It can be applied to younger children, since it concerns none dangerous activities and since it is limited to a low level of working hours. It can be quite in relation with some cultural traditions if they do not present danger for children. The second aspect is an effect of training in a professional perspective. Therefore, in this case, the age must be absolutely the highest as possible. Indeed, the aspect of training is not the same nature as the dimension of socialisation. It involves a defined trajectory of the child's activity for his future and in this sens or strains his space of future freedom. The assimilation of these two effects without any precaution drives the defenders of cultural specificities to admit any type of activity in name of the respect of traditions. In reality, they refuse to accept economic constraints affecting childhood. This pressure is not only the prerogative of developing countries, as confirms it the legal measures taken recently by several industrialized countries in favour of a reduction of the age of apprenticeship which is viewed as a violation of the convention 138. Therefore, what is behind apprenticeship is not really in relation with the question of childhood.

Cultural norms study reveals the opinion and attitude of the particular community regarding any concepts. In this study community norms study has been conducted by the method of *focus group* interviews with the selected community members who have been carefully selected from the different sections of the society. It is important to note that community members are not exclusively aware of the concept of childhood and rights of children. One can say that these concepts do not exist in the form of simple words or phrase among the studied communities. Also, discussing life or any other experiences with the community members is not a common occurrence, so some methods and approaches needed to be developed. A point, among others, is that 'to date children have not been absent but have been silent in the study of childhood'

Despite the challenges in communicating the concepts and other methodological issues, this ethnographic study could able to learn some good informations regarding childhood concept from the samples. It is found that the community is more or less completely failed in defining childhood and adulthood concept logically.

Majority (73%) of the community members said 'childhood or adulthood is largely depended not on the age but on the degree of responsibility that children could successfully fulfill'. Community members feel that their responsibilities towards the family and the contributions they make are significant and important while defining the term's childhood and adulthood. Community feels, 'age and responsibility is not proportional to each other'.

Elite's of the community members felt children belonging to the poor families will not have any childhood period because they have to prepare themselves to face the probable struggle in their future life right from the very beginning. According to them children belongs to the poor family will not have any happy childhood at all. It is all-just because of poverty.

Some of the members (37%) feel that working children who are blow 10 years of age can not be considered as a child because he is playing a major role by contributing significant portion of the income to the family. However, this study has found that different culture and tradition of the society have fixed different age thresholds for demarcating childhood and adulthood, and age may not be a sufficient basis for defining childhood. Community will not take physical age criteria while demarcating child from an adult.

Many community members (23%) have agreed that the fulfillment of certain social rites and traditional obligations may be very important requirements in interpreting the concept 'childhood'. Community is not so serious about the safe period of childhood. They consider it just a normal process of the child's development.

Next, community has no logic or more scientific classification of the phases of life *i.e.*, childhood and adulthood. Study has revealed that 3/4th of the community members feel that end of the childhood and beginning of the adulthood in any ones life can be detected based on the following features; 1. starting work to earn money 2. when children can distinguish between right and wrongs in the life 3. after attaing the age around 15 4. when they get intelligence 5. when their voice get changes (some thing from smooth to rough) 6. when they will ready for marriage. It is all in case of boys only. Community is not properly understanding the period and value of the childhood. They are giving more importance to the economic value rather than normative attitude towards the children.

Further, in case of girl's community members unanimously agree that after attaining puberty, she can be considered as an adult irrespective of age, i.e. her childhood periods ends. Since, India belongs to sub-tropical country, girls reaches puberty at an early age when compare to the western girls. But, majority (69%) of the community members categorically rejects this scientific view and they sticked on to their previous opinion. This study has revealed that girl's childhood ends sooner than boy's. The game of planning house fades imperceptivity into a constant responsibility to help mother. By the time a girl attain 10-12 years of age or so, she will become an economic asset to her mother and spends a great deal of time working.

Community feels it is a kind of training to the girls and it is very essential because after marriage, she should be in the position to balance everything in her husband's house. Little boy's, by contrast spend hours playing among themselves and are able to prolong their childhood into their late teens if they so wish. Even in more contemporary accounts of children's lives, this assumption of unquestioned gender division, where girls are socially responsible at a much earlier age, remains important feature.

This discussion has shown that community members consider children an economic entity, thus ascribing childhood with an economic rather than imply a social value. There is no dispute that children inherit a distinctive human nature but expression of that nature depends on another designative inheritance of human society and culture. This study has an opinion that "decision to give a chance to a child to spend happy childhood is not isolated from other aspects of household decision making nor are they purely household based. Community is evaluating the period of childhood of their children from different contexts, which is highly influenced by their inherited cultural pattern of the life and soil". In some cases, it was found that if the parents have had a happy and decent childhood it is more likely of be passing same jester to their present children also. "They reflect the norms and values of the wider community within which the household is located and the social and economic possibilities which local contexts offer to different categorized of households." The community and the presence or absence of community norms and organizations conducive to children's participation in childhood period. Next, community has not understood childhood as a social construction. A new concept on children and childhood is required which attempts to ground explanation and interpretations in the contexts of community and culture in which children are actually living to spend their respective childhood period. It is also noteworthy to say that present day childhood about the perspectives of working children whose development (in terms of skills, social networks, self-esteem and identity) is embedded within working lives.

Childhood is not static, nor is it narrowly prescribed. It is found that each generation reconstructs childhood, structuring children's experiences and channeling human potential to reflect its own goals, values and circumstances. At the same time it is worth bearing in mind that even the widely accepted orthodoxy's about childhood are not immutable.

Children and their childhood are, accordingly, seen as assets under capitalism and linked to their value in the process of production, be it in school or in the workplace. Local culture more or less considers children are economic entities, thus ascribing childhood with an economic rather than simply a social value. Working children find themselves clashing with the childhood ideology that places a higher value on the performance of economically useless work. Although working for pay offers opportunities for self-respect, it also entails sacrifying childhood, which exposes children to the native stereotyping attached to the loss of innocence these sacrifice is supposed to cause.

The convention on the rights of the child represents an instrument of infinite significance which binds peoples everywhere to co-operate for improving the living conditions of children in every country, more particular, the developing countries. The term rights of the children were very new to many community participants. They have not heard this kind of rights especially for the children in their lifetime. But, few members have asserted that each and every child should have that kind of rights and it is very essential for the normal growth and development of the children. Few (21%) community members have unanimously agreed that this kind of legal binding international treaty for children are very important because it saves children from being misused by the elders/employer's.

Further, some of the community members expressed their doubts about successful implementation of this programme despite, diversities in the political, economic and socio-cultural contexts within each country. Some of them said this kind of programmes requires a lot of money and resources and it is more suitable to rich western countries only. Few members said laws, rules, guidelines and principles can be introduced or adapted to match to a nutrition rights and rights of compulsory primary education. Some of them have expressed their opinion that Governament and NGOs should try hard to implement these rights to all children in the country. Some of the members (34%) have revealed that these rights of children and human rights instrument's in themselves establish only soft rights.

Further, elite's of the society feels that Rights can be truly hard only where there is a strong and effective legislation in place. It should be turned into hard rights, which are clearly articulated in the law and have effective implementation and accountability mechanisms. They continue that, "It is the high time that State should take responsibilities leading to knowledge transformation and smooth implementation of the convention of the rights of the children for building a welfare society". However, some of the community member opined lack of strong political will and poor allocation of resources are some of the reasons for the dismal implementation of the rights of children. Next, they add that effective realization of the legal obligations under CRC would be possible only when domestic monitoring systems evolve and ply out their roles independent of the Government or any other pressure groups.

From the discussion it is found that how far the international conventions and the UNO declaration look in to the local social and cultural environments of the children? Child rights are not geographically and culturally specific. The decisions are taken at the global level without giving due consideration to the third world countries having diversities in social-cultural aspects and where still poor people have economic attitudes towards their children.

Any generalization on the present status of child rights by this study is risky, unfair and does not match to realties on the ground despite instance of relative neglect of children's welfare and uneven enforcement of laws in some parts of the city. Researcher found that large number of organisations working with children at the grass roots level do not have the orientation, training and expertise required to be involved in this significant process. However elite's of the society feels the task of monitoring children rights is particularly complex because the CRC is the first legally binding international treaty for the children in the history. This is very new to our society also. Thus, monitoring mechanism should follow a top-heavy model, i.e. a well-defined structure for monitoring at the national level. But it is found that a kind of a vacuum seems at the domestic level, in terms of monitoring structure and process. This study has further found that even though natural Child Rights are culturally assimilated, more reliable approach should be discovered for the prompt and effective implementation.

The empirical studies reveal the fact that childhood is directly and indirectly related to poverty depending on the structures of the economies. The second problem faced by the convention is its objective of "to develop to the fullest". This objective is the main core of the millennium goal led by the United Nations. For the harmonious development of children, the states members of the UN must educate their children, give health services, as well as social services. In most of the low income countries the rate of enrolment is under 50 per cent and the gap between boys and girls enrolment is quite high and particularly in rural areas. UNESCO has implemented in 1992 the programme "education for all" (EFA) in order to attain the millennium goal.

The objective of such a programme is to have 100 per cent of enrolment for both boys and girls. Two difficulties have to be considered to reach this goal. The first one is of economic nature. The reason for non-enrolling children at school is explained by income poverty, lack of parents' education, worst school infrastructures, and lack of schools in rural areas. In such an environment it is very difficult to fulfil the objective of EFA. The second dimension is cultural. Some countries count in the rate of access to education the children who are registered in schools always not offering basic programmes allowing a "normal" schooling. For instance, some Coranic schools only supply Coranic teaching without any consideration of other subjects or disciplines. It is a wrongly cultural feature since these schools, in addition to the Coranic teaching, can also offer basic teachings required for a normal schooling.

Moreover, a number of them and probably the best make it. The third problem addressed by the UN convention is those of exploitation and child abuse. The convention forbids the recruitment of children for the industry of sex, pornography, and prostitution and also for armed conflicts. Lately in 1999, the ILO has adopted the convention on the worst forms of childhood.

The convention challenges the issue of child rights and the ILO makes its priority to eradicate the worst form of childhood as it is detriment to the child development for the fullest. Hence, the ILO distinguishes between childhood and child work. If the former is seen as dangerous for the physical and mental development of the child, the latter is considered as beneficial to children as it can be a way of socialisation (Fyfe, 1989). Acknowledging the possibility for children to exercise a socialising activity (for instance to milk cows in rural area) does not however justify to put them in work during long hours, even if this activity does not present any danger in itself. It is necessary to distinguish what is of the resort of But for a defense of the specificities of the schools in terms of capabilities.

Socialising activity from what dealt with economic constraint affecting the household. The economic conditions such as the lack of family resources, time constraint for women, etc. Often imply children occupations for completing these resources or for freeing women's time. And if some activities, more or less traditional, can be linked to apprenticeship, it is also necessary to distinguish them from the economic constraints. From this point of view, the number of the performed hours, the conditions in which they are executed are significative elements.

It is then obvious, under these conditions of boundary that traditions do not enter in contradiction with the child's rights but can favor their promotion. In the sense, the argument of cultural specificities cannot be opposed to human rights and child's rights. If it is necessary to take it into account, it is because cultural specificities reinforce the implementation of these rights. One of the more interesting aspects is that this research found that community is not in favor of early socialization of the children by sending them to work only. Community asserted that children could effectively be socialized by sending them to the schools and by allowing them to mingle with their peer age group friends. Next it is found that some of the other cultural factors are independently variables with family structure and sex role.

Conclusion

From the current ethnographic study it is revealed that some section of the community members claimed that children who did not work as laboures outside the family were economical unproductive and drain on household income rather than an addition. It was only when the children were older and began to be involved with waged labour that there members began to see their children as actively contributed the household and acknowledge the importance of their contribution. Study further found that since boys were much more likely than girls to undertake aged labour outside the house therefore likely to be perceived as an economic burden on their parents. Hence, the community members feels boys get more acknowledgement than girl child workers.

This study has also found that few community members has of a opinion that examining childhood through the lenses agency, distributive inequality, and harm suggest that not all work performed by children is equally morally objectable. Some work, especially work that does not interfere with or undermine their health or education, may allow children to develop skills they need to become well-function adults and border their future opportunities. Other work, including child prostitution and bonded labour should be the highest priority. Community feels 'blanket bans' on all childhood may drive families to choose even worse option for their children.

While most sociologists and anthropologists have accepted the contribution of women to household economies, the economic role of girls is still under-studied and consequently under valued. There is still, all too frequently, an elision between socialization and economic activity and childcare by girls is routinely commented on without an acknowledgement of the contribution this plays in the home. It is a blindness shared by parents, children and academics and is based on western assumptions about the essential economic passivity of the child. It is an area which demands much more research, as well as a conceptual shift in how we understand children, their role in the family and the expectations placed on them by their gender (Montgomery: (1999).

While ideas about the essential economic incapacity of children are now being challenged, it is rare to find this in combination with the understandings that girls' experiences need to be placed within a conceptual matrix which includes both truly be taken into account. The new sociology of children has succeeded in its insistence on the importance of age and generation but in doing so, gender has been pushed to the margins. The challenge for childhood studies now is to emphasize the importance of the inter-linkage between the study of generation and gender, to get rid of the notion of the 'strange, ungendered isolate' and replace it with a vision of a child as both a young person and a gendered one.

REFERENCES

1. Bhalotra, S. and C. Heady (2001), *Child Activities in South Asia and Sub-Saharan Africa, Africa and Asia in Comparative Development*, eds, P. Lawrence and C. Thirtle, London: Palgrave, Macmillan, September.
2. Carl em Rosen 2001, 'Childhood and Society,' *Journal of Gender Studies*, Vol. 23, No. 10, pp. 123-23).
3. Carre, Oliver, 2001, '*Sociological Prospective of Childhood in India*', Wind Publication, USA).
4. Dak, (Eds.) 2002, *Childhood in India*, Serials Publications, pp. 24-25).
5. Glauser, B. (1990) 'Street children: deconstructing a construct' in James, A. and Prout, A. (eds) *Constructing and Reconstructing Childhood*, London, Falmer Press.
6. Kabeer, Geetha, and Ramya Subrahmanian, 2003, '*Getting Children back to School: Case Studies in Primary Education*', Vimal Ramachandran (Ed.), Sage Publication, pp. 176-215).
7. G.P. Mishra, 2001 "Supply of Childhood: An Investigation", *Labour and Development*, Vol. 1 No.1 July-Dec. 95)
8. Kristoffel and Ben (1997) Economic Importance of Childhood in Traditional Society, *Irish Review of Sociology*, Vol. XXXI, No. 21, pp. 1232-1245.
9. Kabeer, N., Nambissan, G. B., & Subrahmanian, R. (2003). "Needs versus Rights? Child Labour, Social Exclusion and the Challenge of Universalising Primary Education." In N. Kabeer,G. B. Nambissan & R. Subrahmanian (Eds.), *Child Labour and the Right to Education in South Asia: Needs versus Rights?* New Delhi: Sage Publications India Pvt.
10. Myers, W.E. (ed) (1991) *Protecting Working Children*, London, Zed Books.
11. Myers, W.E. (2001) 'Valuing diverse approaches to child labour' in Lieten, G.K. and White, B. (eds) *Child Labour : Policy options*, Amsterdam, Aksant Academic Publishers.
12. Morrow, V. (2003) 'Moving out of Childhood' in Maybin, J. and Woodhead, M. (eds) *Childhoods in Context*, Chichester, John Wiley and Sons Ltd. / The Open University.
13. Munroe, R.H., Munroe, R.L. and Shimmin, H.S. (1984) 'Children's Work in Four Cultures: Determinants and Consequences', *American Anthropologist*, No. 86, pp. 369-79.
14. Nieuwenhuys, O. (1996) 'The paradox of child labor and sociology', *Annual Review of Sociology*, 25, pp. 237-251.
15. Nieuwenhuys, O. (1994) *Children's Lifeworlds: gender, welfare and labour in the developing world*, London, Routledge.
16. Nieuwenhuy, Olga (1998) "Global Childhood and the Politics of Contempt". *Alternatives*. Vol. 23, pp. 267-289. Boulder, Colorado: Lynne Rienner Publishers.
17. Woodhead, M. (2001). 'The value of work and school: A study of working children's perspectives". In K. Lieten & B. White (Eds.), *Child Labour: Policy Options* (pp. 1-11).

18. Weiner, 1999, Socialization of Childhood and Work, *Critique Sociology*, Vol. 23, No. 4, 1999, pp. 45-48.

19. Woodhead, and Martin: "Combating Child Labour Listen What the Children Say". *Childhood,* Vol. 6(1): 27-49,(1998).

20. William M.: *Children Perspective on Their Working Lives*. Stockholm Radda Barmen. (2001).

21. Woodhead.: Combating Child Labour Listen What the Children say. *The Childhood*, Vol. 6(1): 27-49, (1999).

22. Woodhead, M., Burr, R. and Montgomery, H.K. (2003) 'Adversities and Resilience' in Montgomery, H.K., Burr, R. and Woodhead, M. (eds) *Changing Childhoods: local and global*, Chichester, John Wiley and Sons Ltd/The Open University.

Impact of Lifeskills Counseling on Suicidal Depression among Alcoholics: A New Psychological Anthropology

—Manjunatha, P. and Venkateshkumar, G.

Abstract

The aim of the study is to determine the effectiveness of Lifeskills counseling as intervention for reducing the symptoms of suicidal depression among alcoholics. An experimental design, with treatment and control group is used. The sample is selected by using convenience basis, from K.R. Govt. Hospital and JSS General Hospital, Mysore. Alcoholics are diagnosed by qualified medical officials. The sample of 120, both urban and rural adult males with high score on suicidal depression is considered. Catttell's Clinical Analysis Questionnaire Part-II (CAQ) was used to assess the participants' symptoms. General Linear Model Repeated Measures of ANOVA is applied to know the effect of intervention programme. A significant 'F' was observed indicating differential decrease for experimental and control groups in the symptoms of suicidal depression.

In the Asian sub-continent, per capita alcohol consumption increased by over 50 per cent between 1980 and 2000 (WHO, 2002), while India has experienced a 115 per cent increase in per capita alcohol consumption by adults since 1980 (Rahman, L., 2002). In India alcohol addiction has adverse health and social consequences, ranging from shifting the use of resources away from basic necessities, such as food and shelter, to acquit consequences for the welfare of other members of the household especially children and women (Bonu, S., 2004). India is likely to face a heavy burden of medical and social problems due to increased alcohol consumption (Mohan, D., *et al.,* 2001).

The World Health Organization (2004) estimates that there are about 2 billion people worldwide who consume alcoholic beverages and 76.3 million with diagnosable alcohol use disorders. From a public health perspective, the global burden related to alcohol consumption, both in terms of morbidity and mortality, is considerable in most parts of the world. Alcohol consumption has health and social consequences via intoxication (drunkenness), alcohol dependence, and other biochemical effects of alcohol. In addition to chronic diseases that may affect alcohol after many years of heavy use, alcohol contributes to traumatic outcomes that kill or disable at a relatively young age, resulting in the loss of many years of life due to death or disability. Alcohol causes 1.8 million deaths (3.2% of total) and a loss of 58.3 million (4% of total) of Disability-Adjusted Life Years (DALY). Unintentional injuries alone account for about one-third of the 1.8 million deaths, while neuro-psychiatric conditions account for close to 40 per cent of the 58.3 million DALYs (WHO, 2002). The estimates suggest that alcohol related problems to the society are of great magnitude and need urgent attention of social scientists.

Alcohol has implicated in a variety of mental disorders which are not alcohol-specific. However, before the GBD 2000 study no major overview on alcohol-attributable burden of disease has included these conditions (English *et al.,* 1995; Gutjahr, Gmel & Rehm, 2001; Single *et al.,* 1999). While the causality of the relation is hard to define, sufficient evidence now exists to assume alcohol's causal role in depression, a common mental disorder. Adityanjee, M. D. and Wig, N. N. (1989) report that alcohol-related problems made up 17.6 per cent of the case load of psychiatric emergencies in an Indian General Hospital.

In the general population, alcohol dependence and major depression co-occur over proportionally, on both a 12-month and a lifetime basis (Kessler *et al.,* 1997; Lynskey, 1998). Among alcohol consumers in the general population, higher volume of consumption is associated with more symptoms of depression (Graham & Schmidt, 1999; Mehrabian, 2001; Rodgers *et al.,* 2000). Among patients in treatment for alcohol abuse and dependence, the prevalence of major depression is higher than in the general population (Lynskey, 1998; Schuckit *et al.,* 1997). Higher prevalence of alcohol use disorders has been documented for patients in treatment for depression (Blixen, McDougall & Suen, 1997). This suggests that alcohol use disorders are linked to depressive symptoms, and that alcohol dependence and depressive disorders co-occur to a larger degree than expected by chance.

In male alcoholics, major depression has a five per cent lifetime prevalence rate, compared to three per cent for the total male population. In the DSM-IV (APA, 1994), mood disorders must be of sufficient duration and intensity that they cause significant subjective distress or dysfunction in one or more of life's roles (relationships, work, and school). The Epidemiologic Catchment Area (ECA) data (1989), as cited in Frances & Miller (1991) indicate that major depression and dysthymia occur at least one and half times more often in alcoholics than in the general population. In addition, depression is associated with an elevated risk of suicide (Bernheim, 1997). Cattell, R. B. (1973) states that suicidal depression factor centers on thoughts of self-destruction. Individuals report that they are disgusted with life, that life has become empty and meaningless. They entertain thoughts of death as a viable alternative to their present, hopeless situation. In short they have reached the end of their rope. Cattell further says that these factors are common to alcoholics.

People with alcohol dependency need psychosocial interventions for a variety of psychiatric and personality problems in general and suicidal depression in particular. So far, most of the interventions have focused on stress management training, exercise and cognitive therapy to promote adaptation, reduce depression, anxiety and psychological stress to enhance quality of life. A more intensive and focused intervention may be necessary to meet the specialized needs of alcoholics with multiple medical, social, and economic challenges. Lifeskills counseling is more suitable and an intensive intervention that combines individual psychological care to provide intensive on-going support in many factors of depression.

Richard Nelson-Jones (2000), considered that with the knowledge of lifeskills person would possess awareness in each of these areas; responsiveness, realism, relating, rewarding activity, and right-and-wrong. He advocated lifeskills counseling as a "people-centered approach for assisting clients and others to develop self-helping skills". He designed a five-stage lifeskills counseling model DASIE, for helping clients to manage problems. DASIE is not only for managing or solving problems but also for addressing underlying problematic skills. The model provides a framework or set of guidelines for counselor choices.

In the present study it is aimed to determine the effectiveness of lifeskills counseling as intervention for reducing suicidal depression in the people with alcohol dependence. The study utilized the dependent variable of suicidal depression to assess the effectiveness of lifeskills counseling as intervention and gain insight and understanding of people with alcohol dependence.

Method

An experimental pre-and post-test design, with a treatment and control group, is used. The independent variables varied in the two treatment conditions; experimental and control groups. The dependent variable is the participant's symptoms of suicidal depression. There are two groups of participants : (*a*) experimental group for which the Lifeskills counseling is given, (*b*) control group for which no Lifeskills counseling is given.

Sample

The sample is selected by using convenience basis, from K. R. Govt. Hospital and JSS General Hospital, Mysore city—alcoholic dependents as diagnosed by qualified medical officials. They are under treatment for de-addiction. The sample consists of 120, both urban and rural adult males with high score on suicidal depression. The age ranges from 25-53; with the mean age 38.12 years.

Measures

(A) Personal Information Schedule (PIS) is used to know the following information: (1) Gender, (2) Age, (3) Marital Status, (4) Domicile, (5) Educational Level, and (6) Occupation.

(B) Cattell's Clinical Analysis Questionnaire Part-II (CAQ) was used to assess the participants' symptoms of suicidal depression. The CAQ part-II (1973), Questionnaire consists of 144 multiple choice items representing either a symptom or attitude related to clinical factors of personality. It contains 12 factors for which multiple choice responses are given. The participants were asked to select a single answer in each question that corresponds most clearly with his actual condition at that particular time. Each factor describes a specific manifestation of clinical factors of personality. Only one factor is utilized in this paper.

Procedure

The CAQ part-II is administered to a large number of alcoholics. Those scored above the median level on the questionnaire, are selected for further study. The selected 120

Table 18.1. Mean and S.D. of pre-test and post-test scores on suicidal depression of alcoholics of both experimental and control groups.

Group	Domicile	Pre-test		Post-test		Change
		Mean	S.D.	Mean	S.D.	
Experimental	Urban	9.40	.50	2.50	.51	6.9
	Rural	9.80	.41	2.50	.63	7.3
	Total	9.60	.49	2.50	.57	7.1
Control	Urban	9.47	.51	9.53	.57	- 0.06
	Rural	9.40	.62	9.53	.51	- 0.13
	Total	9.43	.56	9.53	.54	- 0.1
Total	Urban	9.43	.50	6.02	3.59	3.41
	Rural	9.60	.56	6.02	3.59	3.58
	Total	9.52	.53	6.02	3.57	3.5

Table 18.2. Summary results of GLM—Repeated Measures of ANOVA within and between subjects for suicidal depression of Experimental and Control groups in pre-test and post-test situations.

	Within-subjects effects				
Source of variance	**Sum of squares**	**df**	**Mean square**	**F**	**p**
Pre-Post test	735.000	1	735.000	2756.250	0.000*
Expt-Control	777.600	1	777.600	2916.000	0.000*
Urban-Rural	0.417	1	0.417	1.563	0.214**
Expt-Control (Urban-Rural)	0.817	1	0.817	3.063	0.083**
Error (Change)	29.867	112	0.267		
Between-subjects effects					
Intercept	14477.067	1	14477.067	53336.567	0.000*
Expt-Control	707.267	1	707.267	2605.719	0.000*
Urban-Rural	0.417	1	0.417	1.535	0.218**
Expt-Control (Urban-Rural)	0.817	1	0.817	3.009	0.086**
Error	30.400	112	0.271		

* HS = Highly significant **NS = Not significant

participants were equally divided into two groups – experimental and control group, randomly. The experimental group was given treatment with the five stages of Lifeskills counseling model (DASIE) developed by Richard Nelson Jones. No treatment was given to control group but was kept under observation including the self-introduction. The time schedule for intervention is one hour duration per session and two sessions per week. Total of 20 sessions are given spreading through two and a half month approximately. After the intervention, the experimental and control groups are measured again on the dependent variable and obtained post test scores.

Results and Discussion

To assure the randomization of the sample the data are subjected to independent samples 't' test in the pre-test. The experimental and control group's mean score and S.D. for suicidal depression are 09.60, 0.49 and 09.43, 0.56 respectively. The 't' values are 1.723 and 'p' is 0.088 indicating a non-significant difference between experimental and control groups. Thus the equating as well as randomization of the groups was taken care of during the pre-test situation. General Linear Model Repeated Measures of ANOVA is applied to the know effect of intervention programme.

Repeated Measures of ANOVA revealed a significant decrease from pre to post test situation irrespective of the groups. 'F' value is 2756.250, found to be highly significant (p< 0.000). Irrespective of the groups in pre-test the mean suicidal depression score 9.52 is reduced to 6.02 with the reduction of 3.5 scores which found to be significant. When reduction in the suicidal depression scores with reference to groups are concerned again a significant 'F' is observed (F=2916.000; p< 0.000) indicating differential decrease for experimental and control groups. From mean values it is evident that experimental group had a reduction of 7.1 scores (from 9.60 to 2.50), where as control group had reduction of only – 0.1 scores (from 9.43 to 9.53). So the decrease in the suicidal depression has basically in the experimental group which can be attributed to the effectiveness of Lifeskills Counseling. However, the interaction effect between domicile groups with respect to change in the scores and domicile groups with respect to groups and change in scores are found to be non-significant. Between-subjects effects between groups (irrespective of conditions) together significant difference are observed (F = 2605.719; p<0.000). However, domicile groups wise and interaction between groups and domicile groups is found to be non-significant.

Conclusion

The Lifeskills counseling intervention has reduced symptoms of suicidal depression in alcoholic dependents. The major implication of this study is that it indicates a need for a possible shift in the thinking of the health policy makers of our country. The study has implications for the public health approach to the care and prevention. The study also has significance for psychological counselors, social workers and policy-makers. Findings can be used by these specialists to design intervention programs aimed at sustaining people with alcohol dependence in good health.

APPENDIX

The DASIE's five stages Lifeskills counseling

D Develop relationship and clarify the problem.

A Assess and restate the problem in skills terms.

S State goals and plan interventions.

I Intervene to develop lifeskills.

E Emphasize, take awz

REFERENCES

1. Adityanjee, M. D., Wig, N. N. (1989). Alcohol related problems in the emergency room of an Indian general hospital. *Australian and New Zealand Journal of Psychiatry*, 23, 274–278.
2. American Psychiatric Association (1994). *Diagnostic and statistical manual of mental disorders* (4th ed.). Washington, DC: American Psychiatric Association.
3. Bernheim, K. F. (1997). *The Lanahan cases and readings in abnormal behavior.* New York: Lanahan Publishers, Inc.
4. Blixen, C. E., McDougall, G. J., & Suen, L. J. (1997). Dual diagnosis in elders discharged from a psychiatric hospital. *International Journal of Geriatric Psychiatry*, 12, 307-313.
5. Bonu, S. (2004). Household tobacco and alcohol use and child health: An exploratory study from India. *Health policy*, 70, 67-83.
6. Cattell, R.B. (1973). A check on the 28 factor Clinical Analysis Questionnaire structure on normal and pathological subjects. In, Samuel, E. Krug (1980). *Clinical Analysis Questionnaire manual.* Illinois: Institute for personality and ability testing.
7. English, D. R., *et. al.* (1995). *The Quantification of Drug Caused Morbidity and Mortality in Australia-1992.* Canberra: Commonwealth Department of Human Services and Health.
8. Frances, R. J. & Miller, S. I. (1991). *Clinical textbook of addiction disorders* (2nd ed.). New York, NY: Guilford Publications.
9. Graham, K., & Schmidt, G. (1999). Alcohol use and psychosocial well-being among older adults. *Journal of Studies on Alcohol*, 60, 345-351.
10. Gutjahr, E., Gmel, G. & Rehm, J. (2001). Relation between average alcohol consumption and disease: an overview. *European Addiction Research*, 7, 117-127.
11. Kessler, R. C., *et al.* (1997). Lifetime co-occurrence of DSM-III-R alcohol abuse and dependence with other psychiatric disorders in the National Comorbidity Survey. *Archives of General Psychiatry*, 54, 313-321.
12. Lynskey, M. T. (1998). The co-morbidity of alcohol dependence and affective disorders: treatment implications. *Drug and Alcohol Dependence*, 52, 201-209.
13. Mehrabian, A. (2001). General relations among drug use, alcohol use, and major indexes of psychopathology. *Journal of Psychology*, 135, 71-86.
14. Mohan, D., Chopra, A., Ray, R., & Sethi, H. (2001). Alcohol consumption in India: a cross-sectional study. In, Demers, A., Room, R. & Bourgault, C. *Surveys of drinking patterns and problems in seven developing countries.* Geneva: World Health Organization.
15. Nelson-Jones, R. (2000). Lifeskills Counselling. In, Stephen Palmer (ed.). *Introduction to Counseling and Psychotherapy.* New Delhi: Sage.

16. Rahman, L. (2002). *Alcohol prohibition and addictive consumption in India*. London: London school of Economics.

17. Rodgers, B., *et al.* (2000). Non-linear relationships in associations of depression and anxiety with alcohol use. *Psychological Medicine*, 30, 421-432.

18. Schuckit, M. A., *et al.* (1997). The life-time rates of three major mood disorders and four major anxiety disorders in alcoholics and controls. *Addiction*, 92, 1289-1304.

19. Single, E., *et al.* (1999). Morbidity and mortality attributable to alcohol, tobacco, and illicit drug use in Canada. *American Journal of Public Health*, 89, 385-390.

20. World Health Organization (2004). Global Status Report on Alcohol-2004. Geneva.

21. World Health Organization 2002. The World Health Report 2002—Reducing Risks, Promoting Healthy Life. Geneva.

Individual Autonomy of Muslim Working Women in Mysore—India: A Sociological Perspective

—Nahid Sarikhani

Abstract

Women construct part of labor sources in societies, and they have a major role on development of communities. According to census 2001, the work participation rate of Muslim women in India is 14.1 per cent while in Karnataka it is 19.9 per cent. The proportion in Mysore district is 16.1 per cent, and in the urban areas, it is 15 per cent. The present study reports individual autonomy of Muslim working women in government office in Mysore city, and the factors that can increase individual autonomy of Muslim working women in their family. Simple random sampling technique was used in the selection of sample for the present study.

Total sample consist of 150 Muslim women who work in government office sectors. They were assessed by using a questioner. The results revealed that individual autonomy of Muslim working women is less, but we can observe that women are not totally ignored and men consult with them in matters such as education, marriage and occupation of their children, but unfortunately a majority of men members control economic power structure and family income especially economic autonomy of women as nearly half of them have referred to lack of economic autonomy than their salary. Of course high education of men seems to play a major role in the increasing of individual autonomy of Muslim working women in family's structure and society.

Introduction

In Oxford dictionary "Autonomy" means the right of a person, an organization, a region, etc. to govern or control his/her/its own affairs (Steel, 2006). In other words, the condition or quality of being autonomous; especially the power or right of self-government was called autonomy. It can be extended to cover the smallest group in society: the group of one, the individual. Most people live their lives constrained by family, clan, religion, etc. People spend their whole lives following the course that their station in society dictates. (ACC Niagara Archives) They had to ignore their individual autonomy.

For example, in Islamic society one can see this problem. In spite of this, Islam has given men and women equal rights in every aspect of life and gives them equality in the idea of creation of human beings (Engineer, 1992), but unfortunately, traditional societies couldn't utilize its principle correctly. These societies, with wrong interpretation have given men superiorities in every field, especially in the economical, social and political situations. Also, in a society or family as dominated by men, and men became the main decision-makers in the structure of the family. Women's role and their freedom depend on him a lot. In this society, men decide about women's education, their work outside home, their property rights, and so on. In other words, individual autonomy of women was limited.

One of these societies in Indians Islam, came in form especially with purdah. It limits public activities of women. It has also restricted the Muslim woman to make significant economic contributions and in education. As per the 2001 census, Muslim constitutes 13.4 percent of India's population that women consist 48.4 per cent of population. In addition, illiteracy rate for the Muslim women is higher than the Muslim men.

In India many studies have indicated that Hindu and Christian women work participation is higher than other religions; especially Muslim working women are very low. According to 2001 census, the work participation rate of women is only 25.6 per cent in India, the position of Muslim women is worse. As the work participation rate of these women in India is 14.1 per cent.(Census of India, 2001).

Therefore, the majority of Muslim women have been pushed into seclusion and segregation. They are not only suffering from the purdah system but also the authority of men. Moreover it restricts individual autonomy of Muslim women and girls.

On the other hand, excessive dependence on men has deprived them of enjoying many privileges like the pursuit of higher education, taking up jobs, developing self-identity, etc. meanwhile, the involvement of Muslim women in decision-making process was seen to be minimal (Azim, 1997).

Of course, however modernization and development of India caused several changes in the status of Muslim women, but those are not sufficient. Because observations have indicated that working women who take up a job out of home, their autonomy in the family's structure is low and they deprive from more social activities.

In the present study, 'individual autonomy" has been defined as the freedom enjoyed by a person in decision-making relating to household maintenance, shopping, marketing, marriage and occupation of children, traveling, divide income family, buy and change house, freedom to own earning and expending, looking after own property, participate in political and social activities. Meanwhile, it was attempted to explore individual autonomy of Muslim working women in Mysore city and also what factors can increase individual autonomy of Muslim women in family and society.

Objective

- To study the socio-economic status of Muslim working women.
- To study individual autonomy of Muslim working women in family structure.
- To study factors that can affect to increase individual autonomy of Muslim working women.

Hypotheses

- There is a significant difference between individual autonomy of women and their academic qualification.
- There is a significant difference between individual autonomy of women and kind of their occupation.
- There is a significant difference between individual autonomy of women and academic qualification of their husband.
- There is a significant difference between individual autonomy of women and their head of family.
- There is a significant difference between individual autonomy of women and their marital status.
- There is a significant difference between individual autonomy of women and their property status.

Methodology

Simple random sampling technique was used in the selection of sample for the present study. Total sample consist of 150 Muslim working women who work in government office.

Tools

Primary source of information will be collected from Muslim working women in their workplaces by administering a questionnaire.

Results

The results of socio-economic factors of Muslim working women indicated that of the total of Muslim working women 22 per cent are in age group of 18-28, 23.3 per cent are in age group of 29-38, 30.7 per cent are in age group of 39-48 and 24 per cent are in age group of 49-58 respectively. Moreover age mean them is 39.9 year old with minimum and maximum 18 year old and 58 year old respectively.

Findings reveal that of the total target population 4.7 per cent have certificate of PhD, 11.3 per cent have M.A. certificate, 41.3 per cent have B.A. certificate, 27.3 per cent have certificate of SSLC and 3.4 per cent of them are illiterate or lower primary school. Of the working women 28.7 per cent are never married, 65.3 per cent married and the rest divorced or widowed (6%). Some of them have expressed that they are single-wage earners, and they don't have other sources of income. Meanwhile 49.3 per cent of women have begun their job or their economic activities before married. The minimum age of a Muslim woman for beginning to work is at the age of 15 years.

The average salary of working women is Rs. 9948. The average of working experience of women is 13.9 years, and their minimum working experience is 3 months and maximum 38 years. 3.3 per cent of Muslim women work in university, 8.7 per cent of them work in college, 76 per cent work in school, 4 per cent women work in pre-university, 4.7 per cent of them work in hospital and the rest of them work in other government offices (3.3%). Hence, most of the female have selected teaching job to reasons such as high security and acceptance of teaching job from Muslim family especially their elder person and their husband.

On the other hand, the most important reasons of working women who take up a job is economic factors such as their economic necessity, to supplement family and to improve the standard of living. The results have shown that 76.7 per cent of Muslim women wear veil (Burqa). In addition 86.9 per cent of women who practice Purdah, remove it at their working place and they express reasons such as to emphasis by elder person, Islamic tradition and culture and to be Muslim.

The Extent of Participation of Muslim Working Women in Inside and Outside Home

The results reveal that less than half of the respondents (45.7%) do the household duties lonely such as cooking food, serving food, washing clothes, fetching water, looking after the children, cleaning utensils, caring aged persons, sick persons, etc. Moreover 8.4 per cent of women have expressed that their husbands cooperate with them in home, 9.7 per cent of them have presented that they use from servant and 36.2 per sent of them have to use from their children, mother-in-law, sister-in-law and others. According to above data, few of the Muslim men have extended support and cooperation to their wives by sharing some of household duties, and this condition can enhance with increasing Muslim men aware-level in family's structure.

In addition, decision-making and the distribution of power within the family is a basic element. Based on Edmund Dehlstrom "one of the most important objectives of the feminist movement has been to remove various external barriers to equally influence and participate in decision-making by women in the family, in working life, in organization and in public life." (Menon, 1981). Therefore we want to know how much decision-making power a Muslim working woman have in family's structure. In this study, we want to know how a Muslim woman enjoys decision-making power in family's structure. The results reveal that 42.7 per cent Muslim working women go to market to buy vegetables and grocery. Of course, less than half of them constitute never married, widow or divorced women that their male members are not available at home. Moreover, in families that male members were available, men did this duty as in this study 49.3 per cent men members in role of husband and father go to market. Hence we can express that an active role of woman in shopping/marketing returns more to non-availability of male members at home.

The data show that a proportion of married women have expressed that their men involved them in decision-making within family such as marriage and occupation of children (36.1%), traveling (32.7%), divide income family (27.6%) and buy and change house (25.5%), and in some respondent's families husband, father or other adult male members are also involved in taking decisions, so according to above results we can observe a change in the attitude of Muslim men towards their wives and their role in decision-making. Meanwhile the results indicate that economic autonomy of Muslim woman than other matters (marketing, marriage and occupation of children and traveling) in family's structure is low. As we asked "who controls the finance in your home?" that 70.3 per cent of married women have expressed their husband or male members in family (father or father-in-law). Furthermore 58.2 per cent of married women have expressed that they have freedom on their own earnings and 41.8 per cent of them have referred to lack of economic autonomy on their salary. On the other hand, we asked "does/did your husband expect your salary to be handed over to him?" the response was 61.2 pr cent "yes", 37.8 per cent "no" and 1 per cent "sometimes". Besides 6.7 per cent of them give their full salary to their husbands, 36.7 per cent of them their part of salary and 56.7 per cent of them whenever is required.

Hence according to above analyses, most of the working women give their salary to their husbands or in-laws and they can not spend it without the consent of their husbands. It is evident that it can affect the economic autonomy of Muslim working women. Goldstein found in her sample that 77 per sent of educated women turned over more than half of their earnings to their families. Urmila Patel stated that in some cases they are not given even the pocket allowance or the amount to buy things even for their personal use. They have to demand and are given some money as a grace granted to them (Upreti, 2000).

Hence a working woman has to give their full salary or part of salary to their husbands in the most of time, but as a matter of fact Muslim working women could obtain more economic autonomy than before, because 28.5 per cent of them are not totally ignored and they are being consulted in finance matters by their husbands. In the other words, today some of the men involved women in taking decisions especially in finance matters, and they also realized the importance of consulting their wives before taking family decisions.

On the other hand, the results show that a majority of the married women who possess personal property could not look after their personal property, and they have to depend upon their husbands, and they emphasis on skills and experience of their men. As in this study, it was found that there were several women who own houses (75%) and other forms (land and garden 25%) of wealth, but male members in the role of husband (78.2%), father (1.8%) and son (3.6%) look after their personal property.

Moreover take part in political activities also can raise individual autonomy of Muslim working women and it can give to women a better status. According to Krishna Hutheesing "if a nation is to be developed on the right lines to enable it to achieve something, its women must share the burden of planning and shaping its destiny side by side with the men, sharing the rough side of life as well as the smooth. Again, if we wish to achieve rapid and effective progress and to maintain a status of equality with other nations, women must have a definite role and can not be left out of the affairs of their country." (Menon, 1981).

In this study, we asked these questions from women "do you support any political party? And "do you like to become candidate for president/prime minister?" The responses were interesting as 97.3 per cent of women have presented that they don't support any political party, and also 81.3 per cent of them have expressed that don't like to become candidate for president/prime minister, and they have referred to reasons such as hard responsibility, not like cup of tea, not necessary, not time and was faced with men. Besides, it was attempted to find out whether Muslim working women possess membership of any professional organization/union. The results show that 12 per cent of women (18 women) were the members of professional organization/union that only 4 females were participating in organizational activities but not regular in a month.

While in the Islamic history there were no restrictions in women's full participation in the economic, political, and social spheres of society (Shamley, 1985), but as India is a traditional society, women have to practice existent traditions and customs. Hence political and social participation of a woman is low.

Effective Factors on Individual Autonomy of Muslim Working Women

In this study, we attempted to explore the factors that can affect to increase individual autonomy of Muslim working women. The results show that there are significant difference between individual autonomy of Muslim working women and kind of their occupations. In the other words, since the calculated X^2 value (41.938) is higher than the tabulated X^2 value (20.090) for 8 df at 1% level, then the null hypothesis (H0) is rejected (Table 19.1). Hence women who engage as faculty or head of the department and school have higher individual autonomy than the others.

Table 19.1. The Results of Chi-Square Test between Individual Autonomy and Occupation of Muslim working women

Variables	The Calculated X^2 Value	The Tabulated X^2 Value	df	Result
Individual Autonomy & Occupation of women	41.938	20.090	8	Significant

Sources: Primary data survey, 2007.

Moreover, Table 19.2 reveals that there are significant difference between individual autonomy of Muslim working women and their marital status. In the other words, since the calculated X^2 value (67.051) is higher than the tabulated X^2 value (16.812) for 6 df at 1% level, then the null hypothesis (H0) is rejected, and the results that divorced and widowed women have higher individual autonomy than the others.

Table 19.2. The Results of Chi-Square Test between Individual Autonomy and Marital Status of Muslim working women

Variables	The Calculated X^2 Value	The Tabulated X^2 Value	df	Result
Individual Autonomy & Marital Status of women	67.051	16.812	6	Significant

Sources: Primary data survey, 2007.

Table 19.3 reveals that since the calculated value of X^2 for 6 df at 1% level is 39.095 which exceeds the tabulated value (16.812), and the null hypothesis (H0) is rejected. Hence there are significant differences between individual autonomy of Muslim working women and their husband's qualification. As, male members that studied up to MA or Ph.D have given a higher individual autonomy to their wives. In other words, we can present that men's qualification could create a change in the attitude of male Muslims toward increasing of women individual autonomy.

Table 19.3. The Results of Chi-Square Test between Individual Autonomy of Muslim Working women and their Husband's Academic Qualification

Variables	The Calculated X^2 Value	The Tabulated X^2 Value	df	Result
Individual Autonomy & their Husband Qualification	39.095	16.812	6	Significant

Sources: Primary data survey, 2007.

Table 19.4 indicates that the calculated x^2 value is 41.168. The tabulated X^2 value at 1% level of probability is 16.812 for 6 degrees of freedom. This shows that the tabulated X^2 value is less than the calculated X^2 value. Therefore, the difference between the observed and the expected frequencies is significant. Hence, the null hypothesis is not accepted. Results stated that women who have higher academic qualification can obtain higher individual autonomy in their family's structure.

Table 19.4. The Results of Chi-Square Test between Individual Autonomy of Muslim working women and their Academic Qualification

Variables	The Calculated X^2 Value	The Tabulated X^2 Value	df	Result
Individual Autonomy & women Qualification	41.168	16.812	6	Significant

Sources: Primary data survey, 2007.

Table 19.5 reveals that there is a significant difference between individual autonomy of Muslim working women and their head of family. Since the calculated 't' value is significant, and it exceeds the tabulated 't' value. Meanwhile it indicates that the mean of individual autonomy rate among women who are the head of family are higher than the others. Hence the null hypothesis is rejected at P=%1, and the difference between variables is a real difference.

Table 19.5. The Results of T-Test between Individual Autonomy of Muslim Working Women and their head of family

Variables	The Calculated 't' Value	The Tabulated 't' Value	df	Result
Individual Autonomy of women & their head of family	4.018	2.374	113	Significant

Sources: primary data survey, 2007

The result of table 6 presents that there is not a significant difference between Individual Autonomy of Muslim Working Women and their property status. Since calculated 't'value is less than the tabulated 't'value. The null hypothesis was accepted at %5 level of significant. In the other words, the results express that women who possesses house, land, garden etc could not obtain suitable individual autonomy in family's structure.

Table 19.6. The Results of T-Test between Individual Autonomy of Muslim Working Women and their property status

Variables	The Calculated 't' Value	The Tabulated 't' Value	df	Result
Individual Autonomy & women property status	1.699	1.960	148	Non-significant

Sources: Primary data survey, 2007

Conclusion

Muslim working women in India constitute an important segment of society. They take up job out of home and have proved their skills and abilities in all the spheres of work, yet cultural and norms constrains have hindered their path of progress. Meanwhile patriarchal system have prohibited them to come equal with their male counterparts. Moreover they have to obey their male members in family. Though increasing education and consequent impact of modernization is gradually reducing the gender difference, but economic activity of women can not guarantee individual autonomy to them. In other words, education with employment has facilitated women to move a few steps ahead in social hierarchy but for raising individual autonomy of women need to be the other factors. As the results reveal that the individual autonomy of Muslim women has improved, but it allocates more to education, employment and marriage of their children etc and economic power structure in the family and control on family income was done by male members, and males are sharing less with their wives, but in fact we can find that the involvement of Muslim women in the decision-making process was begun. In addition, there are several factors that can affect on the individual autonomy of Muslim working women such as academic qualification of men as high education has certainly enabled men to understand the abilities and feelings of their wives. Another factor is marital status of women as most of the divorced and widowed women take decisions independently in management of household, of course women are head of family. Kind of women occupation is impact on their individual autonomy as most of the women who take up a high job in social structure can obtain experience in the field of management. As a matter of fact, high job and education among women lead to an increase in the development of social skills and self confidence and among men lead to increase their percipience and their aware level.

Therefore it is evident from the above discussion that a change is created in the attitude of Muslim men towards women and their role in individual autonomy, and women are not totally ignored and they are being consulted but for rising individual and economic autonomy of Muslim women need to increase aware level of men members in family's structure. Education of men seem to play a major role in the involving of Muslim women in the decision-making process, and also it can reduce error traditions among Muslims.

REFERENCES

1. Azim, Saukath.1997. *Muslim Women Emerging Identity*. Jaipur and New Delhi: Rawat Publications, pp. 148-166.
2. ACC Niagara Archives. http://www.niagara.com/~freedom/accniag/auto.htm.
3. Census of India 2001-2004. The First report on Religion Data. New Delhi: Registrar General & Census Commissioner. India.
4. Engineer, Ali Asghar. 1992. *The rights of Women in Islam*. New Delhi : Sterling Publishers Private Limited. p 44.
5. Menon, M. Indu.1981. *Status of Muslim Women in India: A Study of Kerala*. New Delhi: Uppal Publishing House, p. 81
6. Shamley, Zieba Shorish.1985. In http://WWW.afghan-web.com/articles/womenrights.html.
7. Steel, Miranda. 2006. *Oxford Wordpower Dictionary for learners of English*. New York: Oxford University Press, p. 38.
8. Upreti, H.C and Nandini, Upreti. 2000. *Women and Problems of Gender Discriminiation*.India: Pointer Publishers, p. 19.

Indigenous Veterinary Practice: A Case Study of Malekudiya Tribal Group of Coorg District., Karnataka

—Venugopal P.N.

Aim of the Paper

In the tribal areas of Karnataka, pastoral people keep alive the traditional veterinary practices based on the curative power of medicinal plants. The author present the most common remedies for the curing of diseases to the animals and analyze the data, concluding with a recommendation for a thorough pharmacological validation. This might be useful for the economic improvement of tribal societies.

Flora of Karnataka

The rich and diversified flora of Karnataka provides a most valuable storehouse of medicinal plants. The curative properties of herbs have long been known and are documented in ancient manuscripts, such as the Sanskrit *Rig Veda, Garuda Purana* and *Agni Purana*. These treatises focus on the potential of plants and herbs to cure human ailments and diseases. But the botanical wealth of Karnataka also offers the people who tend livestock a rich reservoir which they can tap in their efforts to treat the diseases and ailments of the animals they have for so long depended upon.

Indigenous Veterinary Knowledge

Given that Indian communities are traditionally tribal in nature, a great deal of knowledge in this field has been accumulated over the years. And this indigenous veterinary knowledge is also worth recording. There are no ancient manuscripts comparable to those mentioned above, but scientists are now documenting the various ethno-veterinary practices based on plant drugs. The present article is intended to contribute to this growing body of knowledge by supplying information on the plant-based ethno-veterinary curative techniques found in Coorg district, Karnataka (India).

Methodology

Description of the Study Area

Coorg or Kodagu district is located in the state of Karnataka, south India. It is a hilly and heavy rain fall area and habitat for more than 7 different types of natives. Altitudes ranges from 220-2400 m above the sea level. The annual rainfall in Coorg district may be anywhere from 400 to 1230 mm, and temperatures ranges from 5 to 30 degrees centigrade. Parts of the district are covered with green forest, resulting in subtropical to temperate areas alternating with evergreen forests (Western Ghats). The area of investigation approximately lies between 75°0′ to 79°0′ longitude and 21°0′ 34° to 0° latitude. Male Kudiya's are found in different elevations from 300 m to 2,200 MSL in Coorg district. There are a number of hill ranges in the study area. Temperature ranges from 18° to 25° during March–April in high hill ranges and averages between 20° during December and 38° during April–May.

Agricultural Economy

The seasonal crops grown in the Coorg district are—rice coffee and spices, cardamom, potatoes, black pepper, and ginger. These are the major economics crops of the district.

Ethno Botanical Survey

The fieldwork was conducted in several villages around Kodagu district forest areas as part of a study of ethno-botanical wealth of Male Kudiya tribals in Karnataka. More than 30 families and nearly 100 members of Male Kudiyas are found in the study area. During the stay, their daily activities were closely observed and interpersonal contacts were established by participating in several of their social and religious ceremonies such as marriages, rituals and curing sessions. There were 17 informants (14 males and 3 females) between the ages of 35 to 68 year in the study area. Among them 11 were farmers, 8 were housewives and 5 regular tribal practitioners.

Day-to-day Practice

Various types of livestock play a vital role in the agriculture-based economy of many Coorg tribes. In Male Kudiya tribal group normally goats, chickens, buffaloes, cows and pigs plays a vital role in the economy. The people of Male Kudiyas considered expert goat breeders and best pig breeders. Since this groups have to deal with various health problems among their domestic animals, including fractures and diseases like abdominal discomfort, flatulence and convulsion they are largely depend on their traditional way of curing various common aliments.

The Knowledge Required

Some livestock ailments require the assistance of a specialist. Since the government veterinary dispensary is far away, people have to rely on traditional veterinary practices as a first line of treatment. The traditional knowledge of plant-based remedies for the treatment of animals rests with the medicine men, all of whom belong to one family of hereditary indigenous practitioners. Skills and experience are passed on from one generation to the next by word of mouth, and are guarded like secrets. The medicine-man collects the plants needed for a particular veterinary application, either directly from the forest or from the local shops.

Practice and Treatment

The following alphabetical list contains the correct botanical name (genus and species) of each entry, with family name (in brackets and italics) and, when known, name in common English [in square brackets]. The local name (in inverted commas) is followed by a brief botanical description. Finally, the therapeutic uses for specific livestock diseases are given.

Aegle marmelos (L.) Correa (*Rutaceae*) [bael or bel fruit] 'Vilvam', 'Vilva'. A deciduous, armed tree. Flowers white, fruit immature green, mature yellow; commonly cultivated.

The fruit is roasted and the contents carefully removed. A paste is prepared with water and used as a poultice to treat swollen and painful joints in cattle.

Allium cepa L. cv. group Common Onion *(Liliaceae* or *Alliaceae)* [onion] 'Vengayam'. An erect bulbous herb with white flowers; cultivated for its edible bulbs.

A mixture of 250 g onion bulbs and 250 g solidified jaggery (unrefined brown sugar made of palmwine derived from fruit of the toddy palm *Borassus flabelifer* L.) is pounded into a dry paste. This is administered orally each morning for ten consecutive days, to stimulate the virility and reproductive performance of bulls.

Ceiba pentandra (L.) Geartn. (*Bombacaceae*) [kapok, white silk-cotton tree] 'Elavam', 'Ilavamaram'. A large, branched deciduous tree; cultivated.

The leaves are pounded together with fermented boiled rice water and the extract is administered to cows orally as a remedy for reproductive problems. Dose: approx. 500 ml three times a day for three consecutive days.

Calotropis gigantea (L.) Dryander (*Asclepiadaceae*) [gigantic swallow root, ginat milk weed, swallow wort] 'Erukku'. An erect, branched herb or subshrub with milky latex. Flowers purple; common in waste places.

A handful of leaves are crushed and given orally to cattle to make them more alert and active.

Cissus quadrangularis L. (*Vitaceae*) [quadrangular cissus] 'Perandai'. A climbing shrub with tendrils. Stem quadrangular. Flowers greenish-yellow; common along hedges in fields.

The whole plant is crushed into paste and given orally to newborn calves to facilitate removal of the placenta. After swallowing the paste, the calf will start to vomit.

Datura metel L. (*Solanaceae*) [hindu datura] 'Karu-oomathai', 'Oomathai'. An erect herb or subshrub. Flowers white; common in waste places.

A seed paste mixed with water is applied to the patella (knee cap) area in cattle, to relieve pain and swelling. The paste is also used to treat eczema and other skin problems.

Erythrina suberosa Roxb. *(Leguminosae)* 'Mullu Murungai'. An armed, deciduous tree with trifoliate leaves. Flowers dark red; cultivated.

The leaf paste is mixed with water and given orally to cattle as a cure for severe coughing and bronchitis.

Lablab purpureus (L.) Sweet *(Leguminosae)* [hyacinth bean] 'Avarai'. A climbing herb with trifoliate leaves. Flowers pinkish violet; cultivated.

The leaf paste is applied to boils and sores to draw out the pus.

Leucas aspera (Willd.) Link *(Labiatae)* 'Thumbai'. An erect, hirsute herb. Flowers white; common on wasteland.

The leaf paste is applied to wounds to promote healing.

Luffa acutangula (L.) Roxb. *(Cucurbitaceae)* [Chinese okra] 'Pekenkai'. A climber with tendrils. Flowers yellow; cultivated for its edible fruits.

The leaf paste is applied to the neck region of cattle to treat the swelling and sores of yoke gall.

Musa xparadisiaca L. or ***Musa*** (AAB group) *(Musaceae)* [French plantain] 'Vazhai'. An erect, tree-like herb, with large leaves. Inflorescence paniculate, bract spathaceous, large and green; cultivated.

The flowers and fruits are crushed and made into a paste with dry ginger *(Zingiber officinale)*, pepper (*Piper nigrum*), black myrobalan (*Terminalia chebula*), nutmeg *(Myristica fragrans)* and karanda (*Carissa carandas*); this is given orally to cattle for all forms of severe diarrhoea.

Piper betle L. (*Piperaceae*) [betel pepper] 'Vethalai'. A climbing herb with cordate leaves; cultivated.

Ten betel leaves and 20 g of dry black pepper are made into a paste and given orally to cattle as a cure for digestive disorders and flatulence. This is repeated two to three times.

Solanum surattense Burm. f. (*Solanaceae*) [nightshade] 'Kandakathiri'. A diffuse, prostrate, armed herb. Flowers purple, fruits globose, immature green; common.

The leaves of this plant are made into a paste with hot water. The extract is mixed in neem oil (*Azadirachta indica*) and given orally to cattle as a remedy for all types of chronic cough.

Tamarindus indica L. *(Leguminosae)* [Indian tamarind] 'Puli'. A large, branched tree. Flowers light-yellow; cultivated.

The leaf paste is applied as a poultice, to reduce pain and swelling in the joints of cattle.

Tribulus terrestris L. *(Zygophyllaceae)* [ground burnut] 'Nerunji'. A prostrate herb with yellow flowers; common on wasteland.

The seed paste is given orally to newborn calves to facilitate removal of the placenta (cf above, Cissus quadrangularis).

Zingiber officinale Roscoe (*Zingiberacea*) [ginger] 'Ingi'. An erect herb with rhizome; cultivated.

A paste is made up which consists of 10 g each of dry ginger, pepper, asafoetida (*Ferula asafoetida*), and sweet flag (*Acorus calamus*) in hot water. This extract is administered orally to cattle as a cure for gastric problem.

Conclusion

After reviewing the present status of usage of medicinal plant cultivation in Karnataka for the various animal aliments and local demand, I feel there is ample room for improvement. The sector has traditionally occupied an important position in the socio-cultural, spiritual and medical arena of rural and tribal lives of India. In recent years, due to growing recognition of natural products and process in sustaining human and environmental health, the economic as well as environmental importance of the medicinal plant resources have increased tremendously. These improvements can be done by government organizations as well as by NGOs.

Perception of Disease and Curative Measure: A Case Study of Koraga Tribe of Karnataka

—Nanjunda D.C., Venugopal P.N., Annapurna, M.

Abstract

Health education sometimes fails to demonstrate an in-depth understanding the existing cultural meanings that indigenous people associate with health behavior. Health education programmes must be based on sacred values so as to make them culturally acceptable. The proposed study will examine indigenous medicine from an emic prospective, taking into consideration cultural symbols and meanings and their integration with the culture. The findings of this study will help explain the reasons for lack of complete acceptance of different medical systems, including modern medicine. This is some preliminary observation based on the filedwork done so for

Introduction

The origin of Koragas is associated with a few legends such as rise and fall of certain dynasties and empires in the pre-historic period of northern Kerala. Thus Koragas are believed to be the ancestors of a defeated dynasty, which was driven to forests and subsequently became slaves to the mighty. Another legend is regarding the issues of a Brahmin woman by a sudra. It is said that the social unacceptability of their children in the caste-dominated society was so rigid that the children were looked down upon with contempt and their future generation was named as Koraga.

The area of habitation of Koraga is Kasaragod district. According to the PTG survey 1996-97, the population of Koragas is 1349. Their population during 1981 Census was 1098. A study undertaken during 1988 by KIRTADS, the State's Tribal Research Institute, shows that the Koraga population during 1998 is only 1330. The diminishing trend is not much significant as in the case of Cholanaikans. Considerable number of Koragas is seen in Karnataka state also.

Due to their unhygienic way of life all other communities used to observe untouchability with Koragas. In earlier days they used to remove carcasses and ate the decaying flesh of dead animals. Even now a section of the non-tribals treat them as unapproachable and untouchable and all of them were slaves till the state banned slavery through the Bonded Labour Abolition Act. The Koragas speak a language of their own with resemblance to Tulu and Kannada. They have very little interaction with other communities.

In Kasaragod district, Koraga live in 52 settlements distributed in Kodagu, Daksin Kannada districts of Karnataka state. A large faction of the Koragas is engaged with basket making. In olden days a few were engaged in scavenging. They used to beg rather than undertaking agriculture activities or minor forest produce collection. Koragas were experts in crocodile capturing and they used to eat its flesh. Now none of this occupation could give them the subsistence level income for their livelihood. The conventional Koraga houses are thatched huts with grass or leaves, with open sides. Now more than 80 per cent families have received departmental houses. The traditional God of Koragas is Sun. *Mariarnma* and *Kata* (swami) are their popular gods. However, the new generation is interested in worshipping the Hindu gods. They bury the dead.

Health Concept

Every society, advanced or primitive, has its own beliefs and practices regarding health and diseases. Perceptions of illness, customs and practices direct the health-seeking behavior of a community. The socio-cultural pattern of a community is one of the major factors influencing the availability and use of different kinds of treatment. Health and disease are related to the sociological and cultural resources of a community in a specific environment health status is not determined just by the availability of health services or pharmaceuticals. It is the result of an interwoven tapestry of factors, such as socio-economic status, education, community and spiritual wellness, cultural and family support systems, and employment opportunities etc.

The study of such ethno-medical forms of therapy constitutes an extensive and important arena of study. It includes both magic-religious, mechanical and chemical procedure studies conducted on practise regarding therapeutic knowledge. Studies conducted in indigenous society have documented an impressive array of medical practices that demonstrate empirical therapeutic knowledge that includes bone setting and inoculation. A small number of studies have also explored cultural factors and situations that determine the ways in which symptoms are defined by those participating in the healing process like medicinal man. In addition, studies have shown that ethno-medical therapies are not employed simply.

Koraga tribe believes in supernatural powers, they have strong feeling those different deities, and spirits are responsible for causation of different diseases. The spirits of dead ancestors are also believed to play a vital role in ensuring good health. There is a strong belief that persons emanating evil, having mystical powers like evil eye, and evil touch can also affect or deteriorates the health of a person. These people do not associate disease and epidemics with their insanitery condition of living but associate them to the wrath of the gods and goddesses.

Koraga believe that diseases and misfortunes are caused by hostile spirits, ghosts of the dead or by the use of evil powers by enemies, that a diseases caused by evil spirits can only be cured by spiritual powers, this is the main idea behind their system of treatment. In case of illness a person who could not move, is bed ridden, has physical discomfort, has a loss of appetite, is unable to perform daily activities, is having certain physiological disorder, then a person is considered to be ill by majority of Koraga population. Koraga also believe that certain diseases take time to reveal physical mal-functioning.

Therefore, for all aliments they go to the traditional heeler. These medical practitioners are valuable resources for providing primary care to community. They are more readily accepted by their own people than the health workers and allopathic doctors. Traditional medicine system is widely prevalent among Koraga tribes. In adoption to the magic-religious, herbal and indigenous methods of treatment few folks also follows allopathic system of medicine.

Their attitude towards the God is one of fear and dread. The Koragas deities are regularly worshiped and their divine rites are performed as and when situation demands, They feel failure to perform certain divine ceremonies and rituals may result into health hazards and terrifying climates. The Koragas beliefs in spirits and ghosts are not very different from those of the plain farmers, they believe evil spirits are responsible for bringing about trouble and sickness.

The state of illness according to the Koragas is an intermediate stage between life and death. They think it occurs due to an imbalance, co-ordination and disharmony between body, mind and soul. Further they believe illness occurs due to the disruption of man's relationship with his fellowman, other social groups, evil spirits, cosmic forces and entitles and the natural agents. Koraga think illness experiences and ritual healing are also an expression of the problems faced by the cosmic, supernatural, and ancestral beings, which are solved by humans beings through the process of ritual healing at spiritual level. Healing ritual symbols reveal cultural reality. Traditional medicinal men play vital role in case of various illness problems treatment according to the age, gender and severance of the patient. Koraga also respect people who are experts in different types of magic. It was also observed that the Koraga believe that people die as a result of becoming victims of witchcraft, sorcery, wrath of gods and evil etc. To prevent this certain rituals are performed to please these malevolent folks that take away life.

Conclusion

It is required to establish a Traditional Medicine Initiative to foster formal relationships between local service units and traditional healers, so that cultural values and beliefs, as well as traditional healing practices, are respected and affirmed by the people as an integral component of the healing process. The correlation between health and beliefs has been shown in many studies and has a large influence over the behavior choices that can result in improved health. The wide spread prevalence of unique health seeking behavior, poverty, illiteracy, malnutrition, absence of safe drinking water and sanitary conditions, poor maternal and child health services, ineffective coverage of national health and nutritional services, etc. have been found, as possible contributing factors of dismal health condition prevailing amongst the primitive tribal communities of the country. Many of the infectious and parasitic diseases can be prevented with timely intervention, health awareness activities.

REFERENCES

1. Anand (2005) "Primitive Medicine and its Scope", *Medical Anthropology Quarterly*, Vol. 3, No. 5.
2. Ailion, (1991) "Illness, Culture and Meaning: Some Comments on the Nature of Traditional Medicine", Medical Anthropology Quarterly, Vol. 21, No. (2-3), pp. 21-34.
3. Bhasin, V. (1990) "Habit, Habitat and Health in the Himalayas: A Comparative Study of the People of Sikkam and the Gaddis of Himachal Pradesh", *Journal of Human Ecology*, New Delhi, Vol. 8, No. 2, pp. 32-40.
4. Kumar (2004) "Health among the Indian Tribes", *Indian Journal of Anthropological Society*, 39:57-66.
5. Srider, (2005) "Medical World of Selected Tribes of Karnataka (India)", *Medical Anthropology Review*, Vol. 21, No. (5-6), pp. 32-39.

Miracles of Religion and Spirituality: Anthropological Analysis of Faith Healing

—Aneela Sultana

Introduction

Faith is the trust, or belief in the truth of revealed religions. Healing is cure, to treat or to remedy. Faith healing is the system of belief that sickness may be cured without medical application, if the prayer be accompanied in the sufferer by true faith. Faith healing is performed by faith healers in their own specialized field of knowledge through their own strong belief. All religions to some degree have commonalities and provide guidance to a balanced social order through a cross system of unquestioned beliefs. So faith healing revolves around belief which is the main ingredient of religion. Faith healers act as preachers and parishioners of religion. Faith healing is also the exercise to control by religious means what cannot be controlled by other ways through prayer, sacrifice and ritual activity. Faith healing is—related to spirituality through which one seeks heightened effect from the divine to remedy bodily and mental disabilities without medical care to satisfy the biological and psychological needs. Spiritual healing is a concept of intense degree of belief in the power of Divinity to the extent of total dependence for any kind of treatment or solutions to problems. Spiritual healing is the healing of soul through a frame of mind that is highly refined in thoughts, feelings and free from sensuality.

This paper draw its finding from anthropological six-months fieldwork which was carried out in Burhan, district Attock, tehsil Hassan Abdal, with a population of about 8,000. The socio-economic survey was conducted from 80 households only and the total population of the selected households was 616 persons comprising 56 per cent males and 64 per cent females. Anthropological research methods (Participants observation, in-depth interviews, focus group discussion) were used for data collection. The principal objective of this paper was to describe the significance of traditional healing practices which are popular among the community. The main research question was to explore the role of faith healers in recovering social, economic, physical and psychological problems of the people and also to discover the spiritual aspects of healing in relation to the belief system of community.

The data reveals that people consider faith healers as their guide, and teacher, who resolve their social, medical, economic and other problems. They justify their belief that they need someone for direction and to rely on in difficult times. According to them, faith healer is a person who is gifted to have direct communication with the supernatural powers of universe, from where he derives knowledge, belief and strength to help those who are in pain and misery. In this way, faith healers strongly influence the behaviour of their believers. But the status of faith healers depends on their reputation and success. Reputation is achieved through finding solution to problems by healing the people with or without medical treatment. If the faith healer is popular among the people he can bring significant changes in the lives of his followers.

Faith healers are locally known as *Pirs*. *Pir** is the persian word literally means as "old man" or "elder". The term is usually applied to the religious guides and saints. *Pir* is one who achieves this status through his personal spiritual qualities and knowledge of religion, which gives him the spiritual power to cure people with his spiritual strength and faith. There are two types of *Pirs*. One is the living *Pir* whose physical presence matters cures people with the spiritual knowledge and physical touch through faith in divinity. Most of living *Pirs* dedicate their lives for the welfare of their followers. The second category is the deceased *Pir* who resides in the heart and mind of his followers. His grave normally has a shrine or *Ziarats*** status. Due to his displayed spiritual qualities in his life time his name is remembered for good through the shrine built by his followers. They pray for the diseased *Pirs* believing that the Pir is closer to God. So showing faith to faith healers will eventually please God

In developed countries medical problems are first addressed into the medicalcare and health system and serious problems where the hope is lost are addressed to faith healers who work on providing the psychological strength to the patients to accept the medical administration (as in case of HIV and Cancer). However, in our rural communities where mostly people are not literate and the healthcare facilities are lacking, poverty level is high, people seek help from the faith healers first and if no remedy is effective and patient gets serious, then they go to the doctor. People visit shrines to cure their ailments. Cure is achieved by contacting the saint, living or dead, touching the saint's clothes or body. Oil or wax from the light of shrines is used to recover from pain and infections. Barren women mostly take shower at shrine and leave all their accessories over there. After ritual bath, they eat something sweet to recover their infecundity and to have healthy children.

Shrines are also contacted for the cure of diseases related to the supernatural powers and specifically treated by the faith healers whom people believe. In local terminology, they are known as *saya, athra* and *parchawan*. The interpretation of these diseases is that supernatural takes revenge for any kind of mistake a person has done. Such treatment are taken as beyond human control and can only be cured by faith healers with proper

---

*Holy person and saint.

**Shrine.

knowledge of detection and treatment of such diseases, using supernatural powers to hold the supernatural being.

*Saya**: in this disorder, the person sees scary nightmares with weird evil deformed faces of humans and animals, to be frightened out of sleep. It is believed that females are more prone to this disorder because they are comparatively weaker and more sensitive. Another popular notion is that evil spirits get attracted by women's beauty. Spirit possession, is sometimes used as a tactic to express latent and oppressed wishes which are not acceptable in normal social circumstances.

Sometimes spirit possession can develop into schizophrenia, a statement given by Ruth S. Freed. If we see spirit possession from the psychological point of view, it is some form of mental imbalance and derangement, and some of the patients of spirit possession did how symptoms similar to schizophrenic cases. Mental worries, anxiety, depression and frustration, all are effecting the mental health of the individual, leading possibly to mental illness. According to Ruth S. Freed the primary gain of an attack of spirit possession is in fact to relieve the tension; the patient's second benefit is to draw attention and sympathy from influencing relatives, which is obviously not possible under normal circumstances.

Moreover, Linda Giles in her work on the Swahili discusses how people who are possessed do not necessarily belong to marginalized groups; in the case of the Swahili she feels it is a central group of people (often educated, wealthy and westernized) who are part of the cult; also possession for them does not lie outside the realm of Islam. Giles discovered that people from all ethnic backgrounds and social status were present in the possession cults; moreover, although women formed the majority of membership, men also did feature to a considerable extent in the cults (Giles, p. 243).

It is interesting to note that Gluckman for example asserts the fact that spirit possession in effect, contributes to conserving a stable society, echoing the approach of Radcliffe Brown. Another factor is that these cults are allowed to exist even by the men, despite the fact that they reflect the sexual tensions in society. Lewis argues that this may underpin the contradiction between the peripheral status of women in society and their biological role/ commitment to it. Spirit possession is also seen as a way of classifying disease, while ignoring the explanations provided by modern science.

Spirit possession seems to have been substituted by psychoanalysis in the contemporary era. Lewis draws an analogy between spirit possession and psychotherapy, stating that both follow the same 'affective' and contextual logic (Lewis, p. 51). According to Levi-Strauss the functions served by the Shaman for the sick are linked to reinforcing belief within the community; as a spiritual authority, the Shaman's diagnosis and cure locate the patient's ailment in a spiritual context, thereby providing a 'metaphor for personal healing', which gives meaning and cause to his suffering. 'The Shaman provides the sick woman with a language, by means of which unexpressed and otherwise inexpressible, psychic states can be immediately expressed'. By providing a context to the ill, the Shaman 'renders acceptable to the mind pains which the body refuses to tolerate' (Levi-Strauss, p. 197).

---

*Spirit possession.

*Athra** and *Parchawan**: Athra* is the disorder of pregnant females and it causes premature delivery. It causes still birth or immediate death after birth. In this disorder, mother goes through a big physical and psychological trauma and it also causes many matrimonial problems and affects her respect and status in the family. In *parchawan*[9], it is considered that a woman who has miscarriages or had a abortion or still birth will transfer this disorder to another pregnant women due confinement period. So during 40 days of confinement she is kept isolated and is not supposed to talk to anyone.

For the treatment of *saya*, faith healer recites specific verses from Quran to destroy the effect of evil spirit's power. *Taveez* and *dam darood* follow this. The minimum time for the cure of such ailments is from one to two months to years, depending upon the severity of disorder. The patients of saya also wear black thread around their neck, wrist, and anklet. The disorders of *athra* and *parchawan* are also treated by faith healers in addition to prayers at shrines. In *athra* the local remedy for the woman is wear a black thread around neck, wrist or anklet throughout the pregnancy. She has to drink the *taveez* twice a month with specific Quranic verses written on them.

Social and domestic problems are also treated by faith healers. The typical social problems encountered for which the help is sought from faith healers include, good proposals for daughters, to get rid of economic misery, to make annoyed husband happy, to have control over in-laws, to recover infertility, to have sons, and to ward off the effects of evil eye.

Persons visiting the healer for social problems are given a patient hearing in complete privacy, while the ones with medical problems are treated in front of others to prove his skills. In fact, the faith healer asked the other followers present at the time to pray for the medically sick person. There are different ways of treatment used by the faith healers. Their most common practicing medium of treatment include *Dam Darood*, wearing and drinking of *Taweez,* use of different kinds of *taveez* for different applications and involvement of magic in *taveez* and other procedures related to it.

*Dam Darood**** is the most common technique used by the *pir* is *dam* (literally, breath). In this method, the saint simply recites Quranic verse with mind concentration and then blows on the patient. If a person has pain in his/her specific part of body then the saint focuses his breath on that aching area. By uttering a specific verse of the Qur'an, the powers of this verse in the form of blessings are also transferred to relieve the pain.

Dam is most popular for common ailments. Another way of performing of this practice is known as *dam-pani* (literally, breath-water). Here, the saint utters a Qur'anic verse on water instead of blowing directly on the aching body part of the patient. Then he stipulates the procedure of drinking this blessed water. Usually, the water is to be drunk for a specified number of days in specific timings. Specific Quranic verses for specific aches that are recited. The same procedure of dam is performed on other things such as sugar and salt.

---

*Local term for a disease which causes premature delivery.

**Evil shadow.

***Spelling a charm.

Wearing and drinking *Taveez* is another technique used in faith healing. *Taveez** is a piece of paper with written Quranic verses, folded in clothe, leather, polethene paper or in silver or gold wrappings. There are specific *taveez* for different problems. Some are worn around neck and some are tied with arm or thigh. Some amulets are advised to be worn around the waist. Sometimes, *pir* recommends keeping taveez in the room or house of sick person. Some *taveezs* are to be dipped or mixed with water to drink or bathe, and are used until all the writings on the *taveez* is dissolved or washed from the paper. Some taveez need to be put on fire and sometimes they need to be hung from the trees or to be nailed on wall. Mostly, it is recommended to keep taveez under a heavy object to increase its effectiveness. But the fact is that faith or the will-power is pre-requisite in this method of faith healing.

There are different types of *taveez* for each problem such as for *Jumla Amraz* which means various types of diseases and it includes *taveez* for headache, earache, stomachache, backache, toothache, foot ache, etc. *taveez* for *Jumla Maqasid* are related to all types of desires like good proposals, control over husband and in-laws, for economic prosperity etc. *Taveez* for *Hifazat-e-Hamal* (safe pregnancy) and *Aaṣani-e-Bacha* (Safe delivery) are given to married and pregnant women.

Taveez also plays an important role in magical practices. Such *taveez* can be for good or bad purpose, so are named accordingly as positive and negative *taveez*. Positive *Taveez* is used in white magic applied for positive results. White magic is known as *nuri'ilm* (Luminous knowledge) and it meant to eliminate miseries, dilemmas, evil eye, illness, effects of negative *taveez* or removal from passion of evil spirits and beings like *jin, churail,* evil shadow….such positive *taveez* or white magic bring prosperity, good health, benefits and good fortune.

Healing through Negative *Taveez* in local terminology is known as *kala'ilm* or *'kala jadoo'***. This type of *taveez* reflects sin because in such type of *taveez* Quranic verses are written in reverse, using blood, urine or other body discharges, depending on the person's target. This is considered as an unpardonable act as it can cause fatal diseases and death. It is used against enemies and rivals to bring them difficulties like illness, financial loss, family disputes or fatal diseases leading to death. These *taveezs* are placed secretly in victim's house. Sometimes people realize the presence of *taveez* so they consult the faith healer to eliminate the effects. If the effect is illness it may be incurable even by the *Pir*, but if he get to know the presence of *taveez* early enough, precautionary measures are taken to reduce the effects. The impression is that the positive *taveez* can reduce the effects of negative *taveez.*

Few *taveez* are also used to ward off evil eye or as a precautionary measure. Such *taveez* are worn by young boys and girls, little children, pregnant women, even milk giving animals, fruitful trees, crops, prosperous living families, happily married couples, newly constructed houses, etc as are adorned with *taveez* to ward off evil eye.

---

*The literal meaning of taveez in English is "Amulet". According to the oxford dictionary, amulet means 'a thing worn as a charm against evil.'

**Black magic.

Conclusion

Faith healing is the process of preventing and curing illness or disease through a belief in an omnipotent force or creator (God) of the universe. It is a healing process that focuses on both the body and the mind. An important foundation for successful healing in a spiritual context is faith, which has always been at the core of spirituality and religion. Faith healer is a person who is gifted to have direct communication with the Supernatural power of universe, from where he derives knowledge, belief and strength to be communicated in different expressive and non-expressive forms including magic. The research findings reveal that whenever a man is in problem and despair he needs someone who can console and give guidance to his problem. In such circumstances, faith healers are the most reliable persons with whom people can share their socio-medical and spiritual problems.

NOTES

1. Ahmed, Imtiaz, 1975. *Religion and the Rituals among the Muslims of the Sub-continent*. Vunglar Press: India.
2. Claude Levi-Strauss, 1993. *Structural Anthropology*. Stanford University Press: Stanford.
3. Findings from Fieldwork
4. Foster, G.M., Anderson. 1978. *Medical Anthropology*. John Willey & Sons.
5. Ian Lewis., 2000. *Religion in Context*, Harper Collins: Australia.
6. Linda Giles. 1987. *Possession Cults on the Swahili coast: a re-examination of theories of marginality*. Africa.
7. Stanely and Ruth S. Freed, John Middleton. 1967 eds. *Magic, witchcraft and curing*. Natural History Press: Garden City.

Life in Slums: An Anthroplogical Study of Bahawalpur, Pakistan

—Rana Ejaz Ali Khan and Tasnim Khan

Abstract

One of the United Nations Millennium Development Goals (MDGs) is to achieve significant improvement in lives of at least 100 million slums dwellers, by 2020. The MDG target 11 set by Government of Pakistan to improve the lives of slum dwellers is to regulate the 95 per cent of katchi abadis (identified by the cut-off date of 1985) by 2015. Along with it, under Poverty Reduction Strategy Paper (PRSP) and Mid-term Development Framework (MTDF) the target was/is to regulate the 60 and 75 per cent of katchi abadis by 2005-06 and 2009-10 respectively. To see the implications and prospects of these targets the paper probes the life in slums of Bahawalpur as a case study. In this data-based micro study we assess the situation of living conditions (potable water supply, sanitation, public utilities, sufficient living area, household with durable material), household characteristics (compositions, headship, type of employment and educational status, etc.) social safety nets (transfer payments and micro-finance), women laborforce participation and their contribution, health and educational status of children and child labor. To identify the slum areas, an operational definition of slums has been developed, that is slightly different in the part of water availability, sanitation and building material, from that given by UN-Habitat. In this way twelve clusters are taken as sample spreading over whole of the Bahawalpur city. The study provides a micro-view of the standard of living of slum households to the planners and policy-makers along with policy proposals to frame the strategy for improvement of lives in slums. The study concludes that urban slums are the poorest in the urban community from a number of poverty perspectives. They represent poverty pocket and need targeted policies. The multi-pronged, short and medium term policies need attention in the areas of housing, education, health, sanitation and income generating activities. Most of all the social safety nets can play an important role. The district governments may act as identifying and implementing agencies.

Introduction

Over 150 million people currently inhabit Pakistan and despite a reduced population growth rate of 2.28 for 2010-2020, this number is expected to increase to 227 million in 2020. The number of households will increase to 3861 thousands from the current number of 2950 thousands. It is important to note that most of this growth will occur in urban areas as ratio of urban population will increase from 36.9 to 42.4 per cent in 2020. The year of 2020 is the target year for Millennium Development Goals (MDGs) along with others, for improving the lives of at least 100 million slum dwellers. Differences in living conditions, access to services, opportunities for development and ultimately income are seen as major source of many conflicts. These differences can be observed within the country (rich and poor regions[1] as well as urban and rural areas[2]) but also within cities where the gap between wealthy living in gated communities and the poor living in intolerable housing conditions is expanding. Aggregate data at the city level hides such stark contrast of income and living conditions between better-off urban citizens and the urban poor by providing just a single figure. The traditions of providing urban versus rural estimates have further aggravated the crisis that cities are facing. Figures for urban areas average out rich and poor, by providing a single number that overlooks pockets of poverty and destitution in cities. Analysis of data at the city level is fundamental for accurate policy formation. In addition to that, the urban poverty is characterized by a different set of challenges than that of rural ones that is over-crowded areas with insufficient and overused water and sanitation infrastructure, exposure to hazards[3] and crime as well as social fragmentation.

Generally, the concentration of people and activities in cities is regarded as being economically beneficial for a country. However, some complex factors determine the slum incidence in urban areas. One of them is rapid urbanization due to rural-urban migration. Lack of employment opportunities and prevalence of poverty in rural areas push the people to urban areas. Urban areas do not have sufficient employment opportunities for rapidly increasing population[4]. As a consequence, there emerges informal employment opportunities[5], which are unstable and yield low incomes. The resulting poverty in combination with a variety of factors like lack of affordable housing, ethnic politics, inadequate housing program, bad governance, corruption, inappropriate regulation, dysfunctional land market and fundamental lack of political will act as catalysts for the formation of informal settlements commonly known as slums. They offer only sub-standard living conditions to their inhabitants. Along these informal settlements, many established in historical city cores may be classified as slums because they have high residential and commercial densities and over-crowding, as well as have low levels of public utilities. This is especially evident in streets that are too narrow and irregular. In addition, the drains and water supply pipes often leak, and electricity and telephone cables, many of them unofficial, festoon the streets. In many such instances, the original city is separated from the more modern city by its old defensive wall. Slums of such kind are found in Lahore (old walled city of Lahore) and Karachi. These are classic inner-city slums[6].

The term slum simply refers to lower-quality or informal housing. The tracts of squatter or informal housing are connected with perception of poverty, lack of access to basic services and insecurity. The term such as slums, shanty, squatter settlement, informal housing and low-income community are used somewhat interchangeably by authors, agencies and authorities. The coverage of slums becomes more complex when a variety of equivalent words in other languages and geographical regions exists. For instance, *Gharibabad, Merzipura, Khuda Ki Basti* for informal settlement in Pakistani cities[7]. There are slums that are equivalent to cities in size. The example is Orangi in Karachi, with a population of over 500,000. Generally such slums are inner-city squatters[8].

Although little specific survey information is available on slum dynamics at the national level in Pakistan, but it is clear that slums are on the rise. Estimates indicate an increase of slums close to 50 per cent between 1988 and 2000 or from 3.4 to 5 million slum dwellers. In 1985, 5.5 million people were living in 2302 *katchi abadis* comprising 0.86 million households (EUAD, 1987). Currently, there are 3000 *katchi abadis* in Pakistan with a population of 7 million. Some estimates show that slum dwellers are more than 9 million at present. There are 630 slums in Punjab, located on the land owned by government departments like Civil Aviation Authority, Wapda, the Pakistan Railways, the Public Works Department, Irrigation Department, the Lahore Development Authority, the Auqaf Department and the Evacuee Trust Property Board. In Lahore 145 *katchi abadis* are located. Multan, Faisalabad, Sahiwal, Rahim Yar Khan and Gujranwala have 87, 59, 57, 42 and 31 *katchi abadis*, respectively. Accordingly to some other estimates there are more than 900 *katchi abadis* in Punjab (Anwer and Zafar, 2003). By looking at these figures, it seemed a myth that the people in urban areas are automatically better off than those of rural areas. The figures may increase unless development agencies scale up their efforts to improve the living conditions of urban dwellers. The fight against poverty has to take place in both urban and rural areas. Still, urban poverty receives relatively little attention from policy-makers and authorities. In 1985 government of Punjab made efforts to regularize and improve the *katchi abadis*. During 1985-90 Katchi Abadis Improvement Program (KIP) was implemented. The emphasis was on provision of safe and secure housing, potable drinking water, sanitary facilities, basic amenities as well as social services and clean environment[9].

In Pakistan, the first major slum-upgrading and poverty alleviation program at the national level was proposed for the period 1988-93. The program largely failed to meet its targets and it regularized only 1 per cent of the *katchi abadis* per year due to faulty land record, corruption and non-inclusion of gross root organizations. The Social Action Program, 1993 supported NGOs for infra-structural improvements, but failed due to lack of capacity. Even there is lack of effective impact monitoring rather yearly reviews based on the feed back of implementing agencies.

Recently, according to a press release[10], Federal Ministry of Local Government and Rural Development (LG & RD) is working expeditiously for the formulation of a policy to regularize the *katchi abadis* consequent upon Prime Minister 100 Day Plan of Action. Federal Minister for LG & RD has directed the concerned to expedite the finalization of regularization policy making. According to Ministry *kachi abadis* which are socially and environmentally sustainable urge upon the need to involve all stakeholders in the policy formulation. So the policy would be acceptable to all the stakeholders especially *katchi abadis* dwellers. To begin with a total of 20 *katchi abadis* have been selected as pilot for regularization and upgradation of facilities.

The Government of Punjab has also launched a comprehensive Katchi Abadis Development Program under which basic amenities like roads, footpaths, drainage, sanitation, solid waste management, water supply, sewerage waste water treatment and its disposal will be provided. For the financial year 2007-08, Rs. 3 billion have been provided for development of *katchi abadis*. The communities would be involved on principles of component sharing basis within the internal/external distribution. They would also look after themselves in identifying, organizing and executing the lane level works, thus they would own the projects.

It is widely accepted in literature that slums and poverty are closely related and mutually reinforcing. Slum conditions are caused by poverty which reinforce poor living conditions. Monetary measures of poverty do not capture the multi-dimensional nature of poverty. The dimensions of poverty of slum dwellers are assetlessness, poor health of children[11], no-protection by laws and regulations, lack of civil and political, as well as economic, social and cultural rights, discrimination and poor environmental health. To be able to improve the living circumstances of the slums dwellers it is required to identify, quantify and locate slum dwellers at a detailed spatial level, analyze this information and formulate evidence-based urban policies and programs.

Defining and Identifying the Slums

The term slum in a general context is a heavily populated urban area characterized by substandard housing and squalor. The definition encapsulates the essential characteristics of slums, i.e. high densities, low standards of housing (structure and services), and squalor. The first two characteristics are physical and spatial, while the third is social and behavioral. Dwellings in such settlements vary from simple shacks to more permanent structures, and access to basic services and infrastructure tends to be limited or badly deteriorated. The definition also includes the traditional meaning, that is, housing areas that were once respectable or even desirable, but they have since deteriorated. The condition of the old houses has been declined, and the units have been progressively subdivided and rented out to lower-income groups. They are the inner-city slums.

UN-Habitat (2003: 6) defined slums as contiguous settlement where the inhabitants are characterized as having inadequate housing and basic services. A slum is often not recognized and addressed by the public authorities as an integral or equal part of the city. That is why little data is available on slums. Cities Alliance (1999) explained the slums as neglected parts of cities where housing and living conditions are appallingly poor. Slums range from high-density, squalid central city tenements to spontaneous squatter settlements without legal recognition or rights, sprawling at the edge of cities.

The Government of Pakistan has recognized two terms related to unserviced or underserviced settlements: (*i*) *Katchi abadis*: These are informal settlements created through squatting or informal subdivisions of state or private land, and (*ii*) *Slums*: These settlements consist of villages absorbed in the urban sprawl or the informal subdivisions created on community and agricultural land[12].

The *katchi abadis* are of two types: (i) Settlements established through unorganized invasion of state lands at the time of partition and most of them were removed and relocated during the 1960s or have been regularized, (ii) Informal subdivisions of state land (ISD), further divided into: (a) Notified *katchi abadis*: Settlements earmarked for regularization through a 99-year lease and local government infrastructure development, and (b) Non-notified *katchi abadis*: Settlements not to be regularized because they are on valuable land required for development, or on unsafe lands[13].

The slums can also be divided into two types: (i) Inner-city, traditional pre-independence working-class areas now densified and with inadequate infrastructure, and (ii) *Goths* or old villages now part of the urban sprawl, those within or near the city centre have become formal (others have developed informally into inadequately serviced high-density working-class areas)[14].

These definitions meet the common perception of what a slum is, yet they are not associated with operational definitions that would enable one to ascertain whether or not a particular area is a slum. It would be better to have a universal and objective definition, particularly when MDG targets are involved. Efforts to propose a more quantitative definition of slums have only recently been started, not only because of divergent opinions as to what constitutes the key determinants of slums, but because of several features of the concept:

- Slums are too complex to define according to one single parameter.
- Slums are a relative concept and what is considered as a slum in one city will be regarded as adequate in another city, even in the same country.
- Local variations among slums are too wide to define universally applicable criteria.
- Slums change too fast to render any criterion valid for a reasonably long period of time.
- The spatial nature of slums means that the size of particular slum areas is vulnerable to changes in jurisdiction or spatial aggregation.

What is agreed is that the concept of slums, like poverty is multidimensional in nature. Some of the characteristics of slums, such as access to physical services or density, can be clearly defined, and others, such as social capital, cannot be. Even with well-defined indicators, measurement can be very problematic, and acceptable benchmarks are not easy to establish.

UN-Habitat (2002) has devised an operational definition, i.e. a slum is an area that combines, to various extents, the following characteristics[15]:

- Inadequate access to safe water;
- Inadequate access to sanitation and other infrastructure;
- Poor structural quality of housing;
- Overcrowding;
- Insecure residential status.

The identifying characteristics of slums are shown in table 23.1.

Table 23.1. Indicators and Thresholds for Defining Slums

Characteristics	Indicators	Definition
Access to Water	Inadequate drinking water supply	A settlement has an inadequate drinking water supply if less than 50% of households have an improved water supply: • Household connection; • Access to public stand pipe; • Rainwater collection (with at least 20 litres/person/day available within an acceptable collection distance).
Access to Sanitation	Inadequate sanitation	A settlement has inadequate sanitation if less than 50% of households have improved sanitation: • Public sewer; • Septic tank; • Pour-flush latrine; • Ventilated improved pit latrine. The excreta disposal system is considered adequate if it is private or shared by a maximum of two households.
Structural Quality of Housing	(*a*) Location	Proportion of households residing on or near a hazardous site. The following locations should be considered: • Housing in geologically hazardous zones (landslide/earthquake and flood areas); • Housing on or under garbage mountains; • Housing around high-industrial pollution areas; • Housing around other unprotected high-risk zones (e.g. railroads, airports, energy transmission lines).
	(*b*) Permanency of structure	Proportion of households living in temporary and/or dilapidated structures. The following factors should be considered when placing a housing unit in these categories:

Characteristics	Indicators	Definition
		• Quality of construction (e.g. materials used for wall, floor and roof); • Compliance with local building codes, standards and bylaws.
Overcrowding	Overcrowding	Proportion of households with more than two persons per room. The alternative is to set a minimum standard for floor area per person (e.g. 5 square metres).
Security of tenure	Security of tenure	• Proportion of households with formal title deeds to both land and residence. • Proportion of households with formal title deeds to either one of land or residence. • Proportion of households with enforceable agreements or any document as a proof of a tenure arrangement.

UN-Habitat (2003) developed a household level definition in order to be able to use existing household level surveys and to identify slum dwellers among the urban population. A slum household is a household that lacks any one of the following five elements:

- Access to improved water[16];
- Access to improved sanitation;
- Security of tenure (the right to effective protection by the state against arbitrary, unlawful eviction);
- Durability of housing (including living in a non-hazardous location) and
- Sufficient living area (no overcrowding)

Characteristics of Slums

A review of the definitions given by international institutions and government of Pakistan reveals the following attributes of slums.

Lack of Basic Services: Lack of basic services is one of the most frequently mentioned characteristics of slums. Lack of access to sanitation facilities and safe water sources is the most important feature, sometimes supplemented by absence of waste collection systems, electricity supply, surfaced roads and footpaths, street lighting and rainwater drainage.

Substandard Housing or Illegal and Inadequate Building Structures: Slum areas are associated with a high number of substandard housing structures, often built with non-permanent materials unsuitable for housing given local conditions of climate and location.

Overcrowding and High Density: Overcrowding is associated with a low space per person, high occupancy rates, cohabitation by different families and a high number of single-room units. Many slum dwelling units are over crowded, with five and more persons sharing a one-room unit used for cooking, sleeping and living.

Unhealthy Living Conditions and Hazardous Locations: Unhealthy living conditions are the result of a lack of basic services, with visible, open sewers, lack of pathways, uncontrolled dumping of waste, polluted environments, etc. Houses may be built on hazardous locations or land unsuitable for settlement, such as floodplains, in proximity to industrial plants with toxic emissions or waste disposal sites, and on areas subject to landslip.

Insecure Tenure, Irregular or Informal Settlements: Lack of security of tenure is a central characteristic of slums, and regard lack of any formal document entitling the occupant to occupy the land or structure as *prima facie* evidence of illegality and slum occupation. Informal or unplanned settlements are often regarded as synonymous with slums.

Poverty and Social Exclusion: Poverty is considered, with some exceptions, as a central characteristic of slum areas. It is not seen as an inherent characteristic of slums, but as a cause (and, to a large extent, a consequence) of slum conditions. Slum conditions are physical and statutory manifestations that create barriers to human and social development. Furthermore, slums are areas of social exclusion that are often perceived to have high levels of crime and other measures of social dislocation. In some cases, such areas are associated with certain vulnerable groups of population, such as recent immigrants, internally displaced persons or ethnic minorities.

The life in slums consists of a combination of these characteristics. Many slum areas may show only a few of these attributes, while the worst may have them all.

Millennium Development Goals[17]

Millennium Summit of the United Nations in September 2000 established a series of goals for humanity for the 21st century. At the General Assembly session following this Millennium Declaration, a road map was established with a set of 8 Millennium Development Goals (MDGs) and 18 targets (MDG targets) for combating poverty, hunger, disease, illiteracy, environmental degradation and discrimination against women. They were to be measured through 32 indicators (the MDG indicators). Though all goals are generally related with slums but some MDGs are particularly concerned with slums including the one specified for slum dwellers. They are as follows:

Goal 1: Eradicate Extreme Poverty and Hunger

Target 1: Halve, between 1990 and 2015, the proportion of people whose income is less than US $1 a day.

The government of Pakistan has adopted the indicator of proportion of population below the calorie based food plus non-food poverty line for Goal 1. The definition devised is head-count index based on the official poverty line of Rs. 673.54 per capita and per month in 1998-99 prices consistent with attainment of 2350 calories per adult equivalent per day. The MDG target set for 2015 is to reduce the proportion of people below poverty line up to 13 per cent (CRPRID, 2006).

Goal 7: Ensure Environmental Sustainability

Target 10: Halve, by 2015, the proportion of people without sustainable access to safe drinking water and basic sanitation.

Indicator 30: Proportion of population with sustainable access to an improved water source, urban and rural; and

Indicator 31: Proportion of urban population with access to improved sanitation.

The Government of Pakistan has taken the indicator as the population (urban and rural) with sustainable access to a safe (improved) water source. The definition adopted is the rate of population with access to improved water source. The target set by the government is 93 per cent by 2015. For sanitation, the indicator adopted by the government is the proportion of population (urban and rural) with access to sanitation. It is based on the definition of population with access to sanitation. The target set for 2015 is 90 per cent (CRPRID: 2006).

Target 11: By 2020, to have achieved a significant improvement in the lives of at least 100 million slum dwellers.

For the target 11, Government of Pakistan has taken the indicator as the population of registered *katchi abadis*[18] regulated as percentage of those identified by cut-off dates of 1985. The target set is to regulate 95 per cent of the *katchi abadis* (CRPRID: 2006).

National Housing Policy for Slums

There is no specific national housing policy for slums in Pakistan but in the National Housing Policy, 2001, there is a part about *kachi abadis*, squatters and slums describing an effective mechanism to control future growth of *katchi abadis* and squatter settlements and also to alleviate the sufferings of the urban poor. Following are the policy measures concerning slums in the National Housing Policy:

- The process of regularization and upgradation of the pre-1985 *katchi abadis* shall continue as per current policy. However, *katchi abadis*, which are hazardous by virtue of being close to railway tracks or located under high tension power lines, or are on or close to the riverbeds, or on lands needed for operational /security purposes, need to be relocated at appropriate places by land owning agencies (LOAs).
- Formation of new *katchi abadis* shall not be allowed and shall be discouraged by exercising strict development controls in all urban areas.
- There shall be no eviction till *katchi abadis* residents are relocated as per resettlement plans.
- The concerned LOAs will inventorize all *katchi abadis* which have come into existence after 1985 and have an up-to-date information/data for their rational treatment or resettlement at appropriate places.
- Resettlement plans shall be prepared by the concerned LOAs in consultation with affected communities for shifting of *katchi abadis* dwellers who fall within hazardous

or security/operational zones. These plans shall primarily be on a self financing basis. The internal infrastructure and services shall be provided on incremental basis depending on the needs and priorities of the residents to make them affordable and cost-effective. Trunk infrastructure and services shall be provided by public sector organizations and the cost shall be met from government exchequer.

- In all government housing schemes, adequate plots for low-income people shall be reserved to offer them at affordable prices. In addition private developers will also be encouraged to develop low-cost housing schemes.
- City and District Government shall prepare housing plans to cater for the current and future housing needs for low-income groups on incremental basis at affordable cost. *Katchi abadis* resettlement plans and upgradation plans shall be an integral part of these housing plans.
- Building regulations, building by laws, and planning standards shall be revised to permit incremental development and lowering of planning standards to make it cost-effective for low-income groups.
- In the long term perspective, the problems of *katchi abadis* shall be dealt through:
  - (*i*) Forward planning for incremental population;
  - (*ii*) Initiation of low-cost housing schemes and provision of cross subsidy to the poor through auction of commercial plots;
  - (*iii*) Effective punitive and preventive laws; and
  - (*iv*) Regular patrolling of police watch and ward.

Besides the measures, already approved, the following additional measures were recommended for implementation:

- To minimize relocation and resettlement, the concept of mixed development, as internationally practiced, shall be promoted and encouraged by Provincial Government and development agencies, with incentive packages, to ensure effective integrator low-income groups and dwellers of *katchi abadis* and slums in the community and city structures.
- Provincial government shall develop packages in which prime state land within urban centers, occupied by the *katchi abadis*, shall be offered to the private developers for commercial use provided they arrange and finance upgradation or relocation of *katchi abadis* and squatter settlements and slum upgradation (GOP: 2001).

Scope of Study

In order to improve the living conditions of the slums in Pakistan, detailed spatial information is required at the national and local level. Though, local planners, infrastructure agencies and communities know where slums are located, what are the living conditions and what are the daily hardships of slum dwellers to cope with poverty. But more knowledge is required based on detailed data and information on the socio-economic characteristics of the households.

The phenomenon of urban slums rounds about the poverty. The clustering of Pakistan's population close to poverty line[19] implies that households are quite vulnerable to falling into poverty with the slightest rise in price of basic commodities and housing, increase in health and educational cost and unemployment, a fall in wages and income (not only of adult males but also of women and children), and lower provision of social safety nets. A natural calamity can also push a significant number of households into poverty. It needs to see the urban slums from poverty perspective.

In Pakistan many policies at national and grass root levels have been implemented in order to eradicate poverty. For instance, Pakistan Poverty Alleviation Fund (PPAF) was set up in 1997. Asian Development Bank (ADB) has provided $1.1 billion finance during the year of 2002, and $800 million per annum till 2006 for poverty reduction. The Government of Pakistan has launched the anti-poverty programs consisting of five major elements, namely integrated small public works programs, food supplement program, revamping the Zakat system and micro credit banks for improving social indicators. The access of government policies and programs to slums need to be probed.

The slums generally represent the lower section of the society and enjoy lower status in the community. Furthermore, these households have great heterogeneity in economic activities with a wide range of labor productivities, which makes it complex to evaluate the change in socio-economic status of these households. On the other hand economic activities of these households have an important place in economies of developing countries. For instance, they can contribute to economic growth by providing cheap labor force. They should be taken as an agent of change in the urban economy because they are the major part of the country's non-utilized and under-utilized resources. They need the prime and urgent concern of policy-makers.

Pakistan Planning Commission has recommended the level of 2350 Kcal/Day as the food poverty line. In the monetary terms the official poverty line of Pakistan is Rs. 944.47 per capita per month (GOP: 2008). Poverty when applied to human being is the notion of a life situation that should not exist. Amartya Sen aptly sums up many dimensions of poverty as lack of capability, i.e. capability to overcome violence, hunger, ignorance, illness, physical hardship, injustice and voicelessness. The World Bank argued that poverty often lies in the absence of opportunity, empowerment and security, and not just the absence of food on the table[20]. Instead of using simply per capita income or calorie/day as a parameter of poverty, it is preferable to take socio-economic variables to assess the dimensions of poverty and to see the living standard of slum dwellers. Another justification for not to use the per capita income as the parameter of living standard is the inability to calculate the accurate income of these households due to casual or informal nature of their economic activities.

The assessment of standard of life of slum dwellers is necessary, may further be summarized as:

- To advance understanding about the urban slum households
- To highlight the gender dimension of these households

- To increase visibility about those who live in slums
- To inform the designers of policies and programs about slum dwellers
- To see the reach of policies and programs to these households.

Objectives of Study

Facts on the households of urban slums in Pakistan are needed in many aspects. Nevertheless, to keep the study within a meaningful and manageable frame of analysis, the study has been narrowed down to analyze the following aspects:

- Living conditions of slum households
- Social security nets and micro-credit availability
- Household and head of household characteristics
- Women laborforce participation and their contribution
- Labor force participation of children and their contribution
- Health and educational status of children.

Methodology

Different definitions of slums are presented in the literature, given by sociologists, criminologist, anthropologists, economists, NGOs and pubic sector authorities depending upon their tasks. More dominant is the definition given by UN-Habitat. To see the life in slums, we have devised a definition taking five elements of identification of slum households given by UN-Habitat. The elements are: access to improved water, that is a dummy variable showing whether the potable water is available in the household or not; access to improved sanitation, that has two dummy variables, (*i*) whether the separate toilet/flush toilet is available in the household or not, (*ii*) whether underground sewage facility is available to the household or not; security of tenure, that is whether the land/plot of the household is owned/registered by the owner of the household or not; durability of the household, that has two variables, (*i*) whether the household is *kacha* (made up of mud, hay, mixture of mud and stone, etc.) or *pacca* (made up of cement and bricks), (*ii*) whether the household is located in the hazardous place (by the railway tack, flood and rain water area, by the garbage mountain, by the river bank, under the overhead bridge, etc.) or not; and sufficient living area, that is the persons per room are less than two or two/more than two. A household having two elements is identified as slum household[21].

Household has been defined as group of people who had usually slept in the same dwelling and had taken their meals together. Instead of households we have taken the cluster of households in the sample. So a cluster of at least 40 slum households made the slum area. Taking into consideration the above criterion we identified the slum areas[22]. From these slum areas we have taken the sample of twelve clusters so the study adopted cluster sample technique. From each cluster we have surveyed almost 50 households randomly. The clusters were Aziz Town, Gharibabad, Karna Basti, Hajian Basti, Hurian Basti, Javaid Colony, Allahabad Colony, Baqirpur, Bindra Basti, Tiba Badar Sher, Chrimar

Mohala, and Islampura of urban areas of Bahawalpur. The Bahawalpur city has been chosen as a case study due to the facts: (*i*) Bahawalpur city is not so much urbanized as Karachi, Lahore and Rawalpindi, etc. and not so much backward as far-flung cities of interior Sindh and Balochistan, (*ii*) Ghaus, et al. (1996) ranked Bahawalpur district at number 49 out of 94 districts of the country in terms of social indicators in Weighted Factor Score, and at 28 in terms of z-score ranking, while eleven indicators relating to education, health and water supply were included in the construction of score, (*iii*) Bahawalpur district is at 34 and 65 in water supply and sanitation respectively out of 98 districts of the country (CRPRID, 2006). The city represents the average conditions of the cities of the country.

The personal interview is adopted to collect the data from the head of household. From the target group 550 households are interviewed. The questionnaire covered a wide variety of topics as living condition (access to water and sanitation, building material, security of tenure), household characteristics (family size, employment, income, etc.), social safety nets, women work and contribution, education and health status of children and child labor. Only the physical dimensions of slums are covered under these topics as more complex social and legal dimensions are out of the scope of the country. Simple arithmetic calculations are used for analysis of data.

Results and Discussion

Though we have adopted the cluster sample technique but it is found that most slum dwellers live in areas classified as slums, while a minority lives in by-and-large non-slum areas. It means that non-slum areas are not completely, although to a large extent, inhabited homogeneously by non-slum households. It is very likely that in many cases boundaries of slums are not exactly coinciding with the boundaries of non-slums. In addition to that, small clusters of slum households may exist in better-off neighbors, vice versa, a few number of relatively well-to-do households may exist in slum areas. In the slums the households are living from decades. For a number of times these slums were tried to be vacated and sometimes they disappeared due to natural calamities like floods and heavy rains but again appeared after few months. It is observed that in a single housing unit more than one households are living. Some of the households have illegal connections of gas and electricity. The slums round the city have no roads, even some slums have no roads connecting to other urban localities. The slum dwellers use railway side or pavements to go to other urban localities. The majority of the slums have no utilities like dispensary and schools. The dwellers told that seldom the lady health visitor has visited the locality. Tenure security is available to only inner city slums. The slum households in majority are engaged in a variety of labor categories like employer, self-employed, own account workers, pieceworkers, home-based workers, micro entrepreneurs, employee/hired labor/wage workers, domestic servants and hard labor work, etc. but a few are public sector employees along with organized/formal private employees. The location, time of existence, hazards and land owning agency statistics of the slums of the sample are shown in table 23.2.

Table 23.2. Location, Existence, Hazards and Land Owning Agencies of Clusters and Households

		Slums	Households
Locality	Inner-city Slum	16.6 Per cent (N=2)	15.45 Per cent (N=85)
	Railway Track	50.0 Per cent (N=6)	45.45 Per cent (N=250)
	River-side	33.3 Per cent (N=4)	39.09 Per cent (N=215)
	Total	99.9 Per cent (N=12)	99.99 Per cent (N=550)
Existence	Up to 10 years	16.6 Per cent (N=2)	16.19 Per cent (N=93)
	11-20 years	16.6 Per cent (N=2)	19.15 Per cent (N=105)
	More than 20 years	66.6 Per cent (N=8)	64.64 Per cent (N=352)
	Total	99.8 Per cent (N=12)	99.98 Per cent (N=550)
Hazards[23]	Floods	66.6 Per cent (N=8)	50.00 Per cent (N=393)
	Rain-water	50.0 Per cent (N=6)	37.56 Per cent (N=293)
	To much old building	16.6 Per cent (N=2)	12.43 Per cent (N=97)
Land Owning Agency	Pakistan Railways	41.5 Per cent (N=5)	53.09 Per cent (N=292)
	Old State Land	24.9 Per cent (N=3)	17.09 Per cent (N=94)
	Irrigation Department	8.3 Per cent (N=1)	9.10 Per cent (N=46)
	Revenue Department	8.3 Per cent (N=1)	6.63 Per cent (N=36)
	Owned by Household	16.9 Per cent (N=2)	14.98 Per cent (N=82)
	Total	99.9 Per cent (N=12)	100.89 Per cent (N=550)

In our sample majority of the households, i.e. 45.45 per cent are living near the railway track. The main land owning agency (LAO) emerged the Pakistan Railways, whose land is occupied by 53.09 per cent of the households. The river-side households are comprised of 39.09 per cent. It is estimated that 50 percent of the households in the sample has hazard of floods and 37.56 per cent of rain-water. The inner-city slums are comprised of 15.45 per cent of the households of the sample, while 12.43 per cent of the households of the sample has hazard of much old buildings. Similarly, 14.98 per cent households have tenure security, i.e. they own the land of household legally. Most probably the inner-city slum households own the land of their houses. There are 16.9 per cent households in our sample who are living in slums maximum for the last ten years, while 19.45 per cent of the households are living in the slums from last 11 to 20 years and 63.63 per cent of the households are living in slums for more than 20 years. It means more than half of the slum households come under the cut-off line of 1985 for regulation and upgradation, according to National Housing Policy, 2001. The same households are the target population in MGD given by

Government of Pakistan. Almost 40 per cent of the households come under the action of removal, according to the same policy.

Living Conditions

The living conditions represent the poverty of the household and work as powerful tool to visualize the urban inequalities. The other useful opportunity for the data of living conditions lies in the verification of other data sources or using it as data itself (counting slum households and demographic estimation, etc.). They are represented in Table-23.3.

Table 23.3. Living Conditions of Slum Households

Parameters of Living Condition	Nos. or Percentage
Households having Potable Water Facility Inside the House	21.56 Per cent
Households having Toilet in the Household	41.85 Per cent
Households having Flush Toilet in the Household	13.80 Per cent
Households having Drainage Facility	16.83 Per cent
Households having Hazards	89.68 Per cent
Tenure Scarcity to the Household	15 Per cent
Duration of Household Living in Slums	19.7 Years
Average Persons Living per Housing Unit	9.7
Households Living in Kacha Houses	63.64 Per cent
Households Living in their Own Houses	70.15 Per cent
Households having Gas Connections	5.5 Per cent
Households having Electricity	42 Per cent
Average Number of Rooms in House	1.96
Average Persons Living in One Room	4.59
Households having TV/Radio	35.18 Per cent
Households Living in One Room	67 Per cent
Households Living in Two Room Housing Unit	19.40 Per cent
Households Living in Three Room	3.90 Per cent
Households having Separate Kitchen in the House	6.80 Per cent
Households having Bathroom in the House	18.48 Per cent

The availability of improved water is one of the targets of MDGs[24]. In the national population census and household surveys, the sources of drinking water and sanitation facility are misinterpreted. The census questionnaire inquires the source of water (piped water, pipe stand, river, etc.) and the types of sanitation used by household members (flush toilet, septic tank, open defection, etc.). Many people in slum areas correctly respond to this answer by indicating that they are getting water from a pipe. This, however, means that there is a piped water connection somewhere in the area, from where they bring the water to their houses in buckets or water containers, after queing for hours and by paying up. We have used the variable that whether the drinking water is available in the household (through pipe, hand pump, electric pump, etc.) or not. Similarly, we have used the variable of sanitation, that is, whether the separate toilet is available in the household or not, and whether the toilet is flush or otherwise, irrespective of the number of household members. At the national level 89.4 per cent of the urban households have drinking water source within the dwellings. In the Punjab 92 per cent of the households have access (in the household) to improved source of drinking water. In the major cities[25] the facility is available to 98 per cent households. In the other urban areas of Punjab it is available to 96 per cent and in Bahawalpur to 87 per cent households (Government of Punjab 2004: 46). We estimated that the facility is available to only 21.56 per cent of the slum households. The other relevant problem is that under-ground water-table is salty so the households need piped water.

In Punjab adequate sanitation is available to 58 per cent of the households. In major cities of Punjab and other urban areas the facility is available to 98 and 92 per cent respectively. In Bahawalpur the same facility is available to 41 per cent of the households (Government of Punjab 2004: 46). We have found that more than 58 per cent of slum households have no latrine facility within the housing unit (see also Geetha and Swaminathan 1996 for same type of results for Mumbai slum dwellers). Similarly, almost 80 per cent households have no separate bathroom facility for bathing purpose. The drainage/sewage facility is available to only 16.83 per cent households. In general the housing conditions of these households are very low. There may be a two pronged action for water and sanitation facility, i.e. to develop in the sectors of water supply and sanitation facility and or the selected the action should be at the district, *tehsil* or even union council level with a variety of stakeholders including the residents themselves.

The tenure security is a part of MDG. The land tenure security is available to only 15 per cent of slum households though 70.15 per cent of the households are living in their own houses[1]. The regulation of slums is a part of National Housing Policy, 2001 and provincial government is responsible for upgradation, resettlement and relocation of slums. The average duration of the households of slum life is 19.7 years which shows that after the National Housing Policy, 2001, the slum households have been increased. It also explains that no action for upgradation has so far been taken.

The level of congestion in terms of persons per housing unit reflects the housing conditions as well as the living standard. The average household size per housing unit is 6.6 persons in the country but in our sample of slum households the household size per housing unit is 9.7. Moreover, 67 per cent of the slum households are living in one room housing units (see also Geetha and Swaminathan 1996 for same type of results for Mumbai slum dwellers) and 19.14 per cent in two-room housing units. Furthermore 63.64 per cent of the slum households are living in *kacha* (mud) houses and mean number of persons per room is 4.59. On the other hand, according to Government of Punjab (2004: 56) the mean number of persons per room in Bahawalpur is 3.7, in major cities of Punjab 3.4, in other urban areas of Punjab 3.3 and in Punjab including urban and rural areas 3.4. It reflects the local disparity in living conditions. Furthermore, 93.2 per cent of the households has no separate kitchen in the household and only 5.5 per cent has gas connection.

The housing situation in Pakistan has remained under tremendous pressure due to high population growth. We have found that 70.15 per cent slum households have their own houses though for the majority the land is illegally occupied.

The provision and quantity of electricity use is one of the basic parameters of poverty. In the country 89 per cent of the urban households have electricity connections (ADB 2002: 30). In Punjab 83 per cent of the households have utility of electricity. The same utility is available to 99 per cent of the households of major cities and 98 per cent of the households of other urban areas of Punjab. In Bahawalpur 56 per cent of the households avail the facility (Government of Punjab, 2004). Our estimates have shown that in slums of Bahawalpur 42 per cent of the households have electricity connection that is much lower than the figures given above. The situation represents the worst condition of these households. Provision of electricity enhances the productivity, living standard, information and awareness. The use of radio and TV is assumed to be a part of standard of living and source of information but only 35.87 per cent of the slum households have radio and or TV sets (see also Geetha and Swaminathan for the same type of results for Mumbai slums).

Social Safety Nets and Micro-Credit

Poverty reduction that is a part of MDGs (Goal 1) requires a concerted effort to improve the capabilities of the poor and vulnerable. It also requires well-designed programs that can mitigate the vulnerabilities induced by economic downturns. Due to lower income, the slum households have to depend on social safety nets even some times on informal credit. Zakat is the most comprehensive state-level social safeguard net in terms of resources and organization. It has objective of assisting the needy, indigent and poor. Zakat system provides two main types of support: a monthly subsistence allowance and rehabilitation grant. Other benefits include educational stipends, assistance for medical treatment, and marriage assistance.

Table 23.4. Households Availing Social Safety Nets and Micro-Credit

Social Safety Nets and Micro-Credit	Households
Households Receiving Food Stamps	1.39 Per cent
Households Receiving Zakat	5.19 Per cent
Households Utilizing Credit	3.52 Per cent
Ratio of Households Utilizing Credit from Formal Sector	3.93 Per cent
Ratio of Household Utilizing Credit from Informal Sector	96 Per cent

Social safety nets are especially important for the poor. The positive effect of transfers on the poor can be gauged from the fact that the average consumption in households without transfers was only 64 per cent of the average consumption of households who were recipients of transfers (World Bank, 1995). There are two targeted income transfer programs by the government of Pakistan, i.e. Zakat and Usher Program, and the Bait-ul-Mal Program. The social safety nets and credit availability to the slum households is shown in table 23.4. It is found that only 5.19 per cent of slum households are receiving Zakat. One factor of the worse poverty level of these households is the non-availability of transfer payments to these households. According to SPDC (2001) among the Zakat receiving households 61 per cent were still living below poverty line in spite of having Zakat beneficiaries, while among the transfer receiving household 26 per cent were living below poverty line. That is, the programs had not made a major dent on poverty alleviation. It is needed to not only increase the coverage of slum households under the social safety net of zakat but also to increase the effectiveness for poverty reduction by enhancing the amount disbursed per household. As concerns the food stamp program, only 1.39 per cent of the slum households are receiving food stamp.

Microfinance for short and medium term can be effective instrument for addressing poverty. Non-availability of credit to these households is one of the major causes of poverty. The micro-credit scheme has been operative in Pakistan since 1972. Many financial institutions are providing micro-credit facilities. In our study the access to formal credit from slum households is only 3.93 per cent. The result revealed the fact that the credit services provided by the banking system are normally not available to poor slum households, who are not considered to be credit worthy due to their inability to provide any collateral. Credit is very important service as much as it enables one to expand the size of one's business and income earning capacity. Thus the non-availability of credit facilities to slum dwellers places them at a greater disadvantage, which ultimately enhances poverty. This concern may be shared by donor agencies and particularly non-governmental organizations (NGOs) to become active in the programs of credit and assistance to slum dwellers.

Household Characteristics

Besides location, there are a number of attributes, which characterize the slums. One of the important characteristics is larger than average household size. Other characteristics include low-education and illiteracy, few physical assets and a disproportionate reliance on informal sector opportunities. The household size and its composition are of pivotal importance and they play an important role for household in a poor community, where children especially male children are considered as a major strength for economic wellbeing of the family. The household characteristics of slum households are shown in table 23.5.

The large family size is the characteristic of slums. There are evidences in literature that large households are more likely to be poor than small ones. The incidence of poverty in households with 7 or more members is more than three times than that for households with 4 or less members. The poor households on average have 35 per cent more family members than non-poor households (ADB, 2002: 30). In our sample of slums the average family size of 9.2 against the average household size of 6.4 in Bahawalpur, 6.4 in major cities of Punjab, 6.6 in other urban areas of Punjab and 6.6 in Punjab (urban and rural) represents the relatively larger household size in slums.

Table 23.5. Household Characteristics of Urban Slum

Household Characteristics	Average/Ratios
Average Family Size	9.2 Members
Ratio of Children (under 15 years) in Total Population	68.18 Per cent
Ratio of Children (5-15 years) in Total Population	59.57 Per cent
Literate Head of Household	19 Per cent
Average years of Education of Head of Household	4.7 years
Formally Educated Head of Household	14 Per cent
Head of Households completed 10 years of Education	7 Per cent
Household Per-capita Income	Rs. 567/Month
Ownership of Assets[27]	18 Per cent
Adults Employed	58 Per cent
Informally Employed Adults	89 Per cent
Self-Employed	72 Per cent
Employee	23 Per cent
Income of Head of Household	Rs. 4360/Month
Female-headed Households	14.37 Per cent (Footnotes)

The high population growth results into exacerbation of urban poverty and slums, and poverty results into higher population growth. The high population growth rate affects the poor disproportionately since they bear more children than the rich ones, which perpetuate the intergenerational transmission of poverty by lessening the resource investment of the children (Birdsall, 1994). The poor community maintains an increased demand for children. The poor households have 75 per cent more children under the age of 10 than non-poor households (ADB, 2002: 30). It is found that in slums 68.18 per cent of the population comprised of children less than 15 years of age, and 59.57 per cent of the population is of school-age (5-15 years) (see also Geetha and Swaminathan 1996 for Mumbai slums) which explains the link between poverty and population growth.

At the national level, there exists a strong correlation between illiteracy or the level of education, and the incidence of poverty. At the national level, the literacy rate of the head of household in poor households, i.e. 27 per cent is about half of that in non-poor households. Similarly, the households whose heads had no formal education had about three times the incidence of poverty compared to those households whose heads had completed 10 or more years of schooling (Arif, 2000). For urban areas, education contribute 12 percent reduction in poverty (SPDC, 2001). In the slums, we have estimated that only 19 per cent of the heads of households are literate with average years of education of only 4.7 years. Only 14 per cent of the heads of households have obtained formal education and there are only 7 per cent heads who have completed 10 or more years of education.

People may be poor not just because of low literacy and human capital capacity, but their poverty may depend on inadequate, unstable or risky asset base needed as a cushion to carry them through hard times. At the national level the asset ownership is inversely correlated with poverty. In urban areas physical assets contribute 9 per cent reduction in poverty (SPDC, 2001). We have estimated that 18 per cent of the slum households have asset. According to Government of Punjab (2004) only 9 per cent of the households have no possessions in Punjab, 1, 2 and 28 per cent in major cities, other urban areas and Bahawalpur respectively. It again represents a stark disparity among communities at local level. It may have resulted into disparity in income. Our estimates show that per capita income of the slum households is Rs. 567/month. The official figures by Government of Punjab (2004) have shown the per capita income of Rs. 2259, Rs. 1385 and Rs. 863 per month for major cities, other urban areas and Bahawalpur respectively.

Previous studies concluded that in urban areas, access to employment reduces the incidence of poverty by 45 per cent (SPDC, 2001). According to Pakistan Integrated Household Survey (PIHS), the incidence of poverty was highest among the household's heads with elementary occupations. Elementary occupations include only labor in agriculture, construction, trade, and transport. They are precarious and contain a lot of disguised employment. With regard to employment status, incidence of poverty was high among the self-employed. Our analysis concluded that in urban slums, only 58 per cent of the adults (males) are employed and 89 per cent adults are informally employed (see also Pryer, 2002 for Dhaka slums). Self-employed comprised of 72 per cent and employees 23 per cent. The income of head of household remained Rs. 4360/month.

The phenomenon of women-headed households is common in slums. Typically women have lower levels of education, work longer hours, retain responsibility for child-care as well as productive and community management roles, and have poorer diets and more restricted mobility than men. Female-headed households are more vulnerable to poverty and are more dependent on children' earning than male-headed households. Life is difficult for female-heads, not because of prejudice, but social stigma as well. They have far more difficulty in maintaining their families because they have less access to market economy. The household headed by women are among the poorest. In the urban slums of Bahawalpur, we estimated that 14.37 per cent of the households are headed by females[28]. They need the coverage by social safety nets.

Women's Work and their Contribution

The relationship between dependence of the family on women's labor and poverty is ambiguous. However, studies indicate that for the poor households, there is higher likelihood of dependence on female labor. At the same time, micro-level studies reveal that in these households where women's productive labor is critical for the survival of the family, there is more improvisement due to the low economic value of female labor. This is due to relatively lower skill-base of women generally, and their restricted mobility. As a result they find it difficult to compete for access to social and productive assets on an equal footing with men.

In poor households, the women enter labor market at a very early age due to financial pressure and larger family size. The women living in slums are involved in a variety of activities that may be domestic work or home-based work. It is found that in the slums 27 per cent of the women in the age group of 15-60 years are working. In the households where women are working, they are contributing 41 per cent in the household budget, which represents the household dependence on women labor.

Table 23.6. Labor Force Participation of Women and Their Contribution

Age Group	Labor Force Participation (Per cent)	Contribution (Per cent)
15-25	21.68	30
26-35	24.8	45
36-45	21.72	39
45-60	4.5	31
15-60	27	41

The situation of working women coming from slums is quite different from their urban counterparts because of bad health status, low literacy rate, poor knowledge of know-how and minimum level of skill. Despite these hurdles, they contribute to their household income. We have estimated that women in the age group of 21-35 years are contributing in their household income maximally, i.e. 45 per cent. Even the minimum contribution is 31 per cent which shows the significant contribution of these women in their household budget.

Health and Educational Status of Children

Health is one of the sectors targeted in the Social Action Program (SAP). Health indicators in Pakistan have shown some improvements over the past decade, although they remain lower than the indicators in other developing countries. There has been significant improvement in the rate of immunization at the national level. The percentage of children between 12 and 23 months who were fully immunized reached to 76 in the country (GOP, 2008) based on recall and record measures. However, it still fell considerably short of the 90 per cent coverage target set by Government of Pakistan for achievement by 1998. Nevertheless, immunization rates in children significantly improved across both genders and in urban and rural areas in all the provinces and it remained highest for Punjab, i.e. 55 per cent. The relevant literature revealed that there exist a strong correlation between income and immunization in Pakistan as approximately three quarters of children in the upper income quintile were fully immunized against only one quarter in the bottom quintile.

The situation of health and educational status of children of slums of Bahawalpur has been shown in table 23.7. It explains dismal condition as only 31 per cent of the infants ever have been vaccinated. If we make the comparison, the situation seems very disappointing as 61 per cent of the children (12–32 months) are fully immunized in Bahawalpur, and 66 per cent in Punjab (rural and urban) (Government of Punjab, 2004). Furthermore, in slums of Bahawalpur it is found that only 7 per cent of the children have taken supplementary nutrition and 11 per cent of the children are suffering or have been suffered (in the last one year) from major diseases like, diphtheria, typhoid, acute skin problem, etc. Only 13 per cent of the children (under-5 years) have received the treatment from public hospital/dispensary, which shows the dismal position of use of public sector utilities by these households.

Goal 2 of MDG "achieve universal primary education" expresses to ensure that all boys and girls complete a full course of primary schooling[29]. The human capital emphasizes the quality of the labor force, in terms of education and health, which is very important ingredient for a nation's success and elimination of intergenerational poverty (Romer, 1994). A plethora of international economic evidences suggested that the rate of return on investment in primary education is much higher than on the tertiary education (Behrman 1995). At the national level 35 per cent of school-age children (5–15 years) are out of school. For low-income households, the opportunity cost of having a child in school is fairly high, and parents cannot bear this cost. Despite the efforts by Government of Pakistan since 1992 by Social Action Program (SAP) in which 64 per cent of the budget was allocated to primary education, the education has not improved (ADB, 2002: 4). Our study revealed that 82.19 per cent of school-age children are out of school in slums, that is much higher than the national figure. It stresses the approach that poor pockets need immediate attention. The social rate of return of male primary school is 16.4 per cent (Behrman, 1995). It reiterates that primary education for poor pockets like urban slums should be the main development priority of the policy-makers.

A prominent feature of Pakistan's education sector is the gender gap in schooling. This is evident from gender statistics whereby female literacy is only 29 per cent as compared to a literacy rate of 55 per cent for men. Similarly Gross Primary Enrolment is 106 per cent for urban areas, but it is 110 and 89 per cent for males and females respectively. In the slums of Bahawalpur, we find that the gender gap in school enrolment is highest as only 9.27 per cent of the females and 31.34 of male children are in schools in the age group of 5–15 years. Gender gap in education exists not only because of parent's reluctance to send girls to school but also because of non-availability of appropriate facilities for girls. It is further found that in the school-age children, 53 per cent has ever gone to school, 17 per cent has completed the five years of schooling and only 7 per cent has completed ten years of schooling. Inefficiency in the provision of social services like education and health facility by public sector is one of the causes of poverty in slums (see also Geetha and Swaminathan 1996 for Mumbai slums).

Table 23.7. Health and Educational Status of Children

Education and Health Parameters	Percentage
Children (under 5 years) Ever Vaccinated	31
Children (under 5 years) Ever Take Supplement Nutrition	7
Children (under 5 years) Last Time Rcceived Medical Treatment from Public Hospital /Dispensary	13
Children Suffering from any Major Disease	11
Ratio of school-going Children	17.81
Ratio of school-going Children (Male)	31.47
Ratio of school-going Children (Female)	9.27
Children (under 15 years) Ever Gone to School	53
Children (under 15 years) Complete 5 years of School	17
Children (under 15 years) Complete 10 years of School	7

Child Labor and its Contribution

In slums people face a lot of the problems affecting quality of life. The lack of public sector utilities is the major factor behind them. Along with lower household income, the lack of schooling facilities pushes their children into labor force. The labor force participation of children from these households is shown in table 23.8. In the school-age group 32.39 per cent of children are involved in labor force activities that will transform current poverty into poverty of the next generation. Usually these children work with their parents but even some go to other urban areas for work. These children are forced to join labor force because they contribute a significant part to the household income. The children in these households are contributing 26.11 per cent in their household income.

Table 23.8 Labor Force Participation of Children (5–15 years) and their Contribution (Per cent)

Age Group	Boys		Girls		Overall	
	Participation	Contribution	Participation	Contribution	Participation	Contribution
5–10	10.49	15.84	6.46	10.25	8.67	13.17
11–15	37.54	24.39	31.59	18.42	34.55	28.60
5–15	48.06	23.11	28.27	14.63	32.39	26.11

The boys are participating in labor force more than the girls and their contribution is also greater than girls. The labor force participation increases by increase in age group. To eliminate urban poverty the educational facilities for children need policy attention.

Conclusion

The paper has presented the statistical overview of the households in slums of Bahawalpur. It concludes with important new directions, both substantive and operational, for improvement of slums. Generally there may be two ways for the improvement, firstly to relocate these slums specifically those ones who are at the hazardous places and secondly to improve the living conditions of slums where it is possible due to availability of safe land and sufficient places. The improvement should comprise of physical and human development. The data-based findings are presented here as:

- Almost 50 per cent of the households are facing the hazards of floods and 37.56 per cent of rain-water. Majority of the households, i.e. 63.63 per cent are living in slums for more than 20 years.
- The slum households are poorest of the poor in many manifestations of poverty like living conditions, adult employment, social security nets, tenure security, availability of credit, child labor and women labor force participation.
- There exists very poor living condition in slums. The water supply and sanitation, *kacha* houses and congestion need attention of the government towards housing facilities for slums. Previously, all the efforts of government are focused on urban areas. The national housing policy, 2001 still waiting to be implemented.
- Among the social safety nets, the food stamps are almost non-available to the slum dwellers. As 11.35 per cent of the head of households are females so food stamp program should target these households.
- The availability of micro-credit to slum dwellers is extremely insufficient as 96 per cent of the credit availed come from informal sector. To pull these households out of poverty micro-finance funding is direly needed. Similarly, for the short-run transfer payments, and social security nets are required.
- Ownership of assets is another area, in which slum dwellers are much poor. Only 18 per cent of households have assets (15 per cent of the households have tenure security of land). It forces them to involve in casual labor.
- The female labor force participation is characteristic of the slums but women have lower productivity probably due to lack of skill, know-how and education. They are contributing a significant part to the household income.
- Child labor and non-participation of school-age children are evident characteristics of slum households as 32 per cent of children are doing labor and 82 per cent of children are out of school. Due to these two factors along with poor health there exist a inter-generational cycle of poverty so there is a need for public sector intervention for the provision of education facilities.
- The high population growth emerged as the characteristic of slums. The ratio of the children to total population, i.e. 68.18 per cent expresses the high fertility rate in these households that is playing a role for the present poverty and to generate poverty of future generations.

- The health status of children is poor particularly due to non-availability of public sector utilities and non-coverage of health programs to the slums.

Policy Recommendations

Traditional approaches such as physical infrastructure projects for slums may have a modest impact, especially where projects are not integrated with other aspects of poverty such as employment, education and health. Slum policies should be integrated with urban poverty reduction policies, which have to go beyond the physical dimension of slums.

For physical dimensions, it is recommended to identify the slums within the urban areas and targeted programs for housing, electricity, gas, water supply and sanitation, and other utility services should be launched by the district governments. The devolution of power can be used more effectively for improvement of infrastructure of slums.

The basic needs like education and health services should be provided to slum dwellers on priority basis. Generally, the government should aim to spend more of national income on education and health. More important is the quality and composition of spending. For education focus should be on the provision of free primary education. In health sector the initial aim should be the provision of a basic package of low-cost services for slums to prevent and treat the most common infectious diseases.

Last but not the least the MDGs would only be achievable for Pakistan, if targeted policies towards slums is directed. The disparities in the cities may get increasing trend if regulation, upgradation and resettlement of slums is not done.

Zakat Funds should be used for rehabilitation instead of relief. Pakistan Bait-ul-Mal provides relief to poor. With the help of this institution, schools, vocational center, industrial schools for girls and dispensaries may be established in slums. The fund may be used for providing houses to the slum dwellers.

The federal government should allocate loans and subsidies to local governments for social safety nets for slums. There is also a need for promoting employment generating sectors of small and medium enterprises, given that they enable the poor to acquire or enhance physical assets.

The local stakeholders should be involved to promote the interest of slum dwellers, i.e. by involving in design and implementation strategies to improve the housing conditions in slums, and by engaging in policy dialogue towards making poverty reduction a central objective of the policy reforms for slums.

International development cooperation could play a central role in helping to meet targets for improving heath and education in targeted households. The IMF, ADB and the World Bank should allocate loans and subsidies for slum development.

Micro-credit banks may help construction of houses and to improve the living conditions of the housing units. NGOs can play an important role in education and health sector. The pubic sector program like Pakistan Poverty Alleviation Fund (PPAF), Khushhal Pakistan Program (KPP), Rural Support Program (RSP), and Social Action Program (SAP) is needed to be made effective for improvement of slums.

BIBLIOGRAPHY

1. There are considerable differences in the level of poverty in three regions of Punjab: Nothern Punjab (including Islamabad, Rawalpindi Division and District of Mianwali), Central Punjab (including Sargodah, Faisalabad, Gujranwala and Lahore Division) and Southern Punjab (including Multan, Dera Ghazi Khan, and Bahawalpur Divisions). The incidence of urban poverty is consistently lowest in Northern Punajb and the highest in the Southern Punjab, i.e. 35 per cent and almost three times more than Nothern Punjab. Southern Punjab is the least urbanized region in the province. Similarly, the Poverty Line for Sindh is 45 per cent and 16 per cent higher than for NWFP and Punjab respectively (SPDC 2001).
2. In Pakistan, 10.4, 4.2 and 0.4 per cent of urban population is poor, ultra poor and extreme poor respectively as compared to 19.2, 7.6 and 1.3 per cent of rural population in the same levels of poverty respectively (GOP 2008).
3. For instance, in Karachi there are large disparities in the prices of water. Some get it free, others pay nominal rates, yet others pay 12 times more, and some of the poorest pay up to two-thirds of their incomes in obtaining water. Water quality is very poor and not controlled, as a result there are nearly daily reports of deaths due to water-borne diseases. Leakages and poor state of water and sewerage pipes means large scale contamination (KWP 2007).
4. The annual population growth rate of urban areas is 3.59 per cent and of rural areas is 1.19 per cent (GOP 2008). However, for Karachi, it is 5 per cent where 40 per cent of the population is living in informal settlements or *katchi abadis* (KWP 2007).
5. Informal employment include all remunerative work (both self-employed and wage work) that is not recognized, regulated, or protected by existing legal or regulatory framework and non-remunerative work undertaken in an income-producing enterprise. The informal workers are deprived of secure work, workers' benefits, social protection and representation and voice. They lack legal and social protection and face a comparative disadvantage in production which results into poverty.
6. The Old Delhi, India is another example.
7. In South Asia other terms are *chawls/challis* in Ahmedabad and Mumbai, *ahatas* in Kanpur, *katras* in Delhi, *bustee* in Koltata, *zopadpattis* in Maharashtra, *cheris* in Chennai, *katchiabadis* in Karachi, *watta, perpath, udukku* or *pellligewal* in Columbo.
8. Dharavi in Mumbai, India is another example comprised of same size of population.
9. Anwar and Zafar (2003) have analyzed the impact of KIP and found a positive effect of program on household income, employment and expenditures on health and education by slum dwellers of Rawalpindi, Faisalabad and Multan.
10. Press Release No.150, dated 19th October 2008, Press Information Department, Government of Pakistan, Islamabad.
11. Molla, et. al. (1993) found that a significant number of children (16-60 months) in urban slums have low vitamin A level and may constitute a risk group. Geetha and Swaminathan (1996 for India) concluded that there exists high prevalence of malnutrition, especially among girls, in the slum communities of Mumbai (see also Pryer, et. al. 2000 for such type of results for Bangladesh).
12. No settlement area size is mentioned in this definition, as in slum definition by Municipal Corporation, Kolkata specified area is 700 square meters to be occupied by huts. The Indian Census definition also mentioned 300 people or 60 households living in the settlement.
13. Notified *katchi abadis* have secure tenure based on 99-year leases and the non-notified ones have no security of tenure and are scheduled for removal.

14. *Goths* have secure tenure, while ISD on agricultural lands only have secure tenure if declared *katchi abadis*.
15. They are restricted to the physical and legal characteristics of the settlement, and exclude the more difficult social dimensions.
16. The concept of improved water combines the variable on water resources, availability (a minimum of 20 liters per person per day), time spent daily on collecting water (less than one hour per household per day) and affordability (a maximum of 10 per cent of monthly income spent on water). Only households fulfilling all these criteria are considered to have access to improved water.
17. See www.developmentgoals.org and www.undp.org/mdg/goalsandindicators.html.
18. The registered *katchi abadis* under the definition set by Government of Pakistan.
19. The vulnerable poverty in Pakistan is 20.05 per cent (GOP 2008).
20. Cited by John Wall, World Bank's Country Director for Pakistan, in the daily "The News" July 10, 2006.
21. These thresholds for defining slum households are different from those given by UN-Habitat (see table-1). The thresholds by UH-Habitat are perfectly quantifying but complete applicability of them is not possible here for data collection constraints. However, our thresholds for all the elements explain the slums in the same dimension given by UN-Habitat.
22. We will use the term slum whatever the kind of *katchi abadis* is, notified, non-notified, Goths or inner-city slums, although they are different kinds of slums by Government of Pakistan for the task of regulation and upgradation.
23. The kinds of hazards are overlapping for the slums as well as the households.
24. The target of access to safe drinking water was 76 per cent to be achieved by 2005-06 in Poverty Reduction Strategy Paper for Pakistan. The target to be achieved is again 76 per cent by 2009-10 in Mid Term Development Framework by government of Pakistan.
25. Bahawalpur, Faisalabad, Gujranwala, Sialkot, Multan, Rawalpindi, Sargodah and Lahore are considered as major cities.
26. In Punjab 86 per cent of the households have their own houses with value. The ratios for the major urban cities and other urban areas of Punjab are 75 and 83 percent. For Bahawalpur the ratio is 88 per cent (Government of Punjab 2004).
27. Assets include shop, machinery, automobiles, high value tools, live stock, and agricultural land, etc.
28. In Dhaka slums the ratio of such households is 40 per cent (Pryer, et. al. 1996).
29. Pakistan has taken the indicator of net primary enrolment rate to meet the target of 100 per cent by the year 2015 in MDG. The definition adopted is the rate of children aged 5-9 years attending primary level classes, i.e. 1-5.

REFERENCES

1. ADB (2002) Poverty in Pakistan: Issues, Causes and Institutional Responses. Asian Development Bank (ADB), Pakistan Resident Mission, Islamabad.
2. Anwar, H. N. and M. I. Zafar (2003) "Economic Impact Assessment of Katchi Abadis Improvement Program: A Case Study of Punjab", *Pakistan Journal of Applied Sciences*, 3(6):451-461.
3. Arif, G. M. (2000) "Recent Rise in Poverty and Its Implications for Poor Households in Pakistan", *Pakistan Development Review*, 39(4):1153-70.
4. Behrman, J. (1995) Pakistan: Human Resource Development and Economic Growth into Next Century. Background Paper of Pakistan 2010. World Bank, Washington D.C.

5. Birdsall, N. (1994) Inequality, Saving and Growth. Working Paper. William College Research Center, Connecticut. USA.
6. Cities Alliance (1999) Cities Without Slums: Action Plan for Moving Slum Upgrading to Scale. The World Bank/UNCHS (Habitat), Washington, DC, www.citiesalliance.org
7. CRPRID (2002) Pakistan Human Condition Report 2002. Center for Research on Poverty Reduction and Income Distribution (CRPRID), Islamabad.
8. CRPRID (2006) Pakistan Millennium Development Goals Report 2006. Center for Research on Poverty Reduction and Income Distribution (CRPRID), Islamabad.
9. EUAD (1987) Shelter for Homeless, Pakistan Canvas, Environment and Urban Affairs Division (EUAD), Government of Pakistan, Islamabad.
10. FBS (2000) Pakistan Integrated Household Survey. Federal Bureau of Statistics (FBS). Statistics Division Islamabad.
11. Geetha, S. and M. Swaminathan (1996) "Nutritional Status of Slum Children of Mumbai" A Socio-economic Survey", *Economic and Political Weekly*, 31(14):896-900.
12. Ghaus, A. F. A., H. A. Pasha and R. Ghaus (1996) "Social Development Ranking of Districts of Pakistan", *Pakistan Development Review*, 35(4):593-614.
13. GOP (2001) National Housing Policy. Ministry of Housing and Works. Government of Pakistan (GOP), Islamabad.
14. GOP (2008) Pakistan Economic Survey 2007-08. Finance Division, Government of Pakistan (GOP), Islamabad.
15. Government of Punjab (2004) District-Based Multiple Indicators Cluster Survey 2003-04. Government of Punjab, Lahore in collaboration with Federal Bureau of Statistics, Islamabad and Unicef, Pakistan.
16. LWP (2007) Situation Analysis: Karachi, Water and Sewerage Problem and Challenges Faced by the City. Karachi Water Supply Partnership Launch. Karachi Water Partnership (KWP), Karachi.
17. Molla, A., S. H. Badruddin, M. Khurshid, A. M. Molla, F. N. Rehman, S. Durrani, A. Suria, J. D. Synder and K. Hendicks (1993) "Vitamin A Status of Children in the Urban Slums of Karachi, Pakistan, Assessed by Clinical, Dietary, and Biochemical Methods", *American Journal of Tropical Medicine and Hygiene*, 48(1):89-96.
18. Pryer, J. A., S. Roger, S. Mormand and A. Rehman (2002) "Livelihood, Nutrition and Health in Dhaka Slums", *Public Health Nutrition*, 5(5):673-678.
19. Romer, P. (1994) "The Origin of Endogenous Growth", *Journal of Economic Papers*, 8(1):3-22.
20. SPDC (2001) Annual Review 2000: Social Development in Pakistan: Towards Poverty Reduction. Social Policy Development Center (SPDC), Karachi.
21. UN-Habitat (2002) 'Expert Group Meeting on Slum Indicators, October', Revised Draft Report. United Nations Human Settlements Program (UN-Habitat), Nairobi.
22. UN-Habitat (2003) Guide to Monitoring Target: Improving the Lives of 100 Million Slum Dwellers, Nairobi.
23. World Bank (1995) Pakistan: Poverty Assessment. World Bank, Washington, D.C.

Earthquake in Iran: An Anthropology of Social Work Interventions

—Md. Irvani

Abstract

An earthquake with continuing aftershocks occurred in Iran, causing massive physical destruction, loss of life, and social and psychological disturbances. Iran is situated on one of the active earthquake zones; bearing the most risk, both loss of life and of damage. In the last century, Iran experienced more than 100 quakes and suffered their effects. Disasters create profound changes in humans and their environments. People face various events and react to them differently.

According to Hodgkinson and Stewart (1998), reactions to disaster, complex as they are, can be understood essentially as the reactions of normal human beings to sudden, unexpected and terrifying events in their lives. In disasters, generally, people lose loved ones, relatives and property. Above all, in psychological terms, they lose faith in the fact that life has a certain consistency and meaning. The fabric of everyday existence is torn away to reveal death and precarious survival. For the survivor, the encounter involves a violation of tranquillity. Erol and Oner (1999) indicated that once a disaster has happened to individuals, they believe that life cannot ever be the same again; that they cannot go safely to bed at night and that they must have done something to deserve it. Thus they deal with the question of self-esteem and anxiety.

Introduction

Humans have been coping with the effects of natural disasters and hazards throughout history and in every part of the globe. Both the impact of natural disasters and the ways in which humans have dealt with them have changed over time. This international conference brought together scholars from different disciplines to discuss the cultural strategies used to cope with floods, earthquakes, windstorms, and famine around the world from the Middle Ages to the present. Conference participants analyzed the different ways in which disasters were perceived and interpreted, the ways in which relief measures were organized, and the types of cultural strategies and coping mechanisms that evolved over time. For the first time, all of these issues were discussed in global and comparative perspective. One overarching question was whether national styles or cultural idiosyncrasies in dealing with disasters could be discerned.

Disaster relief is a complicated task that involves emergency and related services. Some of the relief work is done by social workers and should be acknowledged as part of social work practice and profession. Historically, social workers were involved in disaster relief work (Webster, 1995). However, this was not at the center of social work documentation and research (Streeter and Murty, 1996). Furthermore, disaster intervention is not always part of social work education. This article discusses the role of social workers in disaster situations. It is based on the Iran experience. Disasters affect the community at large. Consequently, human services have to address a variety of needs that emerge from the complex situation, whatever its causes are (Becker, 1997). Following a disaster, rescue services are on the scene almost immediately and provide the specific operations they have been trained for. Upon completing their duties, they return to their bases. However, caring for the human outcomes of a disaster only begins. A closer analysis of what transforms a natural event into a human and economic disaster reveals that the fundamental problems of development that the region faces are the very same problems that contribute to its vulnerability to the catastrophic effects of natural hazards.

The principal causes of vulnerability in the region include rapid and uncontrolled urbanization, the persistence of widespread urban and rural poverty, the degradation of the region's environment resulting from the mismanagement of natural resources, inefficient public policies, and lagging and misguided investments in infrastructure. Development and disaster-related policies have largely focused on emergency response, leaving a serious under investment in natural hazard prevention and mitigation. A proactive stance to reduce the toll of disasters in the region requires a more comprehensive approach that encompasses both pre-disaster risk reduction and post-disaster recovery.

Less than ten days ago, a deadly earthquake devastated the Iranian city of Bam, killing more than 30,000 people and injuring another 50,000. It was one of the deadliest natural disasters in modern Iranian history, and similar in destruction to the Roudbar earthquake in northern Iran in 1990. Historical information and all available records show that approximately 130 large earthquakes have taken place in most parts of Iran. Considering the high seismicity of Iran, a comprehensive hazard reduction program was launched in Iran in 1991, but the effectiveness of the measures have been limited by lack of adequate funding and institutional coordination. There is no lack of probabilistic studies on the seismicity of the country as well as fault studies.

Earthquakes : The Most Destructive Force of Nature

Earthquakes are the most destructive among all the natural hazards. Most of the time, they occur without any warning, which makes them most feared and unpredictable natural phenomena. Globally, on an average two earthquakes of magnitude 8 are known to occur every year. Iran is surrounded by tectonically active zones. Earthquakes are regularly felt on all sides of Iran. But the capital, Tehran, has been fortunate enough to avoid a major quake this century. Tehran was shaken in 1830 by a magnitude 7.2 quake.

Earthquakes: Causes

The true nature of the causes of an earthquake must be fairly well understood before adopting any control measure. Two models are being tested to justify these control measures.

1. Dilatancy-diffusion theory developed in the U.S.
2. Dilatancy-instability theory USSR

The first stage of both models is an increase of elastic strain in a rock that causes them to undergo a dilatency state; which is an inelastic increase in volume that starts after the stress on a rock reaches one half its breaking strength. During Dilatancy State, open fracture developing the rocks. So it is in this state the first physical change takes place indicating future earthquake. Here the two models diverge. The U.S. model suggest that the dilatancy and fracture of the rocks are first associated with a low water containing dilated rock, which helps in producing lower seismic velocity, lower electrical resistively and fewer minor seismic event. The pore water pressure then increases due to influx of water into the open fracture, weakening the rock and facilitating movement along the fracture, which is recorded as an earthquake.

In contrast the Russian model state that the first phases is accompanied by an avalanches of fracture that release some stress but produce an unstable situation that eventually cause a large movement along a fracture. Seismic gaps are defined as an area along active fault zones, capable of producing large earthquake but that have not recently produced an earthquake. These areas are thought to store tectonic strain and thus are candidate for future large earthquake. Any fault that has moved during quaternary can be called as active fault. It is generally assumed that these faults can get displaced at any time. Faults that have been inactive for the last three million years are generally classified as inactive fault. Active faults are basically responsible for seismic shaking and surface rupture (Sinha et al., 2000) Like all other natural hazards earthquakes also produce primary and secondary effects. Primary effects include surface vibration, which may be associated with surface rupture and displacement along fault plane. These vibrations may sometimes lead to the total collapse of large buildings, dams, tunnels, pipelines and other rigid structures. Deterministic ground motion analysis is one of the tools to determine the spatial distribution of surface vibration. Secondary effects of earthquake include a variety of short-range events; such as liquefaction, landslides, fires, tsunamis and floods. Long-range effects include regional phenomena such as regional subsidence or emergence of landmasses, river shifting and regional changes in ground water level.

Disaster research in social work has deep roots in the profession's history of disaster relief, social work's mission to create resources and make them accessible to people, and the profession's service to vulnerable populations. Social workers have important and unique contributions to make to disaster research through their expertise in ecological approaches, prevention, stress and coping, and promoting change in micro- and macro-systems. Disaster research in social work borrows primarily from psychology and sociology, and is conducted in clinical, organizational, and community contexts. Further social work research on disaster promises improved theory, measurement, and practice in situations of collective stress.

Social Work Contacts

Social workers seem to be the only professionals who are represented at almost every site that is directly or indirectly linked to the disaster. Contacts between people in need and social workers can begin early. Some begin on site. An initial encounter made during an emergency can develop into a helping contact (Seroka et al., 1986). In some cases, victims and their families may ask the worker who met and helped them on site to continue seeing them. The fact that this social worker was together with the family during its worst moments may help establish a unique professional bond. This of course reassures the family not only of the continuity of the process, but also of being able to rely on a professional who knows the case, and by virtue of the tragedy has become a partner. Indeed, a pertinent question often raised is whether the public will accept social workers intervening in emergencies. Dealing with crisis counseling, Stewart (1989) discusses issues related to selling social work to the community.

Traditionally, 'to be associated with social work is to be associated with failure and low status . . . those working with survivors of disaster have to confront this handicap'. However, in an emergency, people may have to approach social workers, or accept their outreach efforts. Evaluating these efforts after the Lockerbie disaster (1988), it was argued that despite the tragic circumstances 'the residents don't understand social work, and are aware of the stigma attached to utilizing the services of a social worker'. In Iran such reactions have been monitored. On the contrary, the public image of social workers seems to change and their central role in disaster work is acknowledged.

The Iran experience shows that social workers are the professionals best prepared to deal with complex situations resulting from an emergency. First, they have the basic training enabling them to relate to the needs of individuals, families and groups. Second, most social workers have some knowledge and experience in crisis intervention, family dynamics and loss. Third, most social workers are well informed about existing welfare programs and services and can refer people to other agencies for specialized help. Fourth, employed in a large variety of agencies, including hospitals, schools, community facilities and even private and public work places, social workers can easily make contacts, becoming an invaluable helping network. Forming such a network is an essential partnership in facilitating professional, comprehensive emergency relief work. This network is based on formal and informal ties between members of the same profession who know and trust each other.

When this is the case, even sensitive information can be exchanged, formally and informally, within this network. A social worker stationed at one location may contact her/ his colleague and refer a worried relative to that colleague. Having a contact person is reassuring and helpful. Social workers assigned by JET to various stations are equipped with sophisticated communication devices, enabling them to broadcast into the JET radio network and provide everyone with valid information. For sharing more personal information, the same device also serves as a cellular phone. Social workers can therefore share information and contact people personally. Such contacts are important as they help social workers collect and exchange personal concerns and worries. They also help social workers support each other when they themselves feel anxious or depressed.

Politics and Victims

In the aftermath of the earthquake, as I have described it, the state began to impinge on freedoms and autonomy. It took an iron grip by divesting people of property and their property rights and investing heavily in a superabundance of new bureaucracy, which was often uncertain of its proper relationship with the pre-existent bureaucracy. The government became a source of worry and confusion for many people and, as the nostalgia inherent in the separatist agitations reveals, it also became a target for their anger. But there was a glaring paradox here. On the one hand, people were clearly alienated from the government and from their natural and social environments, often quite literally so, and they publicly resented this.

On the other hand, the compensation schemes promised wealth. As a result, access to the government's coffers became highly competitive and a source of jealousy, rivalry and suspicion. In time, the struggle for compensation became a collective preoccupation pursued along non-collective lines. Once the levels and nature of the compensation had been set, there was little option for most people but to claim as much as possible. Any claim was time-consuming, and involved large numbers of documents and numerous trips to various government offices. The amounts available were as large as the levels of corruption that surrounded their distribution.

The social ethics of relief giving (the bases on which relief ought to be given) in *natural disaster* situations are explored through a case study of public reactions to Red Cross activities. Red Cross policies and public reactions to them are reviewed, and survey data pertaining to attitudes toward the Red Cross and toward relief giving in natural disasters of residents of a western NY county are presented. Specifically, public satisfaction with present Red Cross distribution policies is explored, and public perceptions of "loss vs need" as bases for relief giving are examined. Although there are some qualifications, findings show a large segment of the public supporting bases other than "need" for the distribution of disaster aid. Implications are that the public does not always support are distributive role for relief giving, but in some cases, with some populations, expects relief giving to reinforce the status quo.

In the early days after the earthquake local people were not involved in the decision-making and pre-existing support networks were not utilized. Given that nearly two-thirds of the population were either killed or injured in the earthquake, it is not surprising that external agencies found it difficult to identify what remained intact in terms of formal and informal networks. While acknowledging that re-creating social capital is no simple task, Putnam (2000: 402) asserts that a palpable national crisis, such as a natural disaster can make the task easier. However, the sense of national solidarity reported in the Iranian media was only temporary and gradually the survivors began to feel disenfranchised and mistrustful of relief efforts coordinated by non-Bamis. Before the earthquake, Bamhad been an affluent city, the regional centre for date growing and packing.

Yet in the space of just a few minutes, this physical capital was destroyed and the people of Bam were dependent on others to assist them. Genuine survivors of the earthquake found that their immediate needs were not being met because of the rapid poor people from the surrounding unaffected area claiming relief food and goods. Due to the poor construction of the buildings in Bam, there were few human survivors, but even so, there were insufficient tents and blankets to protect them from the severe cold of the Iranian winter. Donated tents subsequently arrived, but many survivors preferred to remain among the debris of their former home to protect it from looting. The key social capital ingredients of trust, mutuality and reciprocity present previously in the city of Bam were becoming less evident in the region at both micro- and meso-levels. Individuals were needed at this stage to bridge communities and link survivors in an organized fashion with those from outside Bam who were in a position to help. A week after the earthquake struck, the official relief effort was still not fully organized or coordinated, a task that should have been undertaken by the regional governor of Kerman Province.

Social work functions in disaster aid have been summarized as follows (Yueh, 2003) :

1. Supporting individuals and families. In Bam this included: providing emotional support, grief counseling and post-disaster support (PTSD) for vulnerable groups like people with disabilities, children and elderly people; motivating victims to join activities; providing emotional support for families in shelters; helping families to arrange for funerals and build tents; visiting homes; and interviewing families of the victims.
2. Linking individual needs with resources and helping people to access resources. This included facilitating contact between local government and voluntary groups; linking social services with the needs of the people; identifying vulnerable people; linking family needs with resources; collecting donations; collecting, delivering and distributing food and materials; and registering the needs of victims for central government officers.
3. Preventing severe physical and mental problems. These included therapeutic interventions for survivors, including various types of counseling, e.g. grief counseling and post-relief counseling, linking patients to therapists and therapeutic centers.
4. Preventing individuals, families, groups, organizations and communities from breaking down. This included providing accommodation, information and support

to individuals and families who were homeless; reducing survivors' lack of interest in life, and feelings of powerlessness and despair; coordinating and organizing responses to groups, agencies and communities effectively.

5. Intervening to change micro- and macro-systems to improve client well-being. This included advocating for change in governmental programs; developing volunteer services; conducting needs assessments; improving service programs; providing distribution centers for the victims; changing welfare policies and recovery programs to improve a community's ability to meet people's needs; developing the capacity of systems to improve the inferior structural status of earthquake victims.

Many countries lie in an earthquake zone. Excluding the Bam earthquake, the nine biggest quakes in Iran during the last century measured 5.2–7.3 on the Richter scale and caused anything between 450 and 40,000 fatalities (Goudarzi, 2004). Despite this, neither social work educators nor practitioners created a specialism on disaster programming. The available literature can help social workers learn what it is possible and/or necessary to do when delivering assistance programs as part of a rescue team giving disaster relief aid. Social workers are an important part of disaster aid and recovery plans at the micro, mezzo and macro levels. They play key roles in earthquake relief by assisting earthquake survivors and are on the frontline of emergency responses, as they were in the Bam earthquake.

There, they not only acted as representatives of the state, but they also joined families who were waiting to pull survivors from the debris, provided emotional support for families in shelters and helped families arrange funeral ceremonies. As government agents, social workers act on its behalf during emergency relief and thus enable it to carry out its responsibilities through their work. The majority of agency administrators who support disaster aid initiatives should have a social work background.

Recommendations

Based on our experience of working in the disaster stricken area, the following recommendations are made to address the subject of caring for those social workers who are deputed to perform relief work in disaster areas:

1. Timely rotation of care providers at regular intervals;
2. Focused briefing about the objectives and role of the care provider in relation to the task ahead;
3. The managers must ensure proper logistic support of the project;
4. A debriefing of the individual care provider and the whole team when relief and support duties have been completed;
5. A break or time off for the care provider, or at least relaxed duties after completion of their duties; and
6. Expressions of appreciation from the management and judicious granting of rewards.

One important implication concerns the channeling of resources to reduce exposure to stress and the resulting consequences. Support and counseling schemes targeted at traumatic stress or provision of additional staff, resources, or reduced workloads should be provided to reduce organizational stresses. Employee assistance programs with individualized interventions, monitoring, and more effective pre-employment screening may be a sound policy. With stress resulting from disaster responses potentially influencing the way an individual perceives and/or copes with subsequent negative life events, practitioners providing services to disaster or rescue workers can encourage their clients to monitor their levels of stress and the ways that they care for themselves both during and following disaster assignments.

The curriculum related to disaster aid services and practices should be studies in social work departments at universities both in Iran and indeed in most other developing countries. Natural disasters such as typhoons, goading and earthquakes are happening frequently and are even getting worse. Social workers need to face up and react to this reality as future members of a team that will work on disserts relief. I recommend that instructors allocate one or two sections of their social work curriculum (about 15–20 sessions) to discussing disaster responses. These should include how social work-students work with survivors, their families and communities; how they apply for all sorts of resources needed by victim survivors, how they help remaining family members cope with the death of other family members and make funeral arrangements. Furthermore, the student's practicum should also emphasize this type of social work and provide opportunities for working through some of the issues of disaster relief operations.

Role of the NGOs in Addressing Disasters Effectively

1. Rehabilitation of neglected children, orphan children and the community at large in coping with the consequences of disaster;
2. Enhancing community's capacities to cope with the future disasters;
3. Investing in people's knowledge-building rather than just physical infrastructure;
4. Improving livelihood options, empowering individuals, so that they can meet their own needs; and
5. Strengthening local institutions using local resources, and transferring appropriate technologies

Conclusions

Since the earthquake disaster affected entire communities, children's, families, teachers and friends were also victims. The Pynoos et al. (1993) study, with earthquake survivors among Armenian children, documented that the impact of a major catastrophe might directly affect an entire child population of a large area. The psychological sequel of this magnitude of disaster may alter the individual and social character of a whole generation of children and their families, and PTSD rates may reach epidemic proportions. Chronic, severe and high prevalence rates of PTSD found in this study of Turkish children support this conclusion. Moreover, professional help was also limited; 69 per cent reported that they had not received any psychological or educational debriefings or any type of individual or group counseling, and 45 per cent felt they might need counseling.

Survivor children developed earthquake related cognitive and physical avoidance: Traumatized children did not want to go to places which reminded them of the earthquake and did not want to see people or survivors who would talk about earthquakes. This phenomenon, that survivors might develop numbing and effortful avoidance, has been previously reported by Foa et al. (1995). Clinicians working with an exposed or at-risk population should consider the nature of chronic severe and high epidemiological rates of PTSD when planning intervention and prevention programs.

Social workers are required to cope with a variety of duty related stresses, including the exposure to traumatic incidents. A corner stone of the effectiveness of mental health support at the scene of operations is establishing a rapport between the mental health team and the command staff, rescue team managers, and social workers. Disaster workers have a deep commitment to working long hours without breaks, and quickly may dismiss suggestions about using time to relax. Understanding the stressors associated with rescue work and its culture can facilitate alliance building. Social workers often have a high capacity for trust among each other, but they tend to be cautious about the competencies of individuals perceived as outsiders.

Rescue workers may demonstrate mental and emotional resilience during an operation, but they may have intense emotional reactions afterwards because of their sensitivity to the suffering of survivors and their families. If social workers tactfully acknowledge this duality, it would help them to achieve the confidence of rescue workers while increasing the workers' willingness to disclose feelings of vulnerability or self-criticism, and to accept emotional support.

Index

H

I